THE WAGNER LEGACY

Printed in the UK by: MPG Books, Bodmin

Published by: Sanctuary Publishing Limited, Sanctuary House,
45-53 Sinclair Road, London W14 0NS, United Kingdom
Web site: www.sanctuarypublishing.com

Original English translation by Della Couling, 1997
Translation revised 1998 and 2000

Copyright: Verlag Kiepenheuer & Witsch, Köln, 1997

Preface: © Rabbi Julia Neuberger, 1998

Photographs: courtesy of the author, except where credited. Author
photograph on the cover by John Foley/Opale

First published in Germany by Verlag Kiepenheuer & Witsch, 1997
First Sanctuary Publishing UK edition: 1998
This edition: 2000

ISBN: 1-86074-251-3

THE WAGNER LEGACY

An Autobiography

Gottfried Wagner

ACKNOWLEDGMENTS

My thanks to Eberhard Wagner, Karl Lubomiski, Dorothea Hug-Lauener, Michael Wieck, Ralph Giordano, Jan G Colijn, Michael Shapiro, Abraham Peck and Christian v Ditfurth.

I also thank my mother, Ellen Drexel-Wagner for allowing me to consult her diaries and photos.

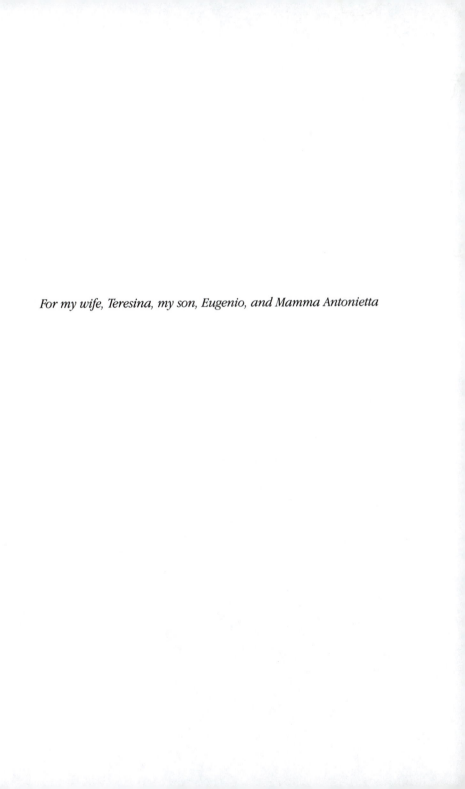

For my wife, Teresina, my son, Eugenio, and Mamma Antonietta

CONTENTS

PREFACE

by *Rabbi Julia Neuberger*

For those, like me, who are convinced that something of Richard Wagner's antisemitism is to be found in his music, this volume of autobiography by his great-grandson brings comfort and hope. Gottfried Wagner was brought up in the overwhelming shadow of Bayreuth and Wagner-worship. Life at home was wholly dominated by productions of Wagner operas by his father or uncle. His grandmother still talked of "Uncle Wolf" (the family's pet-name for Hitler). There was no sense of guilt, no sense of apology, no sense of family warmth. They simply lived an unpleasant legend, with plagued by internecine quarrels within the family.

Meanwhile Gottfried began to doubt the legend, and then broke away entirely – or was dismissed from the "holy" presence of Wagner inspiration. He began to explore his family's role in the Holocaust, and the nature of antisemitism in Richard Wagner's own lifetime. It makes an ugly tale. Gottfried tells the already well-known account of Wagner's writing of 'The Jews In Music', and continues with an account of Wagner's gradual conviction that the racial theorising that became fashionable in the 1880s was right.

No one can argue that Wagner's deeply-held prejudices and hatred led directly to the gas chambers. But the reluctance of his descendants to condemn him for what he said in any way – the desire to continue the great worship and the festival as if the man was somehow a hero because of the music he wrote – needs to be examined closely.

Gottfried has lived since he was born, in 1947. He looked into the Wagner abyss and saw something horrible. He has dedicated his life to the search for dialogue and reconciliation, in recognition of human pain across ethnic divides. He has also made his way as a musical dramaturg as far as he has been able, but his family has tried to prevent his success. This volume, published here in English for the first time, will irritate and anger the Wagner clan worse than ever. More than that: it will upset the very considerable number of English-speaking Wagnerians who have tried to close their eyes to the monster who was their musical hero, the fine artist and pig of a man who was able to put some of his more unpleasant ideas into his music.

One cannot say that one must judge the art by the man, but one can argue that, in deliberate contrast to the noble Teuton, the inclusion of figures such as Alberich and Mime in *Siegfried*, with the strong implication that they were Jews, is more than innocent art. It has a moral message, and that message is a vile one.

In recent years, Israelis and other Jews have conducted at Bayreuth, including Daniel Barenboim and James Levine. Their own motives are left unexplored here, and yet many Jews remain Wagnerians – indeed, my own grandfather was a keen enthusiast. Is it that they refuse to see? Or are they – as I am sometimes myself – so carried away by the animal appeal of the music that they will forgive its creator anything? Gottfried Wagner writes a tale suggesting that we should think again, and that those who perpetuate the Wagner legend need to examine their consciences to establish what they have contributed by their uncritical worship of him.

Gottfried Wagner made his break, and hereby tells his tale. He is a brave man, and is to be congratulated for his courage and understanding. That said, he raises questions he then leaves in part unanswered – about the degree to which it is the duty of the artist to consider how his work might be used, and the duty of the artist's descendants to ensure that the use to which the artist's work has been implemented is noble, or at the very least not damaging to others. His response is that empathy is the duty and individual responsibility of every single human being in their daily lives. Artists such as the Wagners cannot claim some superior status that exempts them from that duty because of their art. Gottfried Wagner's view is that, in "the loss of empathy in our human existence, [we can find]…the reason for all evil".

So far, so good. However, there is more to consider – personal responsibility for what happened, as well as about a failure to recognise the duty of empathy – and here Gottfried Wagner leaves questions unanswered, although his view that we are all responsible for one another – that we all have to sense what it might be like to be in each other's situations, each other's shoes – is a strong statement of his philosophical beliefs.

More compelling is what he doesn't so much spell out as live. The early chapters suggest a young man of a rebellious nature, railing against an impossible family, whom he blamed (rightly, some of us would argue) indirectly for some of what happened during the Holocaust. He has become a man who has taken on part of that responsibility whilst at the same time being refused recognition by that same family. By becoming involved in – indeed, helping to set up – his Post-Holocaust Dialogue Group, he presents himself as someone trying to face the past of his family and his nation and struggling with it. He has accepted an indirect line, an indirect responsibility, even though no one can be held accountable for what was done before their birth. But by his later actions he has shown a realisation that one can play a role in healing, in learning from 'the other'.

There is no doubt that Gottfried Wagner gets under the skin of his Wagner relatives. He doesn't believe the Wagner myth, and plays no part in worshipping him. He cannot sit breathless and silent through a Bayreuth production of *Der Ring*. His story tells us much about the family, and much about the inability of many of its members to see where Richard Wagner's ideas would – or at least could lead. Yet Gottfried Wagner leaves us asking more questions about how far responsibility can be extended. Perhaps, as a man so curious about life and responsibility, it is only to be expected that he would.

Are the children responsible for the atrocities of their fathers? Yes, if they hold to the fatal way of their fathers. But do not all suffer from the atrocities of others? One stumbles by chance over the atrocities of others. Does that mean that all are made responsible for one another? Yes, there, where a man had the power in his hands to protest, and failed to do so.

Based on *Sanhedrin, 27 b*

CHAPTER ONE

VILLA WAHNFRIED

From the moment I was born, in Bayreuth on 13 April 1947, it seems that I was destined to follow in the Wagner family tradition. I was introduced to the world as Gottfried Helferich Wagner, son and heir of Wolfgang Wagner, and the choice of my Christian names was already an indication of role that I was intended to play in the family business. Gottfried is the name of Elsa's brother, the ruler of Brabant, in my great-grandfather Richard Wagner's opera *Lohengrin*, and also the second middle name of my uncle, Wieland Wagner. My middle name, Helferich, was the middle name of my grandfather, Siegfried Wagner, a name Richard Wagner had invented for his only son.

This rather droll manner of naming children was typical of the Wagner family. In a letter to King Ludwig II, dated 9 February 1879, Richard Wagner wrote: "The son, now still so young, shall, when he has reached maturity, know exactly who his father was – nothing more. Then he may decide. This is also more or less the fashion in which we shall raise him. The boy will not be forced to do anything at all; we shall merely support and freely guide his inclinations. We are not at all aiming to turn him into an 'artist'. I have only indicated one direction available to him through the names which I have appended to his surname; two names mark him out as my son, Siegfried Richard (Wagner), but I have added Helferich, ie 'the helpful', to this."[1]

I was christened on 22 May, Richard Wagner's birthday, and my father chose his mother, Winifred Wagner, and my Aunt Verena's husband, Bodo Lafferentz as godparents. Winifred, together with staunch Nazi and general intendant of the Prussian State Theatres Heinz Tietjen, had run the Bayreuth Festival from 1930 until 1945. On orders from Hitler, and as a colleague of Labour Front head Robert Ley, Lafferentz had safeguarded the organisation and finances of the Bayreuth Festival from 1940 to 1944 through the National Socialist organisation *Kraft Durch Freude* [Strength Through Joy].

What looked from the outside to be a peaceful, idyllic family was in reality quite different. Wolfgang and Wieland Wagner were mainly interested in the Bayreuth Festival, which took place for the first time since the war in July 1951. In order that they could to immerse themselves into preparing for this event, my parents took myself and my elder sister, Eva, to the Etzerschlössl children's home in Berchtesgaden, which was a sort of up-market boarding house for the children of well-to-do families. Before leaving us, my father explained the reason for our sojourn: "The festival will be starting soon now, and it's very important. We must all make sacrifices for the future, and you, as a boy, will just have to grin and bear it. If you're good, you'll get some lovely presents."

I have never understood what he meant by these "sacrifices", but I do know that, at the Etzerschlössl, the first of the many places to which I was sent during my youth, I felt miserable. I grew resentful of the hectic activity involved in the preparations for the festival, and even of the presents that my parents bought me to salve their own consciences.

The lives of both of my parents were wrapped up in the Bayreuth Festival. My father was the second son of Siegfried and Winifred Wagner, both of whom had directed the festival – Siegfried from 1904 until1930, and Winifred from 1930 until the war temporarily shut it down in 1944. As a young man, my father assisted Tietjen, the Nazi-influenced artistic director of the festival, and in 1951 he and his older brother, Wieland, became joint directors. Throughout all of his work at Bayreuth, he has remained loyal to the vision of his grandfather, Richard Wagner, and has worked to secure the festival's finances. My mother's life was similarly married to the theatre, although she would rather perform than direct. By her early 20s, she had become a successful ballet dancer, performing mostly in large opera houses. She met my father in Berlin in 1942, and after their marriage she gave up her career and dedicated herself to my father, until their divorce in 1976.

Shortly before the solemn opening of the festival, my sister and I were brought back to Bayreuth, where the public was presented with the image of a happy family. I dreaded the thought of being packed off to the children's home in Berchtesgaden again, and decided that the best way of avoiding it was by behaving well, so I tried to be a shining example of exactly what the grown-up world expected of a Wagner: I didn't answer back, and never interrupted the adults' conversations. In recognition of the sacrifices my father was making for the great idea of the Richard Wagner Bayreuth Festival I didn't bore or pester him with stories of the children's home, and showed nothing but gratitude and admiration for the genius of my illustrious ancestor. The musical and spiritual legacies of the founder of the festival were of global significance, and I was privileged to live at its very centre.

A cult centred on the composer and his ideology imbued nearly every aspect of life in my family and the theatre community surrounding it. This cult placed Richard Wagner at its centre, interpreting his legacy with quasi-religious images – many of which came from his own works – and venerating him as a cultural messiah. My first image of the Wagner cult in Bayreuth was a photograph of the Wagner bust by Arno Breker, Hitler's favourite sculptor. It struck me at once as both heroic and menacing. Zdenko von Kraft, a devoted Wagnerian, offered his own impression in the 1951 poem 'Genius', which he wrote for the programme of the first festival after the war:

> Many have passed on, many will come
> Yet ever faithful a new circle forms,
> What was once flame burns ever hotly
> The glow of the spirit shines undimmed
> For what the best of their time have perceived
> Is close to God, it endures and lasts.

Who counts moons, thankfully counts death;
The unforgettable knows naught of years,
That are, that come and were before us,
Are only leaves on the flourishing vine
That winds about exalted beauty,
That binds us together in a noble way.
For this is the last word of art,
What is common to all is its strength,
What is valid to all creates its works,
What is holy to all feeds its fruitfulness,
And where it inflames a genius,
He has announced himself for the whole world,
Whether the paths of error or pain,
Whether a cobbler's workshop or the trials of gods –
Man's final word means death,
But the seer says a redeeming "Grace!
And so he refines the last things
To a mysteriously beautiful Ring."[2]

I have never understood the New Bayreuth euphoria, but as a dutiful four-year-old boy I managed to appear thrilled by Beethoven's *Ninth Symphony*, under the baton of the famous conductor Wilhelm Furtwängler, and by my uncle's production of *Parsifal*. I was alarmed by the tumultuous applause of the audience: I hadn't been at all prepared for such a spectacle in the *Festspielhaus*, and didn't dare admit how frightened I was of Wieland Wagner's dark world of *Parsifal* and the Holy Grail.

I smilingly acknowledged the constant observations of how much I looked like Richard Wagner, the 'Master of Bayreuth', and the reassurances of what a great future I had before me; but no matter how far I slipped into the role of the young Wagner I couldn't understand the contrast between the devotion demanded by the family to Richard's art and the overwhelming, spontaneous display deemed by the members of the Bayreuth artistic tribe to be appropriate on public occasions. I felt at home neither in the monumental world of the *Festspielhügel* nor in the children's homes I was repeatedly sent to – my own sacrifice for Richard Wagner's "art of mankind". I envied other children, who were allowed to grow up in normal families and in a normal environment.

During those first seven years, when I wasn't being packed off somewhere, I lived with my parents in the gardener's house in Wahnfried Park. We shared the first floor of the small brick house with the gardener, Düret, and his family. The nursery window in our small apartment looked out over the front façade of the Villa Wahnfried. This part hadn't suffered any war damage, and its pictures of Wotan, along with Wagner's house motto ("Here where my fancies [wahnen] found peace [frieden], this house I name Wahnfried"), remained intact.

In front of the Villa Wahnfried, set on a high plinth, was a bust of King Ludwig II, who had financed Richard Wagner's lifestyle as a composer for many years. This statue was surrounded by a pine hedge, where I liked to hide and watch the many tourists passing in and out of the front part of Wahnfried Park. I also waited there for the right moment – once my father had left the Park – to start a conversation with Uncle Wieland's family, or with American officers.

I was forbidden to talk to my cousins or to enter the partly-reconstructed Siegfried Wagner House, where my Uncle Wieland's family lived until 1966. (The house wasn't finally rebuilt and refurbished until 1976, when it was re-opened for its 100th anniversary and made into a museum.) Although the main house (which had been designed by Wilhelm Neumann in 1872) contained a concert hall, a library, a rotunda and eventually an annex for the Führer, the house which my immediate family occupied was modest, and a constant reminder of the animosity that persisted between my father and his brother.

My father gave his orders in a stern voice, and the penalties for disobeying him were severe. He was strong and choleric, and refused to brook any objections to his authority. When he discovered me playing with my cousins he threatened to beat me, and I believed that he would. I learned how to hide – in the cupboard, under the bed, in the hedge, around the statue of King Ludwig – in order to avoid my father's anger. He never discussed his rules: he gave orders and I had to obey. He was a very strong man, and I pretended to agree with him out of a fear of being beaten, cultivating a dissent that I hid from him and the adult world.

He never explained exactly why I was not supposed to play with Iris, Nike, Daphne and Wolf-Siegfried (whom we all called Wummi). He just spoke disparagingly of his brother and his family, especially the children, referring to their bad manners and complaining that they were the wrong company for myself and my sister. I later realised that these accusations were untrue.

In a way I led a double life: with my parents I was the obedient son, but I broke the rules laid down by my father at every available opportunity. As soon as I saw that my father had left Wahnfried Park, I would leave my hiding place in the hedge around the Ludwig II monument, climb over the wall between the Villa Wahnfried and the gardener's house, and enjoy wild games with Wieland's children. I felt possessed of boundless freedom. As soon as my father returned, however, I would clamber back over the wall and scramble back into the hedge. As soon as he had disappeared into the house I would slip across the lawn next to my playground at the driveway entrance. My father caught me now and again during these escapades, despite my precautions, and beat me soundly. However, these beatings only served to strengthen my resolve to leave the family home and escape the Wagner fanaticism that permeated the *Festspielhügel* as soon as possible.

In comparison with the free and easy hours I spent with the Wieland children, our own family life appeared monotonous and regimented. Father dictated the hours during which I could play and which friends I could have. He forbade my friends from entering our garden house or his villa beside the *Festspielhaus*. I began to rebel, lying to him about where I was going, making up stories about school meetings. When he discovered my disobedience he beat me even more severely. He labelled me the "little Russian", as he recognised in me sinister characteristics which he believed were typical of the Russians. My rebelliousness increased when, under my father's orders, my sister Eva tried to control me. If she caught me doing anything wrong, she reported it. She wasn't alone – my mother also blindly subjected herself to her husband's will. I was alone in my own family. My father beat me until I was 16 years old, until I was finally old enough to rebel properly. I told him that, if he beat me one more time, he would never see me again.

There were some bright spots, however. On my fifth birthday my father allowed me to play with Wieland's children. He had given me a heavy, bright blue iron car, equipped with the engine from a moped, and without prior explanation he sat me behind the steering wheel, my sister on the back seat, and started up the motor. The thing tore off around the fountain in the Wahnfried garden, and I lost control, ploughing into the rhododendron bushes near Richard Wagner's grave. Swearing furiously, my father dragged me from the car and the afternoon of birthday games was over. I never got in the car again.

At that time I was already feeling the tension between my father and my uncle, which seemed primarily focused on who did what on the *Festspielhügel*. Their differences of opinion frequently exploded into noisy quarrels, and because even the children heard these angry exchanges, the unity of the family was gradually eroded. The Wieland and the Wolfgang parties grew further and further apart. They eventually refused to meet up at Christmas and Easter, either in Villa Wahnfried or in the spacious house owned by my grandmother, Winifred, in the Fichtelgebirge.

During one of my own illicit visits to Villa Wahnfried, in the Christmas of 1952, I was overawed by a gigantic Christmas tree standing in the hall, decorated with red apples and beeswax candles. I suppose it was at that point that I first wondered why the Wagner family didn't meet together, especially at Christmastime, which, I had always been told in the Bayreuth kindergarten, was a festival of love and peace. I asked my father to pray with me then, but he mockingly refused.

The family was now split between into the Wielands and the Wolfgangs. Wieland denigrated my father as being a simple-minded manager, while he himself was generally regarded as an artist. I began to understand then that there were both gifted and ungifted Wagners. This label persisted for decades, and even coloured media reporting.

To escape from family tensions, my parents, my sister and I began to spend occasional weekends in a small house near Neunkirchen, which was set in beautiful countryside a few kilometres from Bayreuth. These weekends, along with my regular trips to children's homes, were the only escape I had. My parents found mental stimulation enough in championing Wagner's work. They also travelled on festival business outside the season, but even when they were in Bayreuth they rarely told their children anything about it – their work claimed so much of their attention.

In order to escape from such enforced isolation, I disobeyed my father more and more frequently. I felt it ridiculous that I was forbidden to enter the Siegfried Wagner House. In the beginning of the 1950s, extravagant parties were held regularly, at which American officers would celebrate noisily. There was singing, dancing, and always plenty to eat and drink. It was at these parties that I first heard dance bands, jazz and the North American music of the 1940s, which my father dismissed as "nigger music". I enjoyed the warm, lively atmosphere, and instead of listening piously to home-made 'Holy Grail' music, I sat rapturously in the Wahnfried garden, in front of the music-room window of the Siegfried Wagner House, and tapped my feet to the boogie-woogie music of the "uncultured Yanks".

On one occasion, I was spotted by one of the black employees. I went to make my escape, suddenly remembering my father's objections, but the huge, powerfully-built Afro-American saw how afraid I was and approached me. With a broad smile, he handed me a piece of wedding cake and an orange – luxuries, and not just for me – and urged me to have fun. Why should I be against "Yanks" and "Negroes"?

1953 was to be an important year for me, and for two reasons: my father staged his first production, and also designed his first set for the *Festspielhaus*; and I started school. Father had chosen *Lohengrin* for his Bayreuth debut, and during his intense preparations he expected more consideration and respect from his children than ever before. When he was working at home we had to keep absolutely quiet – any noise disturbed him. When rehearsals started in June, there was only one subject of conversation: his production of *Lohengrin*. The sheer fascination of the preparatory work – first on the rehearsal stage, and then on the main stage of the *Festspielhaus* – compensated a little for the fact that the entire family was bent to the cause. The hectic rehearsing and workshopping was fabulously exciting, but the constant grind of having to pose for photographers soon became annoying. I was placed in every conceivable pose next to a *papier mâché* prop of a swan, and forced to smile sweetly again and again.

Giving no reasons, my father categorically forbade me from sitting in on my uncle's rehearsals of *Das Rheingold*, which were taking place at the same time. I couldn't understand the ban, but as I was thrilled just to take part in the theatrical life of the *Festspielhaus*, and reluctant to jeopardise this privilege, I didn't argue. At my insistence, my father briefly told me the fairy tale of the good Lohengrin, a prince who comes down to Earth from the wonderful world of the Grail to free the good Elsa from the wicked Ortrud and Telramund. It struck me as odd that Lohengrin has to leave Elsa just because she asks his name and where he comes from, but after after my father explained this with "the music explains everything", I didn't press him any further, even though I didn't understand what he meant. I also suspected that something wonderful and unearthly was happening in the prelude to the opera, but I couldn't grasp why Elsa dies after Lohengrin returns to his father, Parsifal, in the Grail world, and why her brother, Gottfried, has to go to war as leader of Brabant against the terrible "enemies in the east" after he has been turned into a swan by the wicked Ortrud.

It wasn't so much the fact that I failed to understand *Lohengrin* as the fact that it made me uneasy. I assumed that I would take the non-speaking role of the boy Gottfried, and it was a blow when I learned that my father had given this role to the son of the singer Weber, who portrayed King Heinrich. The boy was only a little older than I, and Father's explanation – "I don't want you getting preferential treatment in getting a role just because you're my son" – did nothing to convince me: my cousin Wummi, four years older than me, was allowed to play one of the Nibelung dwarfs in *Das Rheingold*. Father had decided, however, and that was that.

Looking back, I can see that my father considered me as a potential rival. He was afraid of living in the shadow of both his artistically talented brother and a possibly gifted son. He wanted to be the last Wagner of consequence, thereby securing his place in the history of Bayreuth. Mother told me of how he had hoped for a second daughter, and of his disappointment when I arrived instead.

After the premiere of *Lohengrin* we sat with guests in the festival restaurant, and it was there that I had my first dealings with the press. Until then I had been excluded from public life, unlike my cousins, and I found it unsettling to be suddenly a Wagner scion and a source of interest, and to be quizzed on my opinion of *Lohengrin*. The questions of the tabloids in particular confused me: they wanted to know how I had enjoyed Father's *Lohengrin* and Wieland's *Das Rheingold*. It was natural for me to find my father's production good – in contrast to most of the critics, as it happened, who preferred Wieland's directing. When asked about *Das Rheingold*, I could only say that I hadn't seen it yet.

After the premiere of *Lohengrin*, I was disappointed to find that my father wouldn't let me sit at the same table as Wieland's children. Since then, at all such occasions there was a Wolfgang and a Wieland table, and the hardly spoke to each other. We were paraded as the nice little Wagner children, and instructed to greet those who were introduced to us as members of the Bayreuth Society Of Friends – the festival, that is – particularly nicely. Unfortunately, I didn't always manage this to my parents' satisfaction, instead deciding on who I liked and who I didn't with childlike naïveté, whether they were influential sponsors or ordinary mortals.

I found my grandmother's behaviour on such occasions particularly unpleasant. She couldn't resist theatrically expounding on variations of the theme of familial resemblance. At the core of her always highly-elaborate tales were two sentences: "When you were in my house as a baby, and I had guests, I would ask them if they wanted to see Richard Wagner as a baby. Of course they all wanted to see the infant Richard." Nothing could prevent her from parading this joke. Once, when I cheekily countered with "was I really that ugly?", Omi was amused at my "typically Wagnerian" retort.

After Father's success with *Lohengrin*, my sister and I were once again sent off to Berchtesgaden, in new clothes and laden down with presents, and then, in September 1953, I started school in the nearby village of Maria Gern. This idyllic village school had only two classrooms: grades one to four were taught in one, while grades five to eight were taught in the other. A pretty peasant girl of around twelve, Maria, helped me with writing, reading and arithmetic, and our lessons were broken up with long, happy walks in the countryside, during which our teacher, Losch, taught us the names of the plants. My new schoolfriends (who mostly came from farming families) were friendly and welcoming, and in adapting to the new environment I took on the local upper Bavarian accent. I enjoyed ringing the bell of the little village church with the other boys, jumping up and hanging onto the bellrope tightly, swinging as the bell tolled loudly. In fact, Maria Gern saw me play like other six-year-old boys, and at that time I hardly missed my parents and Bayreuth at all.

This carefree time was short lived, however, and in October I was enrolled in another school, this time in Bayreuth. This heralded the start of a 16-year schooling period which was to be torture, from start to finish. Towns, schools, tutors and teachers changed constantly, and I had to repeat classes three times. The only things to alleviate this were stimulating teachers and the companionship of my fellow pupils.

My very first school experiences in Bayreuth were nightmarish. It quickly became clear to me what it meant to be different from the other children: I was teased because of my upper Bavarian accent and my traditional dress, which I had so enjoyed wearing in Maria Gern, and I was also a long way behind in classes. My first teacher in Bayreuth, the kindly and sympathetic Frau Grohm, tried in vain to defend me, with little help from my parents.

What separated me most from my fellow pupils was the fact that I was a Wagner going to school in Bayreuth. It was inevitable that they should display some envy. At first I tried to make the best out of the situation and played the clown, but that failed to improve matters at all. I gradually withdrew into myself, which only served to make the other children more aggressive. I was once severely beaten up on the way home, and once discovered the words "Gottfried is stupid" scrawled onto the sandstone outer wall of the Wahnfried garden, which amused the passersby no end. My schoolwork deteriorated, and as my parents had neither the time nor the inclination to help they arranged extra tuition for me at home, with nannies and private tutors. The number of tutors who strove in vain to improve my school marks grew steadily. I continued to stand out at school, not only because of my bad marks but also because of my frequent illnesses and absenteeism.

Neither my father nor my mother ever helped me with my coursework; Father was so obsessed with his work for the festival that he had no real friends of his own, let alone time to tutor his son. Dominated by Father, Mother denied her own needs so often that I felt the need to care for her myself. By the age of 13 I felt as if I were her older brother, a role in which I felt only pity for her and the humiliation she endured in my father's house. She cried every time I returned to school, while Father acted as if he was glad to be rid of me so that I wouldn't distract him from his work.

In 1954 my father revived his production of *Lohengrin*. However, this event was less exciting than the meeting with my aunt, my father's elder sister, Friedelind Wagner, who came to see the performance in the *Festspielhaus*. Strange stories about her circulated in the family, and so naturally I had to meet her. My father made the most disparaging remarks about her, telling me that she had been a terribly naughty child and had eventually run away to America. When first I met this brazen American (known in the family as 'Maus') in the *Festspielhaus*, my immediate impression was quite different. She resembled the rest of the family very closely (she had the Wagner nose), and impressed me with her exotic dress and brash, assertive manner. She greeted me very affectionately, becoming the only member of my family who ever inquired about my own interests and treated me like a boy of my age. "Call me Maus, not Aunt Friedelind," she said. She bore none of the Bayreuth affectation or Wagner obsessiveness so ardently demonstrated by the rest of the family, and I listened with fascination as she told me how she had met some Red Indians in the American prairies. I could have talked to her for hours, but my father soon insisted on driving me home, and *en route* he forbade me any further contact with her. This time, however, I didn't accept the edict; I protested, demanding reasons. I didn't get any, however – instead my father stonewalled: "It's a long story, I'll tell you one day."

I didn't give up. "Tell me now," I insisted.

"You wouldn't understand, anyway," Father replied, annoyed.

He dropped me off at home. I began to suspect that there were many secrets about our family I had yet to learn.

Maus knew those secrets, and she was brave enough to expose them in her book of 1944, *The Royal Family Of Bayreuth*, in which she made it clear exactly how close Hitler was to the Wagner family. She was the only Wagner of her generation who opposed Nazi Germany and the Wagner family's elitism. My father despised Maus, both because she was intellectually and culturally superior to him and because she wouldn't let him forget his ties to the Nazi regime. He openly criticised her book, even at her funeral, which he held at Bayreuth against her dying wishes.

After our first meeting, Maus and I only saw each other occasionally between 1959 and 1966, when she was working as director of her Bayreuth Festival masterclasses, which were attended by music students from all over the world. These summer courses comprised discussions on Wagner's operas, and took place in a shed right next to my father's home. Father always made fun of Maus' cultural and intellectual superiority, because she was an expert not only on the works of Richard Wagner but also those of Franz Liszt and Siegfried Wagner, her father, and she was the only member of the family to promote his work. Whenever my father and I talked about her we argued – I couldn't share his cutting opinion of her.

After Wieland's death in 1966, the conflicts between Father and Maus over his style of directing reached such a violent level that, in 1972, she finally left and settled in England. I missed her very much, and during the few conversations we were able to have together until her death in 1991 she was always frank with me, always interested in my professional development, always turning up – with touching pride – to the premieres of most of my productions. Maus helped my mother, too, after she and my father divorced in 1976, showing a great selflessness, which was typical of her adherence to her principles and her courage, and yet so atypical of the rest of the family. Unfortunately, however, she had little luck in her choice of friends, who often exploited her.

I still enjoy reading my letters from Maus. It's clear that, as family outsiders in opposition to the Wagner cult, we actually liked each other, in spite of all the obstacles that beset us. Maus was the only relative of mine who enthusiastically applauded both my journey to Israel and the adoption of my son, Eugenio. I owe it to her to prevent her memory from being dragged through the mud.

In January 1955 we were able to leave the gardener's house and move into a villa on the *Festspielhügel*. My mother, who was worried about the precarious state of my health, was relieved: "At last, we'll be able to live in peace and quiet." Unfortunately my situation failed to improve. Our villa was only a few metres away from the *Festspielhaus* and my father now devoted himself day and night exclusively to his work. The final vestiges of family life soon disappeared: our new home turned into an annex of the *Festspielhaus*, and my father tolerated nothing but the cult of the Wagner legacy. He had the grounds enclosed by high walls, wooden fences and hedges – I often felt as though I were in a prison. I missed the open garden of Villa Wahnfried, the town there and the illicit games I played with Wieland's children.

Moving to another part of the town meant that I had to attend a different school: the Graser school. Here I was confronted with a very strict, very threatening teacher: Herr Schäfer. I impressed him only once, I believe, when I managed to sing a melody which he had played on the violin without a single mistake. Of course, I was also fulfilling the school's expectations that a Wagner would be interested in nothing but music. The most positive thing Herr Schäfer's ever said to me was: "You're not up to much in school, but at least you can sing."

Fortunately, in April 1955 the dreary monotony of school was broken up by my first big trip abroad, when I flew with my parents to Barcelona, where the Bayreuth Festival were on tour with my uncle's productions of *Parsifal* and *Die Walküre*. My first experience of the Mediterranean had a profound and lasting effect on me – not only the luxurious hotels, elaborate gardens, villas and deep azure-blue sea but also the glitterati, both inside and outside the opera house. I found it all fascinating. The Spanish also made much of the Wolfgang and Wieland children. Grandmother Winifred declared at every conceivable opportunity how "these Spaniards stood by us Germans against the Bolsheviks decently and splendidly". She enthusiastically regaled us with stories of Hitler, praised his Spanish ally the Caudillo Francisco Franco, and wallowed in memories of the glory days of the National Socialist dictatorship. The hosts applauded heartily while my father remained silent, and I started shouting with the others "Franco-Hitler! Franco-Hitler!" I didn't even know what it meant.

Barcelona was huge and impressive. The worship of my ancestor went to my head, and I began to believe that I had a great future in front of me. When we returned to Bayreuth I lost interest in my schoolwork completely, and my marks plummeted. I was interested only in the *Festspielhaus*, and I wanted to take part in everything that happened there, even though my parents made it unmistakably clear to me that I could only sit in on Father's rehearsals for his new production of *Der Fliegende Holländer*. I quickly discovered various hiding places in the *Festspielhaus*: over the auditorium, in the orchestra pit, in the prompter's box, under the stage, in the lighting towers, in the flies or on one of the many roofs. From here I not only watched my uncle's rehearsals for his production of *Tannhäuser* in peace but I was also witness to the conflict between my father, his brother and Aunt Gertrud.

Wieland argued like a tyrant, and my father had to submit to him in front of everybody. Wieland's fits of rage, his cynicism and his damning remarks, condemning people who did not agree with his ideas, alienated me just as much as his scornful remarks about my father's productions. Father suffered terribly under this onslaught: he wanted to be his brother's equal as an artist, and although I admired Wieland's directorial work and his sets (in fact, they appealed to me more than my father's stagings), during this time I often felt sorry for my father.

My uncle's open disparagement of my father's productions led to the formation of two rival factions in the *Festspielhaus*, who worked and plotted against one another. The climate became more poisonous, and the rift which split the family grew wider. During performances the children were no longer allowed to sit together in the family box. Only the Wielands sat there now, while the

Wolfgangs sat on the left in the first row of the stalls. Even in official photographs the two families were no longer shown together.

My father's production of *Der Fliegende Holländer* was premiered in these sorry circumstances. Wieland and the press closely allied with him rated it as badly as they had *Lohengrin*. My father, believing that I was on his side, explained the story of the Flying Dutchman to me. It had a similar effect on me as the story of *Lohengrin* had two years before: afraid of the ghostly ship, I couldn't understand Senta's suicide at the end of the opera, and why he should be redeemed by this.

Before this, however, my sister and I were once again packed off to a children's home, this time to the Renée home in Wyk, on the island of Föhr in the North Sea, just off Schleswig Holstein. Leaving my parents and Bayreuth was easier for me than it had been in the past. I didn't feel at home anywhere, and this feeling didn't change after we had got back to Bayreuth. I became ill more frequently.

That Christmas we spent the holidays in the Hotel Wetterstein at Seefeld, in the Austrian Tyrol. It was here that, for the first time, I met people who were proud of being German. I couldn't understand this, however, any more that I could understand the phrase "We Germans are somebody again", which I began to hear with increasing frequency.

At around this time the adults would argue heatedly about German rearmament. When I asked my father what the Federal Army, the National People's Army and the armed forces of the GDR were, he answered: "The Federal Army are our brave soldiers here, who would protect us from the wicked soldiers of the People's Army, if they attacked us." I failed to grasp this explanation, but the People's Army of the Soviet zone did not worry me in particular. While the adults became increasingly anxious about the intensifying cold war, I saw it more as a cops-and-robbers story.

I was now seeing for the first time film news bulletins, newspapers and magazines concerning National Socialism, and I became preoccupied with my country's history. During one film presentation at school we were shown excerpts from contemporary propaganda material focusing on Nazi Germany: the Nuremberg Party congresses of the NSDAP and the World War unleashed by Hitler; goosestepping German soldiers; hysterical mass adulation of the Führer; the war crimes of the *Wehrmacht* – all of it set against Richard Wagner's music.

Shocked by the films, I told my father about the piles of corpses in the concentration camp of Büchenwald, accompanied by the music of my ancestor. "You are still too little to understand all that," he answered. But I refused to be satisfied with this, pestering him until he yelled at me to go away and play, or better still to finally get down to my homework, instead of asking about things I could never understand anyway. If I had persisted any further with my questions I would have been beaten, but I nevertheless resolved to get to the bottom of the matter.

In my next attempt at discovering the truth I interviewed my grandmother, who, when I asked her if there really had been concentration camps in the Third Reich, shot back: "That's all propaganda by the New York Jews who want to make us and the Germans look bad!"

In 1956 I saw Wieland's *Die Meistersinger Von Nürnberg*, which was to influence the course of my life. I had already seen a few illustrations of sets from various earlier productions of *Die Meistersinger*, but hadn't found them particularly interesting. When the opera was staged in the 1956 season, however, I was stunned: before me was a magical set with constantly-shifting lighting before a simple, bright, semicircular horizon, with just a few – but wonderful – changes between acts. (At that time I viewed Wieland as being an artistic genius, and I was determined to become a director. When I told my father of this he didn't say a word.) I was dismayed when aggressive booing broke out amongst the audience when the curtain came down after the last act. Even my grandmother found Wieland's production a besmirching of *Die Meistersinger*.

After these events a stultifying boredom descended on the provincial town of Bayreuth, and the end of the festival was hard to take. The autumn was to bring some diversions, however. At around this time I began to understand that the initials 'USA', which my grandmother quoted on Hitler's birthday on 20 April, meant '*unser seliger* Adolf [our blessed Adolf]', and I secretly began investigating the Wagner family history.

My parents had gone on holiday, as they usually did after the festival period, and so my sister and I were looked after by Gunda Lodes, who worked in the telephone exchange of the administrative centre of the festival. through her warm-hearted, loving kindness, Gunta become a substitute aunt for me, and it was because of her that my childhood in Bayreuth was not a complete nightmare. Gunda's father, the kindly Hans Lodes, had been the caretaker of the Bayreuth Festival for decades; 'Grandpa Lodes' guided the crowds of tourists through the *Festspielhaus* and explained the history of the festival and its connection with Richard Wagner. He provided me with my first snippets of knowledge about the history of my family. His wife, Kunigunde, was small, round and good natured, and like her husband she came from a Catholic farming family. What's more, 'Grandma Lodes' made the most wonderful *Bayreuther glees* (potato dumplings).

At weekends the couple's grandchildren, Werner and Helmut, turned up at the family home, and I was finally able to play with other children. Werner, who is six years older than I, became my best friend. I admired his technical skills, which I – a Wagner training to be an artist – totally lacked. His powers of imagination, demonstrated in the invention of a steady stream of new games in the garden and then later in the *Festspielhaus* as well, were limitless. Neighbouring children soon joined us, including Matthias Röntgen, the son of a painter, who lived in a wooden hut on the other side of the *Festspielhügel*, and Hubert Franz, the son of a forester from the adjoining plot of land.

Before my parents left on their holidays my father had strictly forbidden me to play in the *Festspielhaus*, but of course this was like a red rag to a bull, and I took it as a challenge to slip the master key to the *Festspielhaus* into my trouser pocket and begin my expeditions around the building. I opened all of the doors that had remained locked to me until then, suspecting momentous secrets lying within. Heart thumping, I entered the rooms over the old set-painting workshop, where I found a large plaster model of the *Festspielhaus*, paintings depicting scenes from *Der Ring Des*

Nibelungen, thick tomes on racial theory, festival guides from the years 1933 to 1944, and photographs of my grandmother, Uncle Wieland and my father with the Führer. I also found an enormous oil painting of Hitler with a menacing Alsatian dog, and countless handwritten letters stored in boxes, written partly in the old German script, which I had difficulty deciphering. Although these discoveries were lying around in dusty, wild confusion, or leaning abandoned against walls, I carefully and methodically picked up each one and examined them.

I found the plaster model particularly intriguing, but I was more concerned with who I could ask about the things I had discovered. I dared not turn to my father, because I was in forbidden territory. And besides, his previous reaction to my questions on the Nazi films had made it clear how loath he was to discuss the subject. Grandpa Lodes, on the other hand, seemed a suitable informant. I told him I had heard strange noises over the painting workshop, so that I wouldn't disclose my illicit visit, and he immediately whistled up his terrifying Alsatian, Bodo, and hurried with me to the painting workshop. I urged him to climb the stairs into the lumber room. He contemplated the little footprints on the dusty stairs suspiciously and although when we entered the room I pretended that I had never seen any of it before, he noted drily: "You've already been here." He wanted to know how I had got in, and I finally told him the whole story, swore I would never do it again and started interrogating him.

He answered my questions quite readily: "That's a plaster model of the *Festspielhaus*. After the Final Victory, the Führer wanted to have the old *Festspielhaus* roofed over and only used for very special occasions by very special people. Next to the old *Festspielhaus* he wanted to have another built exactly like the old one, to be used for performances."

"This Führer – was he here often?" I asked.

"The Führer loved Wagner and your family very much."

As Grandpa Lodes talked about him in such a friendly way, I asked him where the Führer was today.

"He's been dead a long time," answered Grandpa Lodes, firmly taking my hand to draw me out of the room. Silently, and with a serious expression, he locked the doors and then said: "I don't want to see you here again without your dad, otherwise you won't be able to come and see us any more." I promised Grandpa Lodes that I would keep my mouth shut, for the sake of Werner and Helmut, but I didn't promise that I wouldn't go into that mysterious room again.

After my parents returned, the family investigations ended, as did my carefree life with the Lodes family. I had a new teacher at school, Herr Popp, who had apparently set himself the task of bringing me up to scratch. He enjoyed coming up very close when talking to me: "Now, *Wagnerchen*, let's just hear what you've been learning." This sentence was the standard prelude to his interrogations, which always left me with nothing to say. With a malicious grin he would slowly curl the fingers of his right hand into a fist and strike the back of my head in short, rhythmic blows. "The Wagnerian musical skull sounds hollow yet again," he would say before pulling the hair over my right temple and, to the delight of my classmates, entering a six in his notebook. Another of his favourite pastimes was to recount his experiences as a soldier in the Second World War. "If we Germans had only had a bit more time the Final Victory would have been ensured, but the whole world was against us," he would moan.

After one of Popp's attacks I would have severe pains in my head. When I complained about his treatment at home my father called me a "crybaby", but he nonetheless sent my mother to talk to the teacher, and from then on he only reminded me once a week about my hollow Wagnerian musical skull.

During this time my father was away more often than usual for the festival, and with his production of *Tristan Und Isolde* in the summer of 1957 he was scarcely approachable at all. He no longer gave me any introductory information on the works he was directing, so I resorted instead to reading the contents of the programme. I understood little of the story, but was gripped by the music of *Tristan* as never before, and attended as many orchestral rehearsals and performances, under the baton of Wolfgang Sawallisch, that I could. To this day, Wolfgang Windgassen's and Birgit Nilsson's performances as the stricken couple remain unforgettable.

My grandmother had time only for my father's productions, and campaigned against Wieland's work. She constantly played my father off against my uncle, and so family tensions continued to escalate. I was not exposed to this unhappy atmosphere for long, though: my grades were bad yet again in that summer, and because I allegedly suffered from an weak heart (because of 'growth problems') I was sent off to the Schliersee to stay with an elderly couple called Zankl. I had no playmates there, but at least I was free of Popp.

In September I returned to the Graser school, and my new classmates welcomed me by chanting: "Wagner, loser, time waster!" Along with this humiliation I also found myself under increasing pressure to perform well, as I had to prepare myself for the forthcoming entrance examination for the *Humanistisches Gymnasium* [classical grammar school]. My grandfather, my uncle and my father had all attended this school, and I was constantly reminded of their example. Frau Moritz was one teacher there who appreciated my situation and encouraging me and providing me with a little relief. It also says much for Frau Moritz that she was obviously uneasy when we had to sing all three verses of the German national anthem. The first verse describes geographic borders that no longer existed for Germany after 1945, and proclaims: "Germany, Germany above all nations [*"Deutschland, Deutschland, über alles..."*]. Since 1952, only the last verse has been officially sanctioned in Germany.

My grandmother, Winifred, had returned to the Siegfried Wagner House in 1957, after the Americans had left. I visited her occasionally, usually finding her sitting at her desk in the anteroom to the dining room, on the ground floor. She would be chainsmoking her filterless North States cigarettes, either writing letters or gazing through the open window out to Wahnfried Park, keeping tabs on who came and went. During one of my visits I told her of Frau Moritz's reservations about the first verse of the national anthem, at which she instantly lost her temper, railing against the school where, apparently, they were now teaching children a profoundly distorted version of German history.

In July 1958 I found that I had passed the entrance exam for the

Humanistisches Gymnasium, although at first I couldn't quite believe it. This news lifted my spirits considerably, while I sat in on the rehearsals of Wieland's first production of *Lohengrin* at the *Festspielhügel*. Like his previous production of *Die Meistersinger*, my uncle's *Lohengrin* enthralled me, and I watched him at work whenever possible. When Father noticed my enthusiasm he forbade me to spend so much time in the *Festspielhaus*, but this had little effect on me. Instead, I would say I that was going to the cinema or swimming, and then creep into the *Festspielhaus* secretly. Wieland understood my situation but didn't comment on it. In fact, my father appeared once during a lighting rehearsal, after somehow discovering that I hadn't gone swimming, and angrily asked my uncle if he had seen me. Wieland had spied me moments before, on the lighting bridge but played dumb, and my father had scarcely disappeared in a fury when he winked at me with a grin and whispered: "The coast's clear."

This was not our only conspiracy. On one day I crept once again into Wahnfried Park, waited until Wieland left the villa, and then approached him, telling him how fantastic I thought his *Lohengrin* was. This praise from the other family camp surprised my uncle; he disappeared back into the villa, returning shortly with an envelope, which he pressed into my hand. I didn't dare open it in his presence, but when he had returned to his car I asked him for his autograph.

"But I'm your uncle," he replied, astonished.

"We can't ever talk to one another, so at least I'll have something from you," I explained.

When I got home I opened the envelope and found a twenty-mark note in it. I had hoped for a more personal present, but I was still pleased. I spent the money on my first record, a Louis Armstrong LP – "nigger music", as my grandmother would say.

After passing my exams I was looking forward to secondary school, but this optimism soon foundered. I fell ill, and was again visited by private tutors in Bayreuth and Berchtesgaden. I wasn't able to attend the *Gymnasium* until April 1959.

In the autumn of that year my father started preparations for his first production of *Der Ring Des Nibelungen*, which he planned to stage in the coming season. My mother had to devote herself primarily to this as well, and as usual her children got in the way. My father became more and more of a stranger to me, and the holidays we took together in Braunwald, in the Swiss Alps, were mainly so that our exhausted parents could recover. On our return from the winter holiday, Froh, our enormous schnauzer, died after a painful death, drawn out over months. He had been my companion for twelve years, and I loved him very much. Of course, Father had no sympathy.

As the 1960 festival approached, my sister and I were once again sent to Berchtesgaden, to the elegant Hotel Geiger. By this time I had come to view the festival solely as a threat to domestic harmony. A visit to the ruins of Hitler's *Berghof*, on the Obersalzberg left me feeling very oppressed, but when I told my father about it he just praised the architecture of Hitler's Alpine home.

The family was really suffering: Father was overstretched, and constantly pressured into competing with my uncle. It lay like a malevolent shadow over my parents' marriage, and I think that it was at that point that my childhood ended. I found the constant feuding of two camps sickening, and yet I was being pulled into these battles more and more. I tried to be loyal to my father, but his productions excited me far less than did those of Uncle Wieland.

In the summer of 1961 I openly opposed my father for the first time, protesting against his constant reprimanding of my mother. It ended in a beating for me and an almighty row between my parents. After the fight, Father threatened to send me to the strictest school in Germany, to finally make a man of me, little wimp that I was.

"Go on then, do it," I shot back defiantly.

A chauffeur promptly delivered me to the boarding school in Stein, near Traunstein. The drive was agony for me, as I was terribly worried about my mother. She was undergoing a crisis at the time, and constantly referred to the festival as being suicidal.

However, in spite of the tensions at home, life in the boarding school proved to be far from punishment. Because of my schooling in Bayreuth I found myself in the novel position of being ahead of my new classmates – indeed, one of the best in the class. So instead of swotting I indulged in everything I was not supposed to do: I smoked, visited girls at night, drank beer, annoyed the teachers and went swimming instead of attending class. The only thing I was worried about was having to go back to Bayreuth.

One day I was thrilled to learn that my cousin, Wummi, was also coming to the school. The everlasting family conflict proved incapable of weakening my affection for Wummi, much to the my father's disgruntlement. We had many things in common: he had also grown up practically parentless; he had also changed schools and tutors frequently; and he had also acquired the reputation of being stupid and lazy in Bayreuth. I hadn't seen him for a long time, and was keen to meet him again. When I met him, he said simply "Hello, Gottfriedla", and I immediately felt that sense of belonging.

At that time we were convinced that we would one day take over our quarrelling fathers' business, but we found this subject difficult to talk about, avoiding it wherever possible. However, I did confess to him how much I admired his father's work. Wummi was always generous to me, and treated me like a younger brother. These were great days, but they ended abruptly as soon as my father learned that Wummi was attending the same school as myself, when I was immediately brought back to Bayreuth. Even then, however, I continued to meet Wummi secretly.

One advantage of my sudden departure from the Stein school was that I was then able to attend Wieland's *Tannhäuser* rehearsals. There was a commotion in the *Festspielhaus* at this time: the beautiful young black singer Grace Bumbry was singing Venus, and Maurice Béjart created erotically provocative choreography for the bacchanale in the Venusberg scene in the first act. The Wagnerian old guard were horrified, declaring: "Thank God she's not singing Elisabeth. That's all we need, a black woman playing the part of a Wagner heroine in Bayreuth."

However, this wasn't the only reason for the uproar. Wieland had joined up with the 'left', although that summer the Ulbricht regime in the GDR had built a wall right through Berlin, to prevent the country from "haemorrhaging" with a mass exodus. The anti-Communist hysteria had also affected the Society Of Friends Of

Bayreuth – there was even talk of war.

Quite beside herself, my grandmother raged publicly: "How on earth could Wieland join up with those left-wing Jews Bloch and Schadewaldt, of all people? And then the Bumbry on top of everything else! Bayreuth is turning into a whorehouse."

My father said nothing. At that time I only had vague ideas of what was meant by the terms left (politically), Jew and Negro, but as a secret fan of Wieland I was angry at my grandmother's provocative comments and my father's silence.

After so much freedom in Stein, and after the thrill of visiting the *Festspielhügel*, returning to the Bayreuth *Gymnasium* became torture. When I became bedridden after suffering a burst appendix, my schoolmates accused me of skiving. After that I became ill frequently, and was once again the outsider in my class, particularly after Tyll Schönemann – my best friend at the time – moved to Munich. I grew to resent the bullying tactics adopted by my teachers, and refused to subscribe to the popularity of some. Once, just before Christmas, Herr Och – one of the most popular teachers – decided to tell us all about his experiences as a soldier in Russia. Sparing no details, he raved about the courage of the Nazi army. After I dared to criticise Herr Och, my other classmates later gave me a thorough beating.

Though instructed in school by a man who used Christmas as a time to glorify his bloody wartime service to the Nazis, I was fortunately also the student of a more righteous Christian man. In the spring of 1962, after a year's preparatory instruction, I was confirmed by Reverend Flotow. Flotow was witty and kind, and he opened my eyes to the splendours of the Bible as a history book and instilled in me an interest in ethics.

My interest in Christianity became yet another point of departure from my family's philosophy. My family hardly ever discussed religion outside the home, but when they did it was to talk about "stupid priests" and "the bloody Church". If pressed to say something positive about religion, my parents would mention Albert Schweitzer, and man who had had contacts with my grandfather Siegfried. However, not even Schweitzer was acceptable to my grandmother, whose antagonism towards

Christianity became increasingly overt. My father branded us "pious heathens" (in Goethe's sense of the phrase). Meanwhile, I was a religious child, always interested in philosophy, and was quickly frustrated by my parents' hypocritical religious posturing. In the end, I think they found religion in the cult of Richard Wagner.

In the summer of 1962 Wieland staged an epoch-making new production of *Tristan Und Isolde*. His set was strongly influenced by the English sculptor Henry Moore, with a lighting design that was clearer and more penetrating than ever before. This production illustrated just the extent of the artistic gulf which separated Wieland and Wolfgang, and my admiration for my uncle's work reached new heights. Unfortunately, my school career didn't enjoy the same lofty successes: in 1962 I had to repeat my fourth-grade year at the *Gymnasium*.

The festival in the summer of 1963 was devoted to the 150th birthday of Richard Wagner. The slogan was "A Life For The Theatre", and the composer was yet again presented unpolitically as a "European genius of the theatre", which was something of a nonsense because Wieland had already moved further to the left through his contacts with Ernst Bloch, provoking some particularly sarcastic comments during rehearsals. He continued to criticise the CDU and the CSU, although this did not prevent him paying court to the ultra-conservative Friends Of Bayreuth and accepting their financial contributions. The more Wieland played the armchair socialist the more conservative my father became. It was only logical, therefore, that my grandmother came to regard my father as the true heir of the Wagnerian legacy.

Wieland's second production of *Die Meistersinger Von Nuremberg* in 1963 included elements of Shakespearean theatre, comprising a basic set that was changed only slightly throughout the performance. Of course, this concept was similar to some of the anti-illusionist elements of the Brechtian stage, such as clearly visible scene changes and the use of mobile screens.

In 1960 the very young Anja Silja had made her debut in Bayreuth as Senta in *Der Fliegende Holländer*. For Wieland she embodied his ideal of the modern singer/actor. As he so wonderfully and provocatively put it, she signified the end of the "bourgeois singing cow", and it was no surprise that he cast her as Eva in *Die Meistersinger* – and promptly fell in love with her! I never found out if he divorced for just this reason, however, because he died suddenly in November 1966, at the age of 49. My father moralised heavily against Anja, who had loosened up the stodgy atmosphere of the Bayreuth Festival with her cheeky Berlin attitude.

We were sent away before the festival, as usual, but that autumn two major events happened in my life. Firstly, my sister, having finished secondary school, was sent to a young ladies' domestic science college, freeing me from her constant supervision, so I was then able to spend much of my time with the kink and cultured Grossmann family from Bayreuth, who, along with Gunda, had kept an eye on me for years. In my new-found freedom, when Father and Mother were on holiday I was able to hold parties on and over the *Festspielhaus* stage, which was empty outside the festival season. I waited for the weekends, when nobody was working in the administration building, and then, using Father's master key, I let my party guests in through the office area, up to a dizzying height above the flies, into a large room over the circle, which we had turned into a dancehall. From there Elvis Presley's 'Jailhouse Rock' boomed out so loudly that passersby alerted the police to the noise in the theatre (known colloquially as the 'Woogna Deooda'). We all hid when Grandpa Lodes turned up with the police, however, and as soon as the coast was clear we rocked on regardless.

At around this time I also became friends with Eckart Grebner and Reiner Heller. Together we kept an eye out for pretty girls and played at dares, one of which was to smear red paint over Arno Breker's bust of Richard Wagner, which had stood in the *Festspielpark* since 1955. I looked on with relish while the fire brigade hosed down the menacing monster. Needless to say, my school grades rapidly went downhill at this time.

Another incident that occurred in the autumn of 1963, and which was to have a lasting effect, occurred when my parents were on holiday, resting after the festival. I took the opportunity to explore a wooden shed next to the garage, where Father's BMW motorcycle and sidecar were housed. I found two cardboard boxes in the sidecar containing lots of round, aluminium cans of various sizes. They were so rusted that I couldn't open them with my bare hands, so I stashed them in my room, scraped off the rust and carefully prized them open with a screwdriver. In each there was a reel of film, and I examined one of the larger reels with a magnifying glass. What I discovered left me stunned. I saw my aunts, Uncle Wieland and my grandmother, together with Hitler, who was dressed in an elegant double-breasted suit, laughing as they strolled in Wahnfried Park. Happy Führer, happy Wagner children, happy Grandmother Winifred! There were also pictures of the Führer in the *Festspielhaus*. Everyone had their arms outstretched in a 'Heil Hitler' salute, glorying in Wagner's art and the Führer's power, a strutting display of members of the 'master race' – laughing comrades, prematurely celebrating the Final Victory. The message behind the film was evident: 'Uncle Wolf' and the Wagners belonged together.

And my father had been the cameraman throughout. From this point on, he, Wieland, and indeed the rest of the adult world, took on a sinister quality. I remembered the pictures of Büchenwald I had seen in cinema newsreels in 1956, and I knew then that I had to keep the films and prevent Father from hiding them again, or even destroying them. I hid them away in my wardrobe, covered the empty cans with dirt again and put them back in the two cardboard boxes in the sidecar. I decided not to tell my parents anything about my find, but resolved to question them about Hitler.

The first opportunity presented itself in Arosa, Switzerland, during the winter holidays in December of that year, whilst on a long walk with my parents and sister. I didn't want to put my father on the defensive, as that would have brought the conversation to an abrupt end, so instead I emphasised that I was interested more or less in the connection between my family and the Führer for purely historical reasons. I asked Father of the impression Hitler had made on him as a human being, and he made no secret of the fact that 'Uncle Wolf' had fascinated him, describing their encounters with restrained affection. He later proudly told me, on numerous occasions, of how the Führer had visited him in the Charité Hospital in Berlin, where the famous surgeon Ernst

Ferdinand Sauerbruch himself had treated Father after he had been wounded in the Polish campaign. "Your uncle was exempted from war service by Hitler – I alone had to serve the Fatherland," he said, and in enthusiastic detail he regaled me with tales of community service and military training, where apparently he developed a unique camaraderie with his fellow soldiers. He recounted how the only friend in his life, Emil, had been killed in a village by "crafty Polacks" as the "brave German army" had conquered Poland.

And Hitler, again and again! After the National Socialists' seizure of power, a Führer annex had been specially constructed on the Siegfried Wagner House, which housed the specially-built Führer fireplace. After a performance of *Götterdämmerung* in the *Festspielhaus*, my uncle and father accepted Hitler's invitation to a lengthy nighttime discussion at the Führer's fireplace on the future of German art in the spirit of Richard Wagner, as an expression of the renewal of the world through National Socialism. I had some difficulty in understanding my father's torrent of words, but didn't dare interrupt him in case he stopped talking.

He continued his story. "We were sitting round the fireplace, and Hitler sketched out his cultural visions of the future. 'Once we have rid the world of the Bolshevik-Jewish conspirators, then you, Wieland, will run the theatre of the West and you, Wolfgang, the theatre of the East.'" I asked Father whom these "Bolshevik-Jewish conspirators" were, but my interruption annoyed him. I was worried that he might stop talking, but instead he launched into a lengthy lecture on German history. It had all started with the "shameful Versailles treaty", which was then followed by mass unemployment in the chaotic Weimar Republic, caused by the incompetent Left and the "bloody liberals". And so he came to the "great achievements of Hitler up to 1939". I wanted to know about this in detail, and Father didn't let me down, answering: "Hitler cured unemployment and restored worldwide respect for the German economy. He freed our people from a moral crisis and united all decent forces. We Wagners have him to thank for the rescue of the Bayreuth Festival."

"But what about the Jews, Father?"

"There's a lot of talk about that," he replied, "and there are a lot of malicious lies told about Germans by left-wing intellectuals about how many, and so on. But that was the only real mistake Hitler made: if he had won over the Jews to his side we would have won the war. After the war, things wouldn't have become as bad as the Allies' propaganda machine makes out."

We continued walking, side by side and in silence, until Mother started talking about Christmas presents.

CHAPTER TWO

NEW DIRECTIONS

I met Maria Kröll, my first great love, after our return to Bayreuth in January 1964. She was possessed of a unique *joie de vivre*, combined with a mental alertness and femininity that I found fascinating, and she freed me from the isolation of my golden *Festspielhaus* cage. Because of her I drove regularly to Creussen, 13 kilometres south of Bayreuth, where she was living with her parents and her younger sister, Dorle, who was in my class. Her father, Professor Joachim Kröll, was extraordinarily gifted in many fields. He taught German, history and geography at the German *Gymnasium*, and his unconventional teaching methods and eccentric manner made him very popular with his pupils. Maria's mother, Ursula, was a kindly, intelligent and cultured woman.

With Maria's help I became more self-confident, and her parents – both active liberal socialists – were keen readers of books on every conceivable subject, and influenced my intellectual development considerably. I soon felt at home with these friendly, open people, and was roused from my provincial *Festspielhügel* sleep. Joachim Kröll, who was the first person to explain German Jewish history to me, also stimulated me to read Heinrich Böll, Günter Grass and other committed writers, and I devoured this reading matter hungrily.

After such influence I found my home life and festival business unbearable. My father couldn't fail to notice that I was becoming critical, and that my interest in German history and politics was growing, not least because I found myself continuing the discussions I'd had with the Krölls at home. For example, while I applauded the way in which Germany was split into two states, my father at that time regarded Franz Josef Strauss as the only decent politician, and reacted to my remarks with fury. The discussion on the GDR's right to exist ended like many others, with my father forbidding any further word on the subject, and cursing Joachim Kröll as a "dirty Leftie" who was having a bad influence on me. Furious, I stormed out of the dining room, slamming the door behind me. My father tried to catch me up on the stairs, but I was faster than him, and raced to my room, locking the door behind me. He hammered on the door, ordering me to open it, but I shouted back at him: "The only answer you've got is giving me a hiding!" I climbed down a rope ladder into the garden and sped off on my moped to Maria's house in Creussen, cigarette gripped furiously in my mouth.

My father couldn't come to terms with my new attitude. Unbeknownst to me, he visited Joachim Kröll and demanded that he ensured that the relationship between Maria and me was broken off, and that the Kröll family stopped influencing me. Maria later described the clash between the two fathers – apparently Joachim was not at all prepared to share my father's views on politics and relationships.

After this episode I threatened to leave for good if my father interfered in my life or ever beat me again. In fact I had already disappeared once before, in the previous year, after another unhappy love affair, and that occasion had become the subject of a scandal in Bayreuth. This time, however, my father thought up a different punishment: at the end of April 1965 I was one again taken to Stein, separated from Maria and her family.

My cousin Wummi had passed his *abitur* [A-levels] in Stein, and the new headmaster, Olf Ziegler, was the son of one of Granmother's friends, so I thought that the school would be a suitable place for me again. The pain of parting from the Krölls – and in particular from Maria – was enormous, and it was even more difficult to adapt to life with a lot of people in a small space.

Gradually, however, I made friends with some kids who, like me, had separated themselves from the main body of pupils, which comprised the arrogant children of 'good' and 'not so good' homes. The majority of the pupils came from 'economic miracle' families, whose parents had no time for them, were divorced, or knew that their spoiled offspring were bone idle, ungifted and probably would never have passed their *abitur* in a normal school. Two descendants of the Bismarck family behaved with particular arrogance, and the constant quarrelling with insufferable show-offs strengthened my urge to read left-wing literature. Henry Hohenemser, a fellow pupil, helped me to come to terms with my family's dark history, and drew my attention to forms of open and covert antisemitism. This was an important time for me, and I started reading the works of Ernst Bloch, Sigmund Freud, Theodor Adorno, Hannah Arendt, Max Horkheimer and Bruno Bettelheim.

In the 1965 summer holidays I sat in on rehearsals of Wieland's new *Ring*. Although the depiction of the mushroom cloud in the finale of *Götterdämmerung* was very effective, its style contradicted that of the set, which was orientated towards the world of Henry Moore, and Richard Wagner's music certainly doesn't end in nothingness.

The contrast between the sponsors, the Bayreuth Society Of Friends, and guests such as Ernst Bloch and the distinguished literary historian Hans Mayer was particularly telling, and even my uncle's halo started to fade. Wieland hardly knew where to draw the line in his relationships with his colleagues – during a rehearsal, he once clouted the electrician of the *Festspielhaus*, his former playmate, around the head in front of the rest of the staff because he had allegedly failed to carry out Wieland's imperious demands. This, coupled with other events, convinced me that Wieland hadn't yet come to terms with his own past, tacking back and forth between Krupp and Siemens on the one hand and Bloch and Mayer on the other. I watched him become more and more opportunistic, leaning to the Left because he vaguely realised that the balance of power in the culture business was heading in that direction.

I returned to the boarding school in Stein after the summer vacation and immersed myself in the early writings of Karl Marx, in particular his essay 'On The Jewish Question'. Later, when I brought up my reading matter in a discussion with my father, he responded with his usual monologue, starting off with the 1935 race laws, for which he believed the Jews had themselves to blame, as they were "the worst racists in history". I countered this by arguing that the Nuremberg race laws couldn't be confused with orthodox Jewish traditions, and he angrily retorted that Jews had themselves contributed to the Nuremberg race laws: "Marx himself was an antisemite, and wanted to emancipate society from Judaism." "But it wasn't exactly the Final Solution," I countered, which effectively ended the discussion.

In the 1966 local elections in Bayreuth, when the neo-Nazis won three of the 42 seats on the city council, my grandmother's hopes for a final victory were re-awakened. Aunt Friedelind was furious when my grandmother slowly started to emerge again as First Lady, entertaining political contacts such as Edda Göring, Ilse Hess, NPD chairman Adolf von Thadden, Gerdy Troost (wife of Nazi architect and Hitler's friend Paul Ludwig Troost), British fascist leader Oswald Mosley, Nazi film director Karl Ritter (who was related to the Wagners), and Hans Severus Ziegler, who was a racist author and former Senator For Culture under the Reich. At her receptions, her guests could finally talk openly about the Führer, after having spent years referring to him as 'USA'. In an interview in a December 1967 issue of *Spiegel*, Aunt Friedelind railed against the return of "fascist demons".

In July 1966, shortly before the festival season, Wieland was admitted to the hospital in Kulmbach and was later transferred to the University Clinic in Munich. My father didn't inform me of my uncle's state of health, but like others I suspected that things were serious. The situation between the Wieland and the Wolfgang camps was now open warfare: Father believed that my uncle's hour had come, and the first cracks were appearing in the Wieland camp. Some toyed with the idea of changing sides, and my father briefly encountered some sycophancy. Quite unexpectedly, he was now the sole director of the festival – for that year, at least.

Even I was hailed with friendly words from people who until then had ignored me. The Wolfgangs were 'in' and the Wielands were 'out' – and I found the new situation just as repugnant as the previous one. Bayreuth, the *Festspielhügel*, the family – the entire situation sickened me. I toyed with the idea of leaving Germany, but how? I had no money and no profession.

On 17 October, while watching the film *The Spy Who Came In From The Cold*, I was told that my uncle was dying. I hitchhiked to Munich and met my father, who embraced me for the first and last time in his life. Not a word was spoken. Mother tearfully told me of Wieland's death.

I shall never forget the funeral ceremony, held in the *Festspielhaus* on 21 October 1966, which was a demonstration of superlative hypocrisy: Grandmother Winifred cried for her poor Wolfgang – "Wolf" – who would now have to bear the responsibility for the Bayreuth Festival all on his own, while the rest of high society professed its love for my uncle. The only bright spot was Ernst Bloch's address.

Flashlights popped and cameras whirred as the long procession moved off to the cemetery, and the relations began vying for positions of power almost immediately – and my father, grandmother and sister Eva held the best cards.

The family spent the following winter holidays together in Arosa, and the discussion turned to a letter, written by Günter Grass, warning against the formation of a grand coalition ("that bad marriage") in Bonn, "which will see the youth of our country split to either the Left or Right". My father was horrified by my move to the Left, and attributed it (not without reason, as it happened) to my reading matter – Bertrand Russell, Erich Fromm and Karl Jaspers. He complained bitterly about my ungratefulness for all of the sacrifices he had made for my education. Were it not for my mother, I would have packed my bags and left – it was Christmas, after all.

I didn't tell him about my grandmother's reaction when I asked her to give me Bloch's book *The Principle Of Hope* as a Christmas present. She had replied: "I'm not giving you any of that left-wing Jewish trash." I had answered that, in that case, she could strike me off her Christmas list: her Nazi attitudes were incompatible with my principles. It was a comment that earned me a number of paybacks.

CHAPTER THREE

"THE WILL TO POWER" I

In 1967 my father began to change beyond recognition. The festival had always been the central focus of family life, but for him it now became an obsession. He began by severing relations with the Wieland branch of the family, except for those who vowed allegiance to him. The productions staged by the Wieland camp were from now on distorted, and my father made strenuous efforts to destroy his brother's reputation. Realising that the pressure of having sole responsibility for the festival and the stress of the final battle over the *Festspielhügel* was threatening to damage our relationship even further, he allowed me to attend the school in Stein as a day pupil.

It was during this time that I first met Dietrich Hahn, a man with an unusual literary gift who is interested in contemporary art, painting, and who at that time had wanted to be an actor. A grandson of the famous radiochemist and Nobel prize-winner Otto Hahn, he had already had a tragic childhood, losing both parents in a traffic accident, after which he was fostered by the Kalkhoff-Roses, a family of industrialists who supported Helmut Kohl. He felt ill at ease in their home, and vacations were always something of a problem for him, so sometimes I invited him to Bayreuth. He had worked in the theatre for only a short time, but like me he was disgusted by its superficiality and hierarchy. A journalist specialising in the history of science, he began working through the considerable body of work his grandfather had left behind after his death, hoping to make these universally available. What drew us together was a common interest in humanitarian activities and German-Jewish history. Neither of us look back on our time at the boarding school in Stein with any fondness.

It was while we were both day pupils there that a whole new existence was available to me. I followed up on reading forbidden matter by disrupting NPD meetings in Upper Bavaria with my friends Norbert and Henry. Norbert and I carefully planned our escape routes before turning up at neo-Nazi meetings disguised as Charlie Chaplin's Great Dictator. We would walk silently through the beerhalls, goading the mob, and then hare off along our escape routes and leap into Henry's ancient VW Beetle, which we always left with the engine running. At that time I could no longer integrate myself in the school, despite a regime that was almost liberal by Bavarian standards, and so I left. In June, the chorus master of the Bayreuth Festival, Wilhelm Pitz, interceded on my behalf with Charles Spencer, the chairman of the renowned New Philharmonic Chorus in London, who offered me a place there. It was a stay which was to have a profound influence on the direction of my life.

The Spencer family welcomed me warmly, and I took full advantage of the concerts and opera that were staged in that season, also attending a language school to improve my English. I was thrilled to be living right near The Beatles' studio. Charles Spencer, a successful choir manager and businessman, was a keen music lover and a discerning Wagnerian, and we often conversed with each other in nothing but Wagner quotations.

However, this happy time was abruptly broken off by a political event of global importance: the six-day war between Israel and the Arab countries in June 1967. I was suddenly confronted by Jewish history more shockingly than ever before, and every night we sat anxiously in front of the television, watching the conflict unfolding. Day and night we had passionately discussed the events, and during this time I discovered that Charles' parents had been Viennese Jews. In 1938, after the *Anschluss* of Austria to Hitler's Germany, they fell victim to the Nazi terror. Only Charles and his sister escaped. Charles' daughter Diana told me further shocking details while we pored over family photos. I felt very uncomfortable: there was I, a child of criminals, living like a son in a family that had suffered terribly under Nazi barbarism. Charles noticed my embarrassment and shame, and I confessed to how oppressive I found the Bayreuth legacy, with its latent antisemitism, and told him about my grandmother's fanatical bigotry. He replied: "Only after the generations of the perpetrators has died will there be any chance of a new beginning between Jews and Germans. However, this shouldn't prevent the possibility of friendships between individual Germans and Jews. Don't feel guilty; learn from your family's mistakes." This wise advice from my 'elective relation' was to be my motto for life.

Charles was an powerful influence on me. Despite suffering great tragedy, he was quite without enmity and hatred, and with quiet modesty he helped people in need as he went about his daily life. During my stay I watched a television programme which had contributions from many countries, including a report from Germany on the 1967 festival, which had opened with my father's new staging of *Lohengrin*. I felt remote from Bayreuth and Wagner, and was relieved when, after the usual boring excerpts from the Bayreuth stage, this report was followed by a song by The Beatles. While talking with my mother on the phone, I told her that I didn't intend to return to Germany for some time, and she said that she understood. I decided to live in France for a while, and was supported by Charles.

Before that, however, I paid a brief visit to Bayreuth. I noted with amazement how my father was acting as the man holding the reins, and my sister, who had just finished training as a kindergarten teacher, was playing the matriarch. My father only tolerated yes men around him, and any form of criticism – particularly that of his production of *Lohengrin* – angered him. It was tacitly understood that Wieland's epoch-making production of the opera in 1958 was the yardstick against which all future productions were to be measured. I refrained from voicing my opinion on the new *Festspielhügel* dictatorship for fear of damaging relations with him even further. While Grandmother Winifred and the chorus of old right-wing Wagnerians rejoiced at the beginning of a new era, I was glad when I could finally leave for Paris.

I was overcome by Paris just as much as I had been by London. I changed from an Englishman into a Frenchman overnight. I tried to deny my German roots, but my accent always gave me away, of which I was often reminded with a certain arrogance. I spent much of my time there at the Sorbonne and at the Alliance Française on language courses, although I didn't actually learn much there as I spoke with my fellow students mostly in English. I often went walking from my home in the sixth *arrondissement*, near the Jardin du Luxembourg, visiting museums during the day and the lively and disreputable Les Halles at night. My Aunt Blandine de Prévaux, a great-granddaughter of Franz Liszt, took touching care of her "*cousin allemand*". She lived in an elegant apartment on the Seine, with portraits of her great-grandfather – who became Richard Wagner's father-in-law – hanging on the walls. I knew hardly anything about the Hungarian composer, piano virtuoso and champion of Wagner's music; my father rated him just as little as Uncle Wieland.

Aunt Blandine told me, without reproach, that the Nazis had murdered her husband, who had been a resistance fighter. After this, our talks became more open, and we overcame the generation gap that stretched between the barely 20-year-old nephew and the 73-year-old aunt. I owe her much – not only did she introduce me to Liszt's work and biography, but she also inspired me to learn something of French painting and literature. She mentioned her cousin Winifred only in passing, but subtly hinted at her lack of education.

In the middle of July, Blandine's daughter, Daniela, invited me to her chateau in the Normandy town of Lessey. While I was there I got to know her daughter, a girl of my age also called Blandine, whose open opposition to her parents' world fascinated me. After a brief introduction, we recognised at once that we essentially held similar views, and on the few points we didn't agree we found the difference stimulating. Cousin Blandine told me a lot about her contact with the film director Jean-Luc Godard – *À Bout De Souffle* – and of the radical democratic circles in which she moved. We spent entire nights discussing how our depraved world order could be changed. She argued passionately, fought social injustice, was courageous and formulated her socio-political ideas in an admirably creative yet concrete way. This close relationship, which is purely intellectual and still continues to this day, is only peripherally concerned with our mutual connections with Wagner and Liszt. How musty the Wagner cult on the *Festspielhügel* seemed compared with all this! Nevertheless, as school beckoned, I once again found myself in its grip. Recognising my father's insecurity, I strove to avoid conflict with him. He was still far from comfortable with his solo role as festival director, and was often severely criticised by the media.

In the autumn of 1967 I had to repeat twelfth grade because of my long absence; I had reached the point where I wanted to get school over as quickly and as painlessly as possible, and I assured the headmaster at Stein that I would keep up an acceptable standard of achievement if in exchange he agreed to allow me to organise my classtime "more freely". This meant that was able to visit Prague and Budapest with Henry Hohenemser, where we sent postcards to the teachers whose lessons we were missing. These excursions weren't just tourist trips, however; when we crossed the heavily-guarded border between East and West we felt the breath of world politics. The Vietnam war and the student unrest in West Berlin and Paris preoccupied our thoughts, dominating conversation. Back at home I defended the students' positions, to the horror of not only my father but also my sister, who was looking for her niche in the establishment.

My father's production of *Die Meistersinger Von Nürnberg* was premiered in the hot political summer of 1968, but after Wieland's productions of 1956 and 1963 I found my father's interpretation unbearably conventional. My grandmother and the majority of the mostly uncultured bourgeois sponsors were thrilled that the opera was finally being staged again as it had been in the good old times. I refrained from commenting on my father's artistic achievement, but reacted heatedly to any glorification of the Nazi past, after which my grandmother introduced me to her "terribly decent friends" with the phrase: "This is Gottfried, the friend of Bolsheviks and Jews", and then give a loud and manly laugh.

A police contingent arrived before the opening of the festival, armed as if they expected terrorists to blow up the *Festspielhaus* and its audience. In fact, it was because a few harmless students chose to protest against the West German industrialists among the festival guests. When I saw the police using violence against the protesters, I swore at them, calling them "pigs", and it was only the fact that I was the son of the boss that prevented my arrest.

After the premiere there was the usual reception in the Neues Schloss, and I discovered that demonstrators had gathered there as well. Although I wasn't welcome at the reception, I sat down at Willy Brandt's table. At that time I considered the SPD Foreign Minister and Vice

Chancellor of the grand coalition in Bonn to be the only credible German politician. In an effort to boost their careers, Bayreuth SPD bigwigs fawned over their chairman and grew nervous when some members of the ballet openly sympathised with the protesting students. They became even more alarmed when the dancers started asking Brandt searching questions on contemporary world politics, on Vietnam and Rudi Dutschke, the leader of the Socialist German Student Federations (SDS). Brandt, however, remained unflappable, inviting the protesters to his table and debating with them, to the horror of the Bayreuth establishment and the guests, including the sponsors, who – like my grandmother – privately referred to the head of the SPD as a 'socialist pig' or called him 'Willy Weinbrand' [Willy Brandy]. My father voiced no opinion on this, and I took his silence as acquiescence.

Although I didn't want to go to Arosa for the Christmas holidays with the rest of the family, I acceded for my mother's sake, because she missed me when I was away at school, which was most of the time. My father complained bitterly about what he viewed to be my communist worldview; he branded my political opinions infantile, and continued to remind me of the great sacrifices he had made in his youth, both during and after the war, and how he had fought to build up the festival. He complained that he had invested heavily into my education, and now had to endure his own son demonstrating as a "parlour pink" against the very people who financed the Bayreuth Festival, and consequently his own life.

My answer was heartfelt and uncontrolled: "You and your bloody ideals from the past! I'm talking here about the criminal war in Vietnam. It's about time you finally took part in a demonstration instead of serving as supplier of luxuries to an international inhuman bourgeoisie."

At the beginning of 1969 I finally understood that the *abitur* was my key to freedom, and I immersed myself in my studies. I was particularly interested in German-Jewish authors of the Weimar Republic, and so, to the consternation of my German teacher, Herr Grütter, I chose Arnold Zweig's novel *Der Streit Um Den Sergeanten Grischa* [The Conflict Concerning Sergeant Grischa] as the subject for an essay. With the Vietnam war in full swing at that time, what interested me in the book was the antiwar theme and the way in which the bourgeois capitalist society was revealed as being the cause of the war.

In a 1930 edition of *Weltbühne*, Zweig wrote about his novel: "How, I ask, does one refute a system, a social order and a war, which is difficult to conceive as not being connected with it? By letting off steam with passionate counter-actions and producing caricatures? In my opinion one refutes a system by showing what its level best might perpetrate, how it forces the average decent person to act indecently...We don't want to expose villains like our friend Schiller, but systems."[3] I told first my grandmother and then my father of my decision to study Zweig, just to provoke them. Grandmother was indignant: "Left-wing Jews – how can you do this to us?" Father's reaction was a predictable, eloquent silence.

At around this time, I heard talk at family meetings of 'foundation statutes' at the *Festspielhaus*. When I asked about this, Father assured me that this was all in my own present and future interests. He mentioned one article of these statutes that set down the regulations for my succession, if I could provide evidence of the appropriate qualifications. This worried me, especially as I was wondering how I could pursue my career once I had completed my *abitur* and left secondary school – I wanted to work in the theatre as assistant director. My father, however, had quite different plans for me. He wanted me to study law so that one day I could become the festival's manager.

Only my mother came to my graduation ceremony in Stein; my father claimed he couldn't possibly leave the *Festspielhügel*. On my return to Bayreuth I found that much had changed. The troop of yes men that surrounded my father had grown even larger. Their drooling servility disgusted even me, the son of the boss; opportunism ruled, and most of this crowd of sycophants kept sharp eyes on changes in the political and cultural climate.

The 1968 revolts had broken down many outmoded structures, and the socialist-liberal coalition, headed by Willy Brandt, was just around the corner. This was before the coalition courageously struck up an accord with our Eastern neighbours, but it was one of the many clear signals that the mood of the country was shifting. In the cultural world, too, the ideological spectrum was gradually shifting to the Left. If you didn't want to find yourself an outsider, you had to change your ideas. In particular, the head of the festival's press department, Herbert Barth, tried adroitly and cautiously to convince my father that a moderate move to the left was now necessary.

My father wasn't ready, however. In 1969 he allocated the first post-Wieland production outside the family to August Everding, who was now general intendant of Munich's theatres. Compared with Wieland's production, however, Everding's staging of *Der Fliegende Holländer* was a depressing continuation of a stretch of prosaic premieres – only the eager gossip was new. To my surprise, this monotonous opera aroused great enthusiasm among most of the festival sponsors and Wagner societies.

Meanwhile, Grandmother had lost what little tact she had. The American conductor Lorin Maazel had been responsible for the musical direction of Wieland's 1968 and 1969 stagings of the *Ring*, and was booked for the next production, staged by my father, in 1970. At one of her receptions, Winifred declared to the amusement of her guests: "Although Maazel is a Jew he does seem to be quite gifted, so in spite of everything Wolf will engage him again next year." I was sitting next to Lorin Maazel and his wife as she said this and almost died of shame. Maazel appeared not to have heard her remark, or perhaps didn't want to hear it. In 1970 he cancelled because of illness.

The official press reports of the 1970 season were manipulated, but even then there was substantial criticism. The media scene – in particular the arts pages – had gone too far to the Left for the Bayreuth sclerosis to be publicly applauded outside the faithful Wagner community – the world was now talking a different language. Father was gradually forced to realise this too; ultimately he had to secure the festival and his own existence financially.

In the autumn of 1969 I yielded to pressure from my father and started studying Law at the University of Munich. While I was there, however, I attended lectures in the humanities, which interested me greatly. In the October holidays I visited my parents in Bayreuth. At that time they were reading Albert Speer's *Memoirs*. Speer had been Hitler's architect, and together with the Führer he had designed bombastic buildings which were to be constructed after the Final Victory. During the war, Hitler had appointed him Head of War Production, and it was in this capacity that Speer saw to it, among other things, that Nazi Germany was able to prolong the war and therefore the machinery of terror. At the war crimes trials at Nuremberg he was sentenced to 20 years' imprisonment, which he served in Berlin Spandau, using the time to write his account of his actions before dying in 1981.

Father quite openly expressed his sympathy for Speer, and repeatedly voiced his admiration for Hitler, along with others who had once been big in Nazi circles. This provoked another spate of quarrelling between us which continued throughout the winter holidays in Arosa. As always, when we were not of the same opinion, I was told that I was too immature to understand the tragic and martyred history of Germany. The atmosphere deteriorated even further when I applauded the appointment of Willy Brandt as Federal Chancellor in Bonn. My father found this unbearable, and consequently suspected left-wing conspiracies everywhere.

As it was, Father was in *Götterdämmerung* mood. The reviews of his 1970 production of the *Ring*, discussions on the future of the festival and the projected foundation had all worn him down. I advised him to just drop the damn festival and finally carve out a decent life for himself, without his band of toadies, and without having to play the entertainer of German high society. Needless to say, this didn't improve the atmosphere.

My sister found these discussions pointless. To safeguard her future in Bayreuth she started to become friendly with Everding, and supported by her "Grandma" Winifred she soon became the darling of influential sponsors and industrialists alike. She was of the same mind as Father, and integrated herself fully in the festival business, regarding everything I suggested as worthless. From time to time she was allowed to play directorial assistant to Everding and Otto Schenk, and thus discovered that the international opera business was destined to be her career, and the intendant's seat in Bayreuth her future. Until 1975, anyone who didn't stay close to her had a difficult or short life on the *Festspielhügel*. The maxim advocated by Wieland – "after Cosima and Winifred, never again a female dictatorship" – no longer applied.

Father and Eva found my way of life quite unreasonable: I was a left-wing idealist, absorbed with contemporary philosophy, psychology and politics – in their view, totally ethereal pursuits which were a complete waste of time. Eva shared our grandmother's opinion that there was no place on the *Festspielhügel* for Marxist crackpots like me (a label I never did quite lose). Even at that time she knew that it would earn her the admiration of the Bayreuth Society Of Friends.

My father's 1970 production of the *Ring*, which was only a technical improvement on his previous cycles, contributed nothing new and relied solely on previous productions. Men at Bayreuth who opposed my father were able to manipulate the media adroitly and show how unreceptive he was to criticism of any kind. The only people whom my father still tolerated on the *Festspielhügel* were those who submitted to his authoritarian rule, a leadership he presented to the outside world as liberal. Anyone who praised the artist Wolfgang Wagner was rewarded with privileges.

But the real masterstroke of Bayreuth power politics cam in the discovery of a "left-wing" Wagner, one that the cultural media would embrace, just in time for the festival's centenary season. I noticed with some unease that the marketing of the 1976 centenary celebrations in Bayreuth had a left-wing image grafted onto it. The architects of this were press department head Herbert Barth; writer and Wagner devotee Martin Gregor-Dellin, who, along with Dietrich Mack, had been appointed editor of the Cosima Wagner diaries; Egon Voss, who later edited the new, complete edition of the critical book *Richard Wagner*; Dorothea Glatt-Behr; and later Oswald Georg Bauer, who is today the general secretary of the Bavarian Academy of Fine Arts.

A typical example of this shift to the left came in the form of the essay 'The Tragedy Of Power', a miscellany discussing Father's and Dietrich Mack's interpretation of the *Ring* in the 1970 festival programme for *Das Rheingold*. There, among other things, I read to my amazement:

"Does this mean afterwards [at the end of the *Götterdämmerung*] an apotheosis, a salvation of the world, a certainty of salvation? Or does it mean an apocalypse, a total annihilation an optimistic tragedy or total tragedy [*Pantragismus*]? ...[It is rather] not a handing on of the legacy, not a continuous transition from one generation to the next, but a radical break, a *tabula rasa*, a smoking ruin. So it is the apocalypse? Yes, but as example, not as an end in itself, for two things have been added. People who...have been demagogically abused with alcohol and drugs to become a dull and stupid mass experience this inferno. They fall prey to lamentation and horror [*sic*]. Enlightenment must be brutal; the world must burn from one end to the other. One funeral pyre alone is not enough to achieve a cathartic effect. Knowledge of this terrible end must be attested to and the realisation handed on, so that perhaps a way can be found out of this void."[4]

No trace of any of these atrocities was to be seen on the stage, however. It was only later that I understood what Father meant by the break between generations: he had unconsciously woven his own family problems into his directorial interpretation.

Under these circumstances I had no intention of becoming Father's assistant, especially as Eva was making it more and more clear that my presence on the *Festspielhügel* was nothing more than a nuisance. In the autumn of 1970 I moved to Mainz to escape the tension, and it was there that I finally began studying what interested me the most: musicology, psychology and German literature. Father disapproved of my new studies, and I could only placate him by promising not to give up my law studies completely. He asked the musicologist Professor Gernot Gruber to keep a discreet eye on me, and tried to find out from him whether I even had the prerequisites for this study. Gruber told me of my father's reservations, and my relationship with my father was jeopardised once again.

In Mainz, along with my other studies I also took piano lessons. In the summer semester of 1971 I studied piano, counterpoint and harmony, first in Graz, in Austria, and then in the Bayreuth *Festspielhaus* under Maximilian Kojetinsky. I studied diligently and with determination, astounding my father, who didn't believe that I could apply myself with such dedication.

The rumour mill had it that I would soon be taken on board in the festival business. Eva vehemently denied this, and rather defiantly I declared that, on the basis of my progress with Kojetinsky, I would continue studying musicology. Gernot Gruber supported me in this, and my father finally agreed to allowing me to give up my loathsome law studies.

In the summer of 1971 I learned from Mother that one of Wieland's closest collaborators, Gerhard Helwig, had been sacked. On 7 August 1971, Helwig handed over all of his documentation from the Wieland period to my father, but Father voiced doubts on the completeness of these documents. It was events such as these that aroused in me interest in my family's history, and at the same time engendered a mistrust of the official methods in which family documents were dealt.

In the winter semester of 1971-2, I continued my studies in Erlangen and started looking for openings as an assistant director. The university there disappointed me; I found the music course too conservative, especially as some professors were so open about their political affiliations, and both students and faculty alike treated me like a museum piece that might prove useful for making a few contacts. Also, the psychology lectures dealt solely with formal analyses. I felt equally uncomfortable in the Theatre Studies department. Although I could get along with the heads of the department, I found many of the students mired in an an outdated ideology, the tail end of the 1968 generation. Anyone not as 'progressively Marxist' as they were was quickly branded a reactionary, and because at that time I was fascinated with Bertolt Brecht, and was attending a course on his theatre work, I was initially ranked among these so-called progressive forces. When the student guardians of pure socialism found out who I was, however, they couldn't believe my fascination with Brecht – how could the reactionary Wagner be compatible with the progressive Brecht? So again I was an outsider. At it happened, I regarded Erlangen merely as a stopgap, a place to obtain the necessary qualifications in order to continue my life elsewhere.

The urge to perform practical theatre work continued to grow, and in the autumn of 1971 I contacted Hans Peter Lehmann, chief director of the Nuremberg Opera House. Lehmann had been one of Wieland's assistant directors, and my father had appointed him chief director in order to preserve some of my uncle's extant productions for the Bayreuth programme. However, the poor man was torn: on one hand he was very affectionately attached to the legacy left by Wieland, while on the other he followed my father, who was in favour of modifying Wieland's works, such as using brighter lighting. Either way, it was certainly in Lehmann's best interests to foster the connection with Bayreuth.

At that time, I believed that Lehmann was interested in my professional development as an opera director. At first everything went according to plan, and in February 1972, in Wuppertal, I was finally able to begin my first job with Lehmann as assistant director on his production of *Tannhäuser*. I threw myself into the work enthusiastically, keeping the prompt book, looking after rehearsals with the second cast, organising rehearsals, making arrangements with soloists, chorus, orchestra, technicians and administration and the media. I realised how difficult it must have been for Lehmann to have been Wieland Wagner's assistant, particularly after his death, when the shadow of my uncle's great example lay over any production of Wagner's music. After the premiere, Lehmann attested in writing that I had done good work, but despite this I didn't get any further work from him, even when I was in difficulties.

Erlangen and Bayreuth are quite close, and I was now occasionally able to visit my parents at weekends. For the staging of *Tannhäuser* at the 1972 festival, my father had engaged the opera director Götz Friedrich, who had been Walter Felsenstein's assistant at the Komische Oper in East Berlin and had earned an excellent reputation. There were therefore no grounds for argument, as far as content was concerned. I had hoped that Everding's 1969 production of *Der Fliegende Holländer* had been a one-off mistake, and that my father would give trying to direct himself. I urged instead to attract distinguished people from other opera houses to Bayreuth, to no avail.

The uneasy truce between my father and me lasted only a short time, ending when the talk turned to Willy Brandt's *Ostpolitik*. I didn't see any alternative to this, whereas my father described the policy of détente as a selling-out of German interests.

I also visited my grandmother during these weekends, mainly to learn more about the time she spent with the Führer. Although she was aware of my 'radical left' attitude, most of the time she answered my questions quite frankly, describing Hitler's wonderful, bright, hypnotic eyes, his gentleness, his good manners, his charming demeanour, his love for Father and Wieland, his plans for the boys in the future of a "better Germany", his profound knowledge of Wagner's works, and his love of nature and of mankind.

At this point I interrupted her, asking her what about love of the Jews? Surely they were part of mankind? In much the same manner as Father, she replied: "You still don't know the Jews. Just wait – one day you'll understand, and Hitler will be seen differently in history."

When these discussions first took place, I made the mistake of reacting obviously to her monstrous statements. "How can you say things like that?" I would ask. "Six million Jews don't seem to be enough for you to stop kidding yourself." But she constantly defended herself with the same sentence: "That's just lies and slander from American Jews!"

At the age of 25, what I had more or less uncritically accepted as a naive nine-year-old boy I now wanted to know in detail. My grandmother's antisemitism was shockingly brutal. I asked her about the fate of Jewish singers who had performed in Bayreuth before the Nazi takeover and later had to emigrate or were murdered in concentration camps, people such as Henriette Gottlieb, Ottilie Metzger-Lattermann, Margarethe Matzenauer, Hermann Weil, Alexander Kipnis, Eva Liebenberg, Friedrich Schorr and Emanuel List. When she found herself caught out, she became particularly aggressive: "You can't understand that!" she screamed. "That wasn't Hitler at all, it was Schleicher and the other criminals who betrayed National Socialism. I always tried to help the Jews who sang in Bayreuth!"

"So you and the family did know about Auschwitz!" I countered.

This effectively ended the discussion. She even employed a blatant distortion of historical truth in order to maintain her view of history: General Kurt von Schleicher had been murdered by the Nazis in 1934, and so couldn't have been involved with the Holocaust – but, of course, my grandmother meant Julius Streicher, the founder of the inflammatory antisemitic paper *Der Stürmer*.

No longer satisfied with this I changed my tactics, and calmly acted as though I were an historian with no personal involvement. It seemed to work: Grandmother answered my questions, and more importantly instructed her confidante, the militant antisemite Gertrud Strobel, to provide me with historical material without my father's knowledge. Gertrud Strobel, who failed to see through my intentions, now regarded me as the only thoroughly decent Wagner and provided me with a wealth of documentation, including all copies of the *Bayreuther Blätter*, festival guides and other documents published between 1850 to 1944. I was particularly fascinated by the correspondence between Hitler, my grandmother, Wieland and Father. The more I read, the more horrified I became: I could never have suspected the scale of my family's involvement with the Nazi tyranny.

CHAPTER FOUR

THE ANTISEMITISM OF THE WAGNER FAMILY (1850-1945)

In 1859 Richard Wagner published an antisemitic pamphlet entitled 'The Jews In Music'. Predominantly ideological, in this piece he expounded on his pathological idea of the Jews as the enemy. This is the keystone of my great-grandfather's future political and artistic concept, which lies at the heart of the idea of the festival and its realisation in Bayreuth. In order to defame the imaginary Jewish enemy and develop this concept, Wagner resorts to terms of simple abuse:

"The Jew is repulsive...he rules and will continue to rule as long as money remains the power before which all deeds and actions must pale into insignificance... In ordinary life, the Jew – who, as we know, has a God unto himself – strikes us first and foremost by his outward appearance, which, regardless of the European nationality to which he belongs, has something about it which is foreign to that nationality and which we find insuperably unpleasant... The Jew, incapable in himself of communicating artistically with us by means of his outward appearance or language, and least of all through his singing, has nonetheless come to dominate public taste in the most widely disseminated of modern artistic genres: music...The Jew has never had an art of his own, and therefore never led a life that was capable of sustaining art...we are bound to describe the period of Judaism in modern music as one of total uncreativity and degenerate antiprogressiveness."[5]

After a denigration of Felix Mendelssohn, Wagner concludes his diatribe with an appeal that sounds like a heralding of what was to come scarcely ninety years later: "Join unreservedly in this self-destructive and bloody battle and we shall all be united and indivisible! But bear in mind that one thing alone can redeem you from the curse that weighs upon you: the redemption of Ahasuerus – destruction!"

Wagner's outbursts against his "enemies" Felix Mendelssohn and Giacomo Meyerbeer, without whose efforts Wagner's stage works would be unthinkable, display disgraceful aggressiveness. He owed to Meyerbeer, his one-time supporter, essential elements of the musical dramaturgy of his early works, and to Mendelssohn a decisive influence on melody and instrumentation. In 'The Jews In Music', Wagner wilfully blurs essential foreign influences on his artistic development. Herein lies a central motive for his pathological antisemitism, which runs through all the composer's writings up to 1882 like a thread.

As was later asserted in Bayreuth, 'The Jews In Music' is by no means the end of Wagner's antisemitism as a politico-cultural concept, but is instead just the beginning. He repeats the ideas of his first anti-semitic pamphlet – and indeed scarcely alters them – in 'Opera And Drama', his 1851 key work on the theory of art. He later revised his revolutionary theory of art in order to avoid distancing himself too much from the taste of the bourgeoisie. His antisemitism remained, however, and was expressed in particular in the writings 'On State And Religion' (1864), 'What Is German?' (1865/78), 'German Art And Politics' (1867), and remained a common theme right up to the regeneration pieces (1879-81). Under the influence of the racist philosopher Arthur Gobineau, Wagner's antisemitism continued to increase. At the end of the 1881 regeneration essay 'Know Yourself', he formulates ideas that today read like a horrifying prediction of Hitler's Final Solution, invoking a Germany free of Jews as the "great solution": "And the very stimulus of the present movement – conceivable among ourselves alone – might bring this great solution within reach of us Germans, rather than of any other nation, if only we would boldly take that 'know thyself' and apply it to the innermost quick of our existence. That we have nought to fear from ultimate knowledge, if we but conquer all false shame and quarry deep enough, we hope the anxious may have called from the above."[6]

Wagner's attitude towards the Jews kept changing, for obvious reasons. He would even claimed to be philosemitic if he considered it helpful in carrying through his ideological-political and artistic goals. But from 1850 onwards, every critic of his art, irrespective of birth, was "an artistic Jew".

The publication of his essay on 'The Jews In Music' provoked angry protests, which also influenced many later reviewers of Wagner's operas and writings. His antisemitic writings read like a constant exchange of attack and counter-attack between himself and the music critics of his time. In them he loses sight of the development of European Judaism in the second half of the 19th century, and increasingly along with it his sense of reality and humanity. So Wagner's art, in spite of all of its brilliant innovations – as manifested in his first works staged in the Bayreuth *Festspielhaus*, the *Ring* and *Parsifal* – also became anti-Jewish, and even anti-art, and the *Festspielhaus* became an anti-Jewish, anti-culture establishment, and was completely in tune with the 'Report On The *Festspielhaus* In Bayreuth' of 1873. In this paper Wagner compares his "new [German] European theatre, taste and morals...to a Parisian whore or a successful stock market speculator" – an allusion to Meyerbeer's operas. So he refers back to his essay 'What Is German?', and the second edition of 'The Jews In Music', which appeared in 1869. The circle that Wagner had already begun to draw in 1850 closes here: the festival was marketed as the 'Bayreuth Festival', which proved to be strong propaganda for Germany. Combined with this, Wagner societies were springing up everywhere and appearing in the nationalistic newspaper *Bayreuther Blätter*. So antisemitism and racism proved to be deeply rooted in the festival's origins, both implicit and explicit. Wagner's own antisemitism was closely connected to this.

Some of Wagner's writings – in particular 'Modern' of 1878, 'Public And Popularity' of 1879 and the reprint of 'What Is German?' of 1878 – encouraged other antisemitic, chauvinist authors to align German culture according to the standards of the Bayreuth. The influence that the bourgeois Richard Wagner had on art is shown in the stage works he realised in his Bayreuth Festival from 1876 to 1882, as both director and impresario. Who is portrayed by Alberich and Mime, the dwarfish exploiters, and Hagen in the *Ring*, Beckmesser in the *Meistersinger* and Klingsor and Kundry, the female Ahasuerus figure in *Parsifal*? If we look at Kundry's baptism in act three of *Parsifal*, in connection with the regeneration writings, we understand how seriously Wagner viewed the conversion of the Jews to Christianity, which had already been demanded in 'The Jews In Music'. The aforementioned "great solution" of 1881, on the other hand, is realised on stage in the dramaturgically superfluous (and therefore ideologically eloquent) death of Kundry at the end of *Parsifal*.

Just as Wagner admits different interpretations in his works of art, in his regeneration writings he tempts his followers to subscribe to 'his' new Christianity. This is a confused blend of antisemitism, antifeminism and Buddhism, mixed with elements of Schopenhauer's philosophy of renunciation. As Nietzsche perceptively writes in his 1878 work *Human, All Too Human*, with regard to his experiences with Wagner and the composer's works:

> "In regard of the knowledge of truths, the artist possesses a weaker morality than the thinker; he does not wish to be deprived of the glittering, profound interpretations of life and guards against simple and sober methods and results. He appears to be fighting on behalf of the greater dignity and significance of man; in reality he refuses to give up the presuppositions which are most efficacious for his art – that is to say, the fantastic, mythical, uncertain, extreme, the sense of the symbolic, the over-estimation of the person, the belief of the presence of the miraculous in genius. He thus considers the perpetuation of his mode of creation more important than scientific devotion to truth in any form, however plainly this may appear."[7]

Liszt's daughter Cosima, who was Richard Wagner's second wife and director of the festival until 1907, was no less antisemitic than her husband. Evidence of this is offered *inter alia* by an entry in her diary of 18 December 1881, in which she records a conversation she had with Richard:

"Then he tells me about a recent performance of *Nathan* [*Der Weise*], at which – when the line was spoken that asserted that Christ was also a Jew – an Israelite in the audience cried 'Bravo!' He reproaches Lessing for this piece of insipidity, and when I reply that the play seems to me to contain a peculiarly German kind of humanity, he says 'But not a trace of profundity.' ...One adds fuel to the arrogance of these fellows by having anything at all to do with them, and we, for example, do not talk of our feelings about those Jews in the theatre in front of Rub[instein], 400 unbaptised and probably 500 baptised Jews."[8]

The attitude and remarks of Richard and Cosima Wagner were to have far-reaching effects even after their deaths. In a few sentences, this quotation from Cosima's diaries sums up what was in effect the Bayreuth tradition until 1945, and is echoed in the writings of her son-in-law, the English racial theoretician Houston Stewart Chamberlain, who was also one of Hitler's mentors.

A quotation from Chamberlain's 1895 biography of Richard Wagner confirms the enduring effect of Wagner's antisemitism:

"At the beginning of his '*Judenthum In Der Musik*' ['The Jews In Music'], Wagner tells us that his purpose is 'to explain the unconscious feeling which in the people takes the form of a deep-rooted antipathy to the Jewish nature, to express therefore in plain language something really existing, not at all by force of imagination to infuse life into a thing unreal in itself.' And how was this really existing thing to be removed? How was the baneful yawning abyss to be bridged? Wagner points to the regeneration of the human race, and to the Jews he says 'Bear your share undauntedly in this work of redemption, gaining new birth by self-immolation; we shall then be one and undivided! But remember that there can only be release from the curse which rests upon you: the release of Ahasuerus – destruction.' What he means by destruction is evident from an earlier sentence: 'to become men in common with us is, for the Jews, primarily the same thing as to cease to be Jews.'"[9]

A direct line runs from Chamberlain to Hitler, whom the writer revered from the very beginning. On 7 October 1923, Chamberlain wrote to the future Führer:

"Dear Herr Hitler...You are not at all, as you have been described to me, a fanatic; rather I would like to describe you as the direct opposite of a fanatic. The fanatic heats heads, you warm hearts. The fanatic wants to persuade, you want to convince, only convince – and that is why you are successful; yes, I would likewise define you as the opposite of a politician...for the axis of all politics is membership of a party, whereas in your case all parties disappear, consumed in the fire of love for the fatherland...You have tasks requiring tremendous force before you, but in spite of your strength of will I do not consider you a man of force. You know Goethe's distinction between force and force! There is a force that originates from chaos and leads to chaos, and there is a force whose essence it is to form the cosmos, and of the latter he said: 'Ruling, it takes on any shape – and even in the great it is not force.' I mean it in this cosmos-building sense when I say that I want you to be listed among the ranks of the uplifting, not the forceful men...My belief in Germanness has not wavered for a moment, but my hopes – I admit it – had reached a low ebb. At a stroke you have transformed the state of my soul. That Germany in the hour of its deepest need has borne a Hitler, that attests to its vitality; likewise the effects emanating from him; for these two things – personality and its effect – belong together. That the great Ludendorff openly allies himself with you and joins the movement emanating from you – what a splendid confirmation! I could calmly fall asleep and would not even need to wake up again. May God protect you!"[10]

In 1915, Richard Wagner's son and my grandfather, Siegfried, married Winifred Williams. She revered Hitler just as much as her brother-in-law, Chamberlain, as documented in her 'Open Letter' of 14 November 1923 in the *Bayreuth Oberfränkische Zeitung*, for example – only a few days after Hitler's attempted *putsch* in Munich:

"The whole of Bayreuth knows that we have a friendly relationship with Adolf Hitler. We happened to be in Munich in those momentous days and were the first ones to come back from there. Understandably, Hitler's followers turned to us for information from eye witnesses…For years we have been following with the greatest inner sympathy and approval the uplifting work of Adolf Hitler, this German man who, filled with ardent love for his fatherland, is sacrificing his life for his idea of a purified, united, greater Germany, who has set himself the hazardous task of opening the eyes of the working class to the enemy within and to Marxism and its consequences, who as no other has managed to bring people together in brotherly reconciliation, has been able to do away with the almost insuperable class hatred, who has restored to thousands upon thousands of despairing people the joyous hope of a reviving, dignified fatherland and a firm belief in it. His personality has had a deep, moving impression on us, too, as on anyone who comes into contact with him, and we have understood how such a simple, physically delicate man is capable of exercising such power. This power is founded on the moral strength and purity of this man, who without ceasing stands up for an idea he has seen to be right, which he is trying with the fervour and humility of divine vocation to realise. Such a man, who is standing up so directly for good, must inspire, electrify people, animate them with selfless love and devotion for his person. I freely admit that we too are under the spell of this personality, that we too, who stood by him in happy days, will remain faithful to him now too in his hour of need."[11]

Siegfried Wagner ran the Bayreuth Festival from 1907 to 1930. He also corresponded with Hitler, but Siegfried's antisemitism wasn't as extreme as that of his wife, Winifred, or that of Cosima. For example, on 6 June 1921, still quite uninfluenced by the later pro-Hitler atmosphere in Bayreuth, he wrote to an antisemitic editor of the *Deutsche Zeitung* in Berlin: "Among the Jews we have very many faithful, honest and selfless supporters who have given us countless evidence of their friendship. You want us to close our doors to all of these people, to rebuff them for the sole reason that they are Jews. Is that humane? Is that Christian? Is that German? No! ...On our *Festspielhügel* we want to produce positive not negative work. Whether a person is Chinese, Negro, American, Indian or Jew is totally immaterial to us. But we could learn from the Jews how to stick together and help one another."[12]

This letter was used after the Nazi period as a pseudo-liberal alibi for the Bayreuth Festival in order that the period from 1907 to 1930 could be presented in the light of the pure art of Richard Wagner. However, the extant documents produced during the period of 1925 until Siegfried Wagner's death show that, even in the 1920s, Richard Wagner's work was serving politico-cultural ends on the *Festspielhügel*. In his letter of Christmas 1923, only a few weeks after Hitler's failed *putsch* in Munich, in the November of that year, Siegfried Wagner wrote to Rosa Eidam: "We got to know that splendid man [Hitler] here in the summer at the German Rally and remain true to him even if it should mean our going to prison. We were never timeservers here in Wahnfried. [Alluding to the political unrest in the 1920s in Bavaria.] The situation in Bavaria is appalling. The times of the Spanish Inquisition have returned. Perjury and betrayal are sanctified, and Jew and Jesuit are working hand in glove to exterminate Germanness! But perhaps Satan has miscalculated this time. Should the German cause really succumb, then I'll believe in Jehova, the god of revenge and hatred. My wife is fighting like a lioness for Hitler – first rate!"[13]

In this light, Hitler's letter to Siegfried on 5 May 1924 becomes equally clear. In memory of his official visit to Bayreuth on the occasion of the *Deutsche Tage* [German Rally] on 30 September 1923, aimed at a future electoral victory, and regarding the Wagner family's open support of him, among other things, Hitler writes: "I was filled with pride and joy when I saw the people's victory in the very city in which, first through the Master [Richard Wagner] and then through Chamberlain, the spiritual sword with which we are fighting today was forged."[14] When comparing the inflammatory anti-semitic writings of Richard Wagner and Chamberlain with Hitler's racist politico-cultural ravings in *Mein Kampf*, there can be no doubt of their historical connection.

The fact that Siegfried Wagner, his wife and his sisters took over the honorary presidency of the national Bavarian Federation Of German Youth (BBDJ) on 1 August 1923 further proves the historical connection. As future objectives, the BBDJ swore "to convey the ideas of Bayreuth, the artistic works and politico-cultural ideals of Richard Wagner to the whole of the German people; to reveal the profound sense of the direct bond between the great German memoir [*Mein Kampf*] of Adolf Hitler and his cultural will and the work of Bayreuth".[15]

Closely connected with this national stock of ideas and the Bayreuth Festival was the *Deutsche* festival, held in Weimar from July 1926, and in which operas by Siegfried Wagner were performed and national poetry was published, including pieces by Hans von Wolzogen, who was editor of the antisemitic and chauvinist *Bayreuther Blätter* from 1878-1938. The Weimar festival, like the Bayreuth Festival, was an aggressive politico-cultural counter-concept of the avant-garde art of the Weimar Republic. After the foundation of the National Socialist Society For German Culture in 1927 and the *Kampfbund Für Deutsche Kultur* [Militant League For German Culture] in 1928, headed by Alfred Rosenberg, the semi-official national socialist philosopher and author of the propagandist *The Myth Of The Twentieth Century*, leading Nazis Hans Frank, Baldur von Schirach, Wilhelm Frick, Hans Severus Ziegler, Hans Schemm and Adolf Bartels and many others were also won over to the Bayreuth cause. As son of the master and cultural inspiration for Hitler as much as through his wife's party membership since 1923 (which has been confirmed by the Canadian Wagner scholar Philip Wults), Siegfried Wagner could ostensibly play the role of the non-partisan artist but still enjoy all of the concomitant advantages brought by the embryonic National Socialist movement.

Shortly before his death in June 1930, Siegfried had recruited Arturo Toscanini to Bayreuth. Toscanini was a man who had doggedly refused to see anything but the artist in Wagner, and his appointment was quoted repeatedly after 1945 as exonerative proof that Siegfried Wagner had opened up to other cultural trends. Quite how Siegfried Wagner would have survived in the Third Reich is pure speculation today: because of his homosexuality, he was viewed as decadent by

Hitler and his propaganda minister, Joseph Goebbels.

After Siegfried Wagner, my grandmother ran the festival until 1944. Her faith in Hitler's Final Victory is evident in her contribution to the *Meistersinger* programme of the 1943 wartime festival:

"If, during the wartime festival in 1943, *Die Meistersinger Von Nürnberg* is chosen, then this has a deep and symbolic meaning, for this work shows us in the most impressive way the creative German man in his nationally conditioned will to create, to which the master gave immortal form in the figure of the Nuremberg shoemaker and national poet Hans Sachs, and which, in the present struggle of the Western cultural world against the destructive spirit of the plutocratic-bolshevist world conspiracy, gives our soldiers invincible fighting strength and a fanatical belief in the victory of our arms."[16]

CHAPTER FIVE

"THE WILL TO POWER" II

In February 1972, my investigations into my family's Nazi past were interrupted by my first stint as assistant director in Wuppertal. After my experiences there I was keen to see how Götz Friedrich would direct *Tannhäuser* in the festival, so in April of that year, a few months before his debut in Bayreuth, I visited him in East Berlin, and he explained his ideas to me. I was thrilled. Afterwards, he invited me to a performance of the Berliner Ensemble's production of *Coriolanus*, which turned out to be disappointing: dry, sterile perfection and robotic acting.

I used the time after Berlin to continue conversations with my grandmother and Gertrud Strobel. Father didn't like this at all – Grandmother had faithfully reported my interest in the political past of Bayreuth, my questioning and note-taking. Father was particularly on edge during these months regarding anything to do with the festival, Hitler or the Wagner family: he wanted to pass his Foundation statutes and avoid anything that might prejudice this great undertaking, so from that point on I had to be even more careful in my investigations. Horrified, Frau Strobel informed me that the left-wing musicologists of the Thyssen Foundation, Egon Voss, Dietrich Mack and Michael Karbaum – people with whom I was to have personal experience – were pestering her about the great 1976 jubilee. The Thyssen Foundation financially supported these and other authors, and they were now working on the project: the festival centenary.

In July 1972, the dress rehearsal for Götz Friedrich's *Tannhäuser* took place in Bayreuth. In East Berlin, Friedrich hadn't built up my hopes in vain. I was fascinated, in particular with how he handled the soloists and the chorus in act two. I expected an uproar at the premiere, when the Wartburg company, clothed in dinner jackets and evening dress, greeted the Landgraf with raised arm and a "Heil Hitler", and later tried to evict Tannhäuser from the Wartburg Nazi style. Grandmother pressured my father to prevent this production from being performed unaltered, but I urged him to let Friedrich work in peace. It says much for him that he agreed.

As it happened there was indeed a furore at the premiere, not in reaction to act two but because of the epilogue, which I had found rather tame. The chorus, dressed in out-of-place leisure clothing, announced jubilantly that Tannhäuser was now redeemed. The majority of the audience misunderstood the final scene, interpreting it as a 'worker-and-peasant greeting' of Friedrich's design. They screamed hateful epithets as fanatically as their predecessors before had cheered the Führer a few decades. The cause of such hysteria was clear: Friedrich had held a mirror up to the audience, and many of the ladies and gentlemen from the land of the economic miracle had quite unconsciously recognised themselves in the Wartburg society. After the premiere, the fascistic behaviour acted out on the stage was repeated in real life in the auditorium.

I was also involved in a scene when Friedrich came to take his bow in front of the curtain. One of the gentlemen standing next to me, a member of the Bayreuth Society Of Friends, shouted "Go back to your dirty communists in the GDR! We don't need you here!" and the audience around us agreed enthusiastically. I asked the heckler his name, but he didn't want to tell me. "Who are you, anyway, to ask me my name here in the *Festspielhaus*?" he asked. Furious, I retorted: "You coward, hiding in a group. Have the courage of your convictions! Tell me who you are."

As soon as I said this he grabbed me roughly by the neck. He evidently wanted to tear off my bow tie and would probably have beaten me up. Quickly, I said: "My name is Gottfried Wagner. I'm the son of the director of this festival, who backed this splendid production. You're still on the private property of my family, and

I'll take you to court for disturbance of the peace and bodily harm. Now come to the police with me." I'd hardly finished speaking when the man fled from the theatre. A few days later someone from the audience wrote to my father, complaining about my "left-wing radicalism".

There was even more controversy after the premiere. Ewald Hilger, president of the Bayreuth Society Of Friends, together with his retinue, was outraged by Friedrich's production. Hilger had succeeded his father – an influential gentleman of West German society and a patron of Arno Breker, Hitler's favourite sculptor – to this position. He consulted the festival administrative department, and later on that evening lost control of himself completely, attacking my father for having engaged Friedrich in the first place. Father scarcely had the chance to defend himself, and as Hilger's attacks became cruder Mother and I were forced to intervene. She jumped up, pointed to the door and, loud enough to silence the whole room, shouted: "Now that's enough! Stop insulting my husband like that. The Friends Of Bayreuth have no right to dictate their opinions to my husband and us." She stood there, still pointing, until Hilger – deeply offended – rushed from the room, threatening: "This will have consequences!" These consequences failed to materialise, however, and Father and he were soon once again bosom pals.

I was thrilled by the way Mother had leapt into action. The atmosphere around us soon became icy, however, a foretaste of what was to come. Even the "left-wing vanguard" around Herbert Barth, the press spokesman of the festival, cautiously drew back. Only a handful of people came to offer words of appreciation to Mother: my sister and my father remained awkwardly silent, but Mother and I had seldom been as close as we were on that evening. The next morning Father approached me and asked me to restrain myself. This concerned me, because until then I had been convinced that Mother and I were fighting for the right cause. All of this lying disgusted me.

Father found himself under such a barrage of criticism that he started questioning the final scene of Act Three. Of course, this sparked off another quarrel between us: I was against any change in the staging, and disagreed with the sacrificing of artistic freedom simply because the sponsors had found themselves unable to live with Friedrich's production. I told Father of the incident in the auditorium, and he looked like he was about to reconsider his decision yet again. He finally caved, however, and the second performance had to make do without the worker-and-peasant greeting. This lame compromise satisfied the Society Of Friends, but in my view it was a cowardly concession.

The reaction of bourgeois society – especially that of Franz Josef Strauss, who had publicly attacked Götz Friedrich's staging and was negotiating with my father on the Foundation statutes – had wounded my father, and probably contributed to him distancing himself from Friedrich's interpretation of the final scene. The liberal and left-wing press, which at first had only applauded his work, now voiced some doubts as well. The two versions of the endings were the subjects of heated debates. Overnight, Bayreuth had been not only *retheatralisiert* ['re-theatralised'], as Friedrich put it, but its politics had been publicly redefined. The alignments of right, liberal and left – which had been blurred since 1951, after Wieland's apolitical, psycho-analytical stagings – became clear again.

The era of the left-wing Richard Wagner had now dawned. The fanatical majority of the audience at the premiere were troubled by such debate, and waited for the reviews of Joachim Kaiser and other well-known Wagner experts to be published before expressing their opinions any further, so that they could then repeat these arguments, even if they were different from the opinions they had held in the auditorium shortly before. It was most important to remain 'in'. Many members of the Society Of Friends who were unsure what to think went to my grandmother for advice. She declared: "I think that this communist Friedrich's *Tannhäuser* is repulsive, too, but think of my son. Anyone can make mistakes, and he's already changing the worst scenes. Our Bayreuth is still our Bayreuth! It just makes Wolf's artistic genius even more obvious!" Soon after, however, the same people who had found her judgment so wise became connected with the "wicked" Friedrich. Grandmother was disappointed: "Fine friends," she muttered.

Father continued to be publicly abused. At the AGM of the Bayreuth Society Of Friends, the members objected to only being allowed to offer financial support to the festival: they also wanted a say over the content as well. The reaction of most of the sponsors to the 1972 *Tannhäuser* concert reminded me of Friedrich Nietzsche's comments in the epilogue to his essay 'The Case Of Wagner':

> "One pays heavily for being one of Wagner's disciples. Let us take the measure of this discipleship by considering its cultural effects. Whom did this movement bring to the fore? What did it breed and multiply? Above all, the presumption of the layman, the art-idiot. That kind now organises associations, wants its 'taste' to prevail, wants to play the judge in *rebus musicis et musicantibus*. Secondly, an ever-growing indifference to all severe, noble, conscientious training in the service of art; all of this is to be replaced by faith in genius or, to speak plainly, by impudent dilettantism (the formula for this is to be found in *Die Meistersinger*). Thirdly, and worst of all: *theatrocracy* – the nonsense of a faith in the presidence of the theatre, in the right of the theatre to lord itself over the arts, over art.
>
> "But one should tell the Wagnerians a hundred times to their faces *what* the theatre is: always beneath art, always only something secondary, something made cruder, something twisted tendentiously, mendaciously, for the sake of the masses. Wagner, too, did not change anything in this respect. Bayreuth is large-scale opera – and not even good opera. The theatre is a form of demolatry in matters of taste; the theatre is a revolt of the masses, a plebiscite against good taste. This is precisely proved by the case of Wagner: he won the crowd, he corrupted taste, he spoiled even our taste for opera!"[17]

In Erlangen, during the winter semester of 1972-3, I suddenly became popular in the Theatre Studies department. The institute had already organised a 'Richard Wagner Music Theatre Seminar', and I invited my lecturers and fellow students to the dress rehearsal of *Tannhäuser*. Wagner was wrongly identified as having been a pioneer of socialism in 1848, and this was very similar to the view of the composer in East German musicology, led by Werner Wolf (assisted, incidentally, by the old and indispensible Wagnerian Gertrud Strobel, who was then working in the Bayreuth archives department). In seminars at Erlangen, authors such as Bloch, Gregor-Dellin, Hans Mayer and Walter Jens were identified among those who interpreted Wagner's work as having left-wing origins. At my instigation, Dietrich Mack – the dramaturg of the Bayreuth Festival, and at that time a close adviser of my father – was also included.

On my flying visits to Bayreuth I was careful not to mention my researches into our family's Nazi past, and I also kept my meetings with Gertrud Strobel secret from Father. Claiming that I had to prepare for a Wagner seminar at the university, I stepped up my investigations in the Siegfried Wagner House. I can still clearly remember hearing my father complaining during one of my visits home that the situation with Gertrud Strobel could no longer be tolerated: she persisted in passing on material that concerned only the family and should not be made public – especially now, with the Foundation charter about to be signed.

I cautiously asked Father what material he meant.

"All those private letters between Hitler and Grandmother, and a whole lot of other things that have nothing to do with politics or the family. If the lefties at the Thyssen Foundation get hold of them, there'll be hell to pay!"

"Everything should come out in the open, or there'll never be a fresh beginning," I replied calmly, if not diplomatically.

This infuriated Father. I remained silent, afraid that he might remember the films from the Nazi period which I had hidden. I occasionally checked to see whether he had taken the empty cans out of the sidecar.

In May 1973 I took a job as assistant director with Götz Friedrich in Amsterdam, but this meant that I now had to combine my theatre work with my studies, while at the same time ensuring that I didn't miss my exam deadlines. I tried to keep up with events in music theatre, and in mid April, at the invitation of the city of Leipzig, I went with Dietrich Mack to the premiere of *Das Rheingold*, directed by Joachim Herz and with set designs by Rudolf Heinrich. The staging was based on the works of Bernard

Shaw, who had interpreted the *Ring* by way of the early capitalism of the 19th century. Alberich and Wotan were depicted as swindling bourgeois businessmen locked in a deadly struggle for world domination. After having seen so much non-committal abstraction in my father's stagings, I was thrilled by such a strong interpretation. The staging designed by Herz and Heinrich became a model on which many other directors later to based their own productions, including Patrice Chéreau in his 1976 production of the *Ring*.

Leipzig itself, however, was a striking contrast to this epoch-making staging of *Das Rheingold*. Richard Wagner's birthplace! The bleakness and mundaneness of my daily routine and the omnipresence of the security police depressed me. I wanted to know more about life in East Germany, but any serious discussions on social or political matters foundered before they got anywhere. Instead, people took refuge in hints or tasteless jokes which I couldn't find funny. For example: "Honecker spoke in our theatre. Then the set fell down and killed him." Rudolf Heinrich's father had scarcely finished the last sentence when those accompanying him burst out laughing, while I waited for the punchline.

I was able to pick up some great stuff in secondhand bookshops, including first editions of books from the 'bad old' feudal and bourgeois days – they were dirt cheap, compared with prices at home. I didn't just buy valuable old tomes, like the famous Gotha peerage guide of 1860, but also East German literature on Brecht and Weill.

On the way back, Dietrich Mack and I discussed the GDR. Like many left-wingers of the time, he defended the social achievements of the system, which I on the other hand rejected as too high a price to pay for the loss of autonomy. When we reached the border my opinion was confirmed: with German thoroughness a border guard searched my VW Beetle, and of course he found the Gotha.

"Why did you buy this book?" he asked.

"I'm interested in German history," I replied.

"Why are you interested in German history?"

"Because I'm a German."

I had to force back laughter, which annoyed the guard. In the end I got fed up and introduced myself, informed the good man of my invitation by the city of Leipzig and said I was going to be making a report of this journey as a journalist. At this, the man transformed from a dour functionary into a thoroughly polite human being, and let us pass through without further ado.

We'd only just reached the Bavarian side of the border when the whole game started all over again, this time with the West Germans. The border guard discovered the East German literature during his inspection, but this time I cut to the chase, repeating what I had told his colleague. Again, within seconds I was witness to a magical transformation. The guard begged for festival tickets (not getting any, naturally enough).

After such trips I felt ill at ease with my nationality, so I was glad when, in May 1973, I was asked to work as assistant director, under Götz Friedrich, on a production of *Aida* at the Théâtre Carré in Amsterdam. Friedrich staged Giuseppe Verdi's opera as a violent political thriller, in which love came into mortal conflict with the State. Unfortunately, this compelling concept was realised with a rather *kitschig* set, and I was really only enthusiastic about the directing. For twelve hours each day I worked like a slave; my feet bled from rushing between stage and auditorium. Friedrich – who was something of a tyrant – found this to be quite acceptable.

I learned much from him about my job. His keen intellect was coupled with a wide-ranging imagination. He directed the chorus and principals with great intensity, and his passion inspired me in my own theatre work. I refused all other invitations to work with him, however, as I didn't want to become the eternal student of one master.

Two events remain particularly memorable from that hectic period. Friedrich was accustomed to behaving in an authoritarian way (a hangover from his background in the GDR), and dealt with the chorus like an army sergeant commanding his troops. On one day the chorus' spokesperson said to Friedrich and I: "You speak like we're still under German occupation – we're not prepared to put up with it." Friedrich dismissed this out of hand, and the atmosphere abruptly worsened. I urged him to give in, which he eventually did.

On the next day I had my first solo rehearsal. It was my enviable task to select 20 slave girls out of 80 hopeful auditionees – beautiful dark-skinned girls from the former Dutch colonies – and to rehearse the scene from Act One in Amneris' apartments with them. So there I stood, lucky boy, surrounded by a crowd of stunning flower girls, feeling like Parsifal in Klingsor's magic garden – I would have loved to have engaged them all! After I'd made my choice, I had to go through the blocking and choreography with these girls in Amneris' chamber. They were only supposed to serve as decorative framework for Amneris, combing her hair, adorning her, waving palm fronds and lying seductively on cushions. I, of course, felt it my duty to insist on frequent rehearsals.

Then I had to go and fall in love with the conductor's sister! Edo de Waart had generously offered me accommodation in his spacious home, and it was here that I got to know Manja. She had a finely formed oval face and an irresistibly sunny smile. We floated hand in hand through nocturnal Amsterdam, visiting the notorious railway station and the museums. With a disarming combination of charm and knowledge, she taught me everything one ought to know about Dutch history, in particular the German occupation in the last war, and about Dutch painting and music. A gifted viola player herself, she was by no means interested only in the world of the arts. A visit to the Anne Frank Museum left me feeling ashamed to be German, but Manja brought me back to the present: "Our generation has to make it better!", she told me, in her attractive Dutch accent, and she was right. It was difficult for me to finally say goodbye to her when the time came for me to return to Germany.

In the summer of 1973 I informed my father that, on the strength of my studies in Erlangen, I intended to write my thesis on the contemporary music theatre of Kurt Weill and Bertolt Brecht. Brecht and Weill were the most notable opponents of Wagner and his Bayreuth shrine, and when Father realised that my choice was not for purely musicological reasons he was cutting: "Can't you think of anything better than this honky-tonk music?"

I was furious. "The pirate Jenny song is a thousand times better that all this fake, bourgeois Wagnerian redemption shit!" It would probably have been better if I'd kept my mouth shut, because Father then went into one of his blind rages and stalked out of the dining room. With a certain relish I also brought the bad news to my grandmother. She reacted calmly and bluntly as I had expected her to: "So you're getting mixed up with the Jews, then, yes? Even the left-wingers! I can understand that your father has to do it to a certain extent in these Jew-ridden times, but you? You wait – the wheel of history will turn for us again, I'm sure!"

"Wieland was right after all!" I interrupted her. "You still believe in the Final Victory."

The only person who encourage me to stick with Weill and Brecht was my friend Eberhard Wagner, editor of the *East Franconian Dictionary* at the Bavarian Academy of Sciences. At that time he was a committed poet, playwright and novelist, and today is the vice-chairman of the Bayreuth Studio Theatre. I became friends with him in Erlangen, and he always proved one of my few genuine friends in Bayreuth. He was always there – even later, when things became difficult.

CHAPTER SIX

THE RICHARD WAGNER FOUNDATION

In May 1973, the Founding Charter of the Richard Wagner Foundation of Bayreuth was signed. The family was represented by my grandmother, my aunts Friedelind and Verena, my father and the children of Uncle Wieland. At the time, I was indignant that I hadn't been informed of the content of the document before it was signed, and that I wasn't invited to be a signatory. Although I had insisted on learning more, I only discovered the content of the charter from Martin Gregor-Dellin's rather superficial account of it in the 1973 festival programme for *Die Meistersinger*. It wasn't until four years later that I received the complete text of the Foundation document from the lawyer of the Wieland children. Of its 14 paragraphs, the second, sixth and eighth concerned me particularly. In paragraph six the Foundation council was defined: according to this, the members' votes were distributed (before the deaths of my grandmother and Aunt Friedelind) thus: Federal Republic of Germany, five votes; Free State of Bavaria, five votes; Wagner family, five votes; City of Bayreuth, two votes; Bayreuth Society Of Friends, one vote; Upper Franconia Foundation, two votes; Region of Upper Franconia, two votes; Bavarian Land Foundation, two votes.[18]

In paragraph eight, this heterogeneous Foundation council – which was only partially capable of making judgments in artistic and cultural matters – was entrusted with decisions concerning the artistic suitability of my father's successor as festival director. This appeared to satisfy certain minimum democratic requirements, except for the second and third clauses in paragraph eight, which stated: "The *Festspielhaus* shall in principle be let to a member of the Wagner family (several members, if applicable), or to another entrepreneur should a member of the Wagner family (several members, if applicable) run the festival. This shall only fail to apply if other, more suitable applicants come forward. With the majority vote in the Foundation council, the descendants of Richard Wagner may make proposals. As soon as it is determined that the contract with a festival entrepreneur has ended, or will end, the Foundation shall indicate the possibility of making a proposal to the representatives of the Wagner family in the Foundation council...Should the Foundation council entertain doubts as to whether or not a member of the Wagner family is better than any other applicant, or just as qualified for the position of festival entrepreneur, then the Foundation council shall seek a decision of a tri-partite committee of experts. This committee shall consist of the intendants of opera houses from German-speaking regions, whereby the intendants shall be consulted in the order of the hereafter named opera houses: Deutsche Oper, Berlin; Bayerische Staatsoper, Munich; Staatsoper, Vienna; Staatsoper, Hamburg; Staatsoper, Stuttgart; Städtische Oper, Frankfurt/Main; Städtische Oper, Cologne."[19]

This also sounds sensible, but is in practice a very difficult concept to realise. It really just boils down to a question of taste, a decision based on whether or not – and to what extent – a member of the family, or another applicant, is suitable to run the festival. Furthermore, in view of the history of the family, it couldn't automatically be assumed that they would agree on one or more candidates. It was also a question of how far the members of the two boards – the Foundation council and, below that, the committee of experts – were able and willing to judge objectively. Nevertheless, for the intendants in the committee, it proved at least possible that they could appoint a non-family member to the post of festival director.

Of course, this sounds quite reasonable, but if examined *in toto* it becomes clear that it leaves the door wide open to despotism. For years my father had tirelessly and publicly written off every other member of the family as unsuitable.

In my view, paragraph two was equally dubious. In connection with the joint will and testament of Siegfried and Winifred Wagner of 8 March 1929, the following four points are cited as being the purpose of the Foundation:

"1. To preserve the artistic legacy of Richard Wagner in perpetuity for the public good;

"2. To maintain the Bayreuth *Festspielhaus* in perpetuity for the public good and make it accessible and constantly subservient to the purposes for which its founder intended – that is, solely for the solemn performance of the works of Richard Wagner;

"3. To promote research into Richard Wagner;

"4. To promote the understanding of the works of Richard Wagner, in particular among young people and the younger generation of artists."[20]

Richard Wagner's legacy should be understood basically not only as purely artistic but also as politico-cultural. Out of the tragic history of the Bayreuth Festival, a special responsibility has arisen in dealing with this legacy. In other words, the present purpose of the Foundation denies the possibility of dealing with matters such as "Wagner, Hitler and the consequences" in a critical and unbiased way. One could counter this by saying that the promotion of research, mentioned in point three, should guarantee this. However, as in point one, only the artistic legacy is mentioned – the "generosity" of point three is hogwash. From a legal point of view there are certainly no objections to point two, but it does indicate how little the authors of the statutes had learned from history: to focus solely on Richard Wagner would mean the perpetuation of the Wagner cult, the horrifying consequences of which have already been shown in the past. In order to counteract a monoculture focused solely on Wagner, the existing concept of the festival should be broadened:

1. All of Wagner's works – including his early operas, symphonies, chamber music and *Lieder* – should be performed in the *Festspielhaus*, as it would then be possible to experience and understand the various artistic influences on his work.

2. The works of those artists who had a particularly long-lasting influence on Wagner should also be staged within the framework of the festival. This would bring about a considerable broadening of the artistic horizon.

3. Throughout his life, Richard Wagner emphasised the open, provisional nature of his concept of the festival. In this sense, contemporary representatives of all forms of art – with the emphasis changing from year to year – should receive a regular opportunity to present themselves to the public.

The following of these three points would also lead to the opening up of the festival to a whole new audience. Or to put it another way, the festival would then, in the words of Richard Wagner, exist not only for the "upper ten thousand" but would have a broad, democratic accessibility in keeping with the modern world.

Such a programme is rendered impossible, however, by paragraph two, which makes my proposals sound hopelessly idealistic. I could live with that, if the logic of the Foundation statutes didn't compel me to take on a dual role: on one hand, my family membership includes me in the "circle of candidates" for the succession, while on the other hand I could only conform to the demands of paragraph two of the statutes if I were prepared to comply with their monocultural claims in everything I did. I played no part in the discussion concerning succession, yet it has nevertheless proved to be a serious obstacle for the development of my career both as a director and music journalist. Apparently a Wagner should only be a trustee of Richard Wagner if he adheres strictly to the letter of the Foundation statutes. The dilemma I face is that, if I suggest any changes, I lay myself open to charges of personal ambition – no matter how ludicrous those charges are within the context of my life.

CHAPTER SEVEN

"THE WILL TO POWER" III

In the autumn of 1973 I enrolled at the University of Vienna, where Professor Otmar Wessely was my doctoral supervisor and Professor Gernot Gruber oversaw my dissertation. They both helped me a great deal with my thesis on Weill and Brecht, and I was glad to escape Bayreuth. The university library was packed with books, and provided a wealth of material both for my studies and for my private research into the history of the Bayreuth Festival during the Nazi period. I also spent a lot of time in the offices of Universal Edition, the music publishing house, where my passionate interest in Weill and Brecht caused much consternation. To my amusement I was addressed, in the Austrian fashion, as "Herr Doctor Wagner." If the subject of Kurt Weill came up, it was always accompanied with a covert antisemitism. Many Viennese claimed that they had had nothing to do with the Nazis – in their eyes the Germans had annexed Austria by force – so they therefore believed that they had nothing to come to terms with. "But Herr Doktor, why go poking around in the past, and about Weill and all that? Wagner's music is so wonderful!" was one of the many suggestions I heard.

Whilst on holiday in the winter of 1973, I wanted to talk to Father about paragraph eight of the Foundation statutes, which struck me as being something of a muzzle. I explained my concerns to him while we were out walking one day. "Isn't it absurd to assume that our family would agree on a candidate from the family? And who decides on which criteria the more suitable candidate would meet? And what interests do the intendants from Munich, Vienna, Hamburg, Stuttgart, Frankfurt or Cologne represent? Surely they'd look after their own interests, first of all. And they'd surely be against conflicts in the family. Anyone from the family who wants to get in there has to get on with everyone, including the politicians, industrialists and members of the Society Of Friends. I don't understand that."

Father replied: "If you stand the test according to the Foundation statutes, you're in with a good chance."

We quarrelled again.

During the Christmas holidays another argument broke out over the inclusion of the Federal Republic and East Germany to the United Nations. I considered the universal recognition of the GDR as a sensible and logical continuation of Brandt's and Genscher's *Ostpolitik*, but Father thought otherwise: "That means the end of the unification of Germany. Not only that, it also means that the communists will be rewarded for the dividing Germany."

Early in 1974 my father set Peter Stein and Patrice Chéreau competing against each other to direct a new production of the *Ring*, which was scheduled to be staged in the 1976, the festival's centenary. Pierre Boulez had already agreed to be the conductor, but negotiations with the directors had progressed little. Father considered directing the *Ring* himself, although I advised him strongly against this, because it would have proved an obstacle towards the modern (if not avant-garde) interpretations of Richard Wagner's works. My knowledge of French meant that I was occasionally called on to assist in the negotiations. Whether Father dangled the carrot of the directorship under the nose of Chéreau or Stein depended entirely on their remarks on the opera, and whether these remarks conformed with his own – especially in relation to the so-called reception history and the subjects of art and power from 1850 to 1945 (Father wanted an ambiguous, apolitical interpretation). Such competition didn't exactly create a good atmosphere – it seemed to me that they were playing with a marked deck. As it turned out, Chéreau finally won.

Once, when I picked up Peter Stein at Nuremberg airport, he told me that my father's constant patronage reminded him of old times.

In July 1974, at the end of the summer semester, I returned to Bayreuth in time to see *Tristan Und Isolde* under Carlos Kleiber's fascinating musical direction. The old Wagnerians and my grandmother's cronies were pleased with August Everding's staging. Eva knew about Everding's growing influence in the German opera and theatre scene, and waxed enthusiastic about him. I, on the other hand, had nothing else to say to him – we ended up talking about the weather. He did his best to be socially accepted, and because of his conservative attitude he was also a welcome guest of my grandmother, who, along with Eva, was taking over more and more representative duties in the Siegfried Wagner House, even though this didn't quite fit in with the new left-wing image my father and his chorus of yes men were keen to portray.

On 1 August 1974 I married Beatrix Kraus, who had been my partner for a long time, and introduced my new wife to my astonished family. They had cold-shouldered her for years, because they believed that she lacked the respect which should have been their due. She had a razor-sharp wit, was socially confident and was well able to defend herself in the festival snakepit. This did nothing to improve her popularity, however, especially among the women of the *Festspielhügel*. We moved into an apartment in the Feustel family's villa on the outskirts of Bayreuth, which was surrounded by a beautiful garden. We entertained many guests, but never people from the *Festspielhügel*, and Richard Wagner was never suggested as a general topic of conversation.

After the wedding the next most important event in these months was Ernst Bloch's visit to our home. After I collected him and his wife Karola from Tübingen, he offered me some important tips for my doctoral thesis, and provided me with important contacts, such as Lotte Lenya, the Austrian-American actress and singer.

It was also because of him that I became involved in a controversy with Bayreuth's SPD mayor, Hans Walter Wild. I had suggested appointing Bloch an honorary citizen of the City of Bayreuth – Hitler had been granted honorary citizenship in 1933, and nobody had objected when, even in as late as 1974, the city still boasted a street named after Chamberlain, the Nazi admirer and Wagner acolyte. In a letter dated 25 April 1974 the mayor wrote back to me, informing me that he could see no grounds for my proposal, and cited the names of other honorary citizens, my grandmother amongst them.

At that time I found Bloch's passionate interest in all things cultural very attractive, particularly his fascinating accounts of his time in the Weimar Republic and at the Kroll Opera in Berlin with Otto Klemperer. Most of all I liked listening to him when he talked about the Devil: he conjured images in my mind from the Old Testament that I shall never forget. When my father, Macks and Herbert Barth invited him and Karola to the centenary production of the *Ring* in 1976, Bloch talked about Wagner as he understood him: as a revolutionary.

That summer, our festival guests included the set designer Roland Aeschlimann, his wife Andrea, and the literary scholar Hans Mayer, who brought with him a publisher's proposal for us to collaborate on a history of the Bayreuth Festival. At the time I found Mayer's interpretation of Wagner stimulating, and also saw in this an opportunity to make myself financially independent from my father. I agreed to the proposal and began working, at the same time filling in the gaps in my own research into Wagner and the *Festspielhügel*.

In the autumn of 1974 Beatrix and I moved to Vienna so that I could concentrate on my doctoral thesis and continue researching the book. I was also able to gain further experience as an assistant director when Joachim Herz and Rudolf Heinrich invited me to work with them on a State Opera production of Mozart's *Die Zauberflöte*. Herz, a pupil of Walter Felsenstein, taught me a lot of things, both theoretical and practical, and it was he who convinced me of what a great – but still largely underestimated – influence Meyerbeer had had on Richard

Wagner's musical dramaturgy.

Working together on a day-to-day basis was often difficult: Herz was always on edge, and expected me to be prepared to work day and night. I went along with it, however, as the results he had already achieved spoke volumes. I also had some equally stimulating talks with the brilliant set and costume designer Rudolf Heinrich, who, with Felsenstein, had brought world recognition to the Berlin Komische Oper (also known as the 'Anti-Bayreuth'). The assistants at the opera house, who mostly allied themselves with the influential director Otto Schenk and the singer Eberhard Wächter, were disgusted that the Saxon Herz dared stage such a critical production of *Die Zauberflöte* in Vienna, and the usual intrigues were soon reflected in the media – how could it be otherwise in the Vienna State Opera? A devastatingly critical reception was systematically prepared. I found that the whole thing nauseated me, and as a gesture of support for Herz's exemplary production I prepared my first interview as journalist for the Vienna newspaper *Die Presse* as a platform for the show.

At the beginning of December, Roland Aeschlimann, Gernot Gruber, Eberhard Wagner, Father and I held a meeting. We were supposed to be discussing Aeschlimann's proposal for a set design for *Parsifal*, and we hoped to give Father some ideas for his first staging of the opera, which was planned for 1975 and again had to measure up to Wieland's production, staged in 1951. Aeschlimann – for whom I managed to secure the position of lighting technician in the *Festspielhaus* in 1974 – had worked out a set based on the work of the avant-garde set designer Adolphe François Appia, who died in 1928. Cosima Wagner had vigorously rejected the set at the time, but we all enthusiastically supported Aeschlimann's model. Unfortunately, although Father acted as though he were interested, and even paid perfunctory compliments, it amounted to a rejection.

I made a big mistake when I tried to talk to him about Kundry and Jewry (key word: "female Ahasuerus"). He said gruffly: "What on earth has Kundry to do with the Jews?" After that I gave up discussing Richard Wagner's art with him. With some justification, the set that he finally used for the 1975 production of *Parsifal* reminded some critics of the work of Albert Speer, Hitler's favourite architect.

CHAPTER EIGHT

WINIFRED'S FILM

On 20 January 1975, my sister wrote to tell me that the film director Hans Jürgen Syberberg wanted to collaborate with me on a film about our grandmother. The idea appealed to me, and I accepted Syberberg's invitation to visit him in Vienna, where he was presenting his film about Karl May. I actually found the film rather boring, but in a conversation after the premiere Syberberg informed me that Ernst Bloch, Hans Mayer and Walter Jens had also reacted positively to the idea of his new film, and he registered my interest in German-Jewish history and the work of Kurt Weill with obvious attentiveness, and applauded my courage in tackling taboo subjects such as my own family's involvement in National Socialism. At out meeting I noticed that he didn't know much about this area, or about my grandmother's role in this period; I consequently not only to procured him with an *entrée* to my grandmother and my father but also placed all of my knowledge at his disposal. As well as participating in the preparation, shooting and editing of the film, I also had a passionate interest in disclosing the darkest epoch of my family's history.

Having informed Syberberg that I was also working on a TV documentary on the subject with the BBC's Brian Large, *The Festival's Centenary*, Syberberg drew up a contract which took this other project into account and cleared important rights for me. I showed the contract to Father, and he agreed that we could begin filming in April 1975. Until then, Beatrix and I used the time to conduct further research for the book with Hans Mayer.

However, it appeared that researching the film wasn't to be that straightforward, as Father had no intention of handing over all of the documents on 'The Wagner Family And National Socialism' that I had found listed in the archive catalogue or that my grandmother had told me about – the correspondence between Adolf Hitler and Winifred, Wieland and Wolfgang from 1923 to 1944, for example, which my grandmother had removed from a secret steel-lined cupboard and allowed me to look at for a short time. The letters were evidence of the great friendship that existed between my grandmother, my uncle, my father and Hitler, and were full of declarations of faith in the Final Victory of the Third Reich. My father, however, ignored inquiries about these letters.

He was also irritated when I broached the subject of the presents that Hitler had given to my grandmother and the rest of the family, such as the 1925 gilt-edged copy of *Mein Kampf* that had been dedicated "From Wolf for Winnie", and categorically refused to make such intimate family documents available for the Syberberg film. He subsequent watched over the preparations and the filming suspiciously, mostly hoping to prevent any of my grandmother's statements from damaging the liberal-left image of the festival which he was keen to promote at that time. I, on the other hand, wanted everything to come out into the open: it was only by exposing fully my family's involvement in National Socialism that it would be made to work through its guilt.

I showed Syberberg the films from the Nazi period that I had found in my father's sidecar, and I stupidly gave him some to take back to Munich. He assured me that he would look after them, and that he wouldn't use them without my permission. However, I found it difficult to believe that he had already devised an artistic direction and concept for the film when he was in Bayreuth, as claimed. Two basic factors were missing: knowledge of the material and any understanding of my grandmother's character.

In fact, Grandmother took over right from the beginning. The result was a film by Winifred Wagner, featuring Winifred Wagner, and with assistance from Syberberg. He fell under my grandmother's control from the moment shooting began. She saw her window of

The Wagner family in 1881 on the steps of Villa Wahnfried, photographed by Adolf von Gross

Top: Blandine von Bülow, Heinrich von Stein, Cosima and Richard Wagner

Middle: Daniela von Bülow, Paul von Joukowsky

Bottom: Isolde von Bülow, Eva and Siegfried Wagner

Richard Wagner, photographed by Joseph Albert, in Munich 1880

A caricature of Richard Wagner which appeared in the magazine *Puck*, Leipzig on 3 September 1876, referring to the opening of the Bayreuth *Festspiele* in the same year

Richard Wagner's home in Bayreuth. L-r: Cosima, Richard, Franz Liszt and Hans von Wolzogen, the editor of the racist journal, *Bayreuther Blätter*. Oil painting by W Beckmann, 1882

Cosima and Richard in Vienna, 1872. Photographed by Fritz Luckhardt

L-r: Cosima, Siegfried and Richard, in Bayreuth 1873, photographed by Adolf von Gross

1872. Richard Wagner's children.
L-r: Eva, Siegfried and Isolde Wagner,
Daniela and Blandine von Bülow

Cosima, in the 1890s

"A week in the life of Wagner" – a cartoon featured in *Der Floh* (*The Flea*) at the opening of the *Festspiele* in 1876

A design by Fantin-Latour in 1883, following Richard Wagner's death in the same year

Richard Wagner as Siegfried. "I will take away the shining treasure." Published in *Schalk*, Leipzig on 5 January 1879

A cartoon published in *Kikeriki* on 18 February 1883 (five days after Richard Wagner died). "My dear angels! The reception is rather nice, but without the timpani and trumpets, you never will have an effect"

French caricature published by *L'Eclipse*, 18 April 1869

"The Jews In Music": their opinion of *Parsifal*, Wagner's last work, was that it had been a "firm, solemn stagework". Published in *Kikeriki* on 13 August 1882

How a Leipzig Jew slowly became Richard Wagner. Published in *Der Floh*, Vienna

Richard Wagner surrounded by Jewish children, one of whom presents him with the day's movement of the Stock Exchange. *Der Floh*, Vienna

A sketch by George Grosz showing his feelings against the Wagner
cult. Published in the newspaper, *Simplizisimus* in 1921

Caricature of Richard Wagner by Olaf Gulbranson entitled 'It can't go
higher' to commemorate his 100th Anniversary on 22 May 1913

Left and right:
Thora Nissen-
Drexel. Gottfried's
grandmother,
born 6 March 1891
and died 22
October 1953

The Berlin Wagner monument erected on
1 October 1903 by Professor Gustav Eberlein
and presented to the public on 3 October 1903

Siegfried Wagner with his dogs in
Wahnfried Park, Bayreuth 1909

opportunity and leapt in immediately. Syberberg acted like a flirtatious sixth-former being bowled over by an older woman, and in doing so he was being absolutely true to his real intentions, which I was only later to learn. When he reported on the filming, he avoided the whole truth – for example, he kept silent about the fact that, during filming, my grandmother turned to me when she was singing "Wolf's" praises. I didn't agree with what she said about Hitler at all; it was very difficult for me to suppress my anger while the cameras were rolling.

During breaks in filming I discussed with Grandmother her statements about the Führer. Syberberg just wanted to let her talk, so he didn't get involved; he was evidently relying on her giving herself away. However, he grew very irritated when I lost my temper with Grandmother interpretation of events. He repeatedly complained that he was being hindered in his art. Because of this, Grandmother went down on record saying such things as (in connection with the 'Jewish question'):

> "We [Hitler and Winifred] never talked about these things...to be frank I didn't feel competent enough. I'm a totally apolitical person, and I was extremely astonished that, in the trial court [during the 1947 de-Nazification] I was continually accused of being political. I said that politics didn't enter into it, and then they all laughed. They said of course I dealt in politics. I didn't deal in politics."[21]

Of course, the members of the trial court were right to laugh: Grandmother was in reality a very politically active woman:

> "In Christmas 1923 I took a collection among the National Socialists here. They all brought their Christmas presents here, and I packed them all in boxes and sent them to the director of Landsberg [Fort Landsberg, where Hitler was imprisoned], requesting that they distribute them. This was done. I had asked him what he wanted, and he said that writing paper was something that he urgently needed, and so I sent him reams of writing paper. Good God, now people are accusing me of

having supplied the paper for *Mein Kampf*, aren't they? Almost as though it's my fault that *Mein Kampf* was written. Whatever you did, you were constantly attacked for it."[22]

My relationship with Syberberg also became increasingly strained. At first I had seen his film as a vehicle for publicly exposing the family past, but as filming progressed I began to mistrust him because of his undistanced and uncritical method of questioning and his slavish adherence to my grandmother. He noticed my mistrust, and with my sister's help tried – unsuccessfully – to keep me happy. I left Bayreuth after the end of filming.

During the summer semester of 1975 I met my cousin Nike Wagner, the second daughter of Uncle Wieland, again in Vienna. After this we met regularly in Vienna, and an enthusiastic dialogue developed between us, far from Bayreuth and the family. Syberberg's film about our grandmother was a popular talking point, and through this we came to talking about our fathers' roles during the Nazi period. The subject proved sensitive, because at that time Nike didn't want to talk about the privileged position her father had held, whereas spoke openly about Father and Wieland. Only at the beginning of the Nineties was she able to talk about Wagner, Hitler, antisemitism and the Wagner family, and she had her own opinions on these subjects. We were agreed, however, that it was necessary to approach Jewish artists in the same the way we had approached them in our theses – she with Karl Kraus, I with Kurt Weill. Wummi probably felt something similar; it was no accident that he was living with Nona von Haeften, who was the daughter of one Hitler's would-be assassins.

My mistrust of Syberberg continued to grow. He kept me only vaguely informed about the film's progress, and even then he would only talk over the phone. Meanwhile, Father persuaded Winifred apply for a power of attorney, according to which he could decide whether to accept or reject the film and how to make further use of the material, such as in books.

At the beginning of June, Father, Syberberg and myself met up in Munich. Syberberg showed us a version of the beginning of the film, with which Father was happy. Immediately afterwards, in an interview on 9 June, Syberberg summarised our meeting from his point of view. On the same day, my father issued a statement in response to Syberberg's account. As he was gradually coming to recognise the way in which his own role took a contradictory position, he suggested "other solutions" for the legal position of the film, which his legal advisers had worked out for him, unbeknown to me. On 10 June Syberberg produced a five-page contract which seemed to sum up everything that had been agreed between him, my father and his lawyers. By this time I had completely lost track of the legal situation; I had no idea that the version Syberberg had shown Father and I bore little resemblance to the finished film, and when I phoned him he told me that Hans Mayer had seen excerpts from the film and was enthusiastic.

Then problems arose over my project with the BBC. Syberberg wanted to market my grandmother exclusively with his own film, which pleased the British production team as little as it pleased me. I asked my father's lawyer to look over my contracts with Syberberg and with the BBC, but despite countless reminders I never saw the contracts again. It was eventually decided that the British were allowed to film Grandmother driving through Bayreuth to the *Festspielhügel* in her old Volkswagen and posing silently in front of the *Festspielhaus*. Brian Large obtained film records of the production of *Die Meistersinger* in 1975, of *Parsifal*, and of the Chéreau and Boulez's centenary production of the *Ring*. My situation did not look very favourable: I was ousted from the BBC project – Large now had his own Bayreuth connections.

At the end of June 1975 I visited Syberberg in Munich, accompanied by Nike and Beatrix, and was shown some insignificant excerpts. I grew even more suspicious when I asked him to show us certain scenes with Hitler and he explained that this was impossible, as those scenes were being edited. By chance I noticed that in another room he was projecting my father's films – the ones that I had found in the motorbike's sidecar – onto a screen, with a stills camera standing before it. It transpired that Syberberg was not only taking stills from these films but had already had complete copies made. Furious, I demanded that he hand over the originals and copies. They weren't returned until the autumn, and I decided to store them with

Beatrix's parents, where they remained until my father's lawyer demanded them back.

The situation had already become confrontational. In July 1975 the world premiere of his film was due to take place in the Cinémathèque Française in Paris. Syberberg had neither informed me about it nor invited me – he quite rightly feared a row if I discovered how he had assembled his film. It was my French cousins who told me, and Nike, Beatrix and I rushed immediately to Paris. The premiere was a nightmare: I found myself in the large auditorium in the middle of a swarm of sensation-hungry onlookers and journalists, all keen to learn everything about Winifred's "affair" with Wolf.

While the film was running I realised with horror that it didn't have much at all to do with the version Syberberg had shown me in Munich. It was in fact a quite different film, with new captions and edits that conveyed a quite different content. My French relations understood at once what had happened; they remained my only relatives who refrained from attacking me. After the premiere, I sat in the Capitol restaurant with Syberberg, Nike, Nikolaus Sombart and Wolf Donner from *Die Zeit*. I was in agony.

While we there there, Syberberg and I had our first serious dispute. I had wanted to talk to him alone, hoping to avoid a public scandal. I was angry not because he had revealed my grandmother's Nazi mentality but rather because he had broken our agreement, and had not only disregarded my right of veto on the use of the films but had also reneged on other agreements. I told him that, before a public viewing of the film, there should have been a private viewing, in front of experts such as Hans Mayer. I particularly resented the fact that, in the film, Syberberg had overlaid stills taken partly from Father's films, which included cynical remarks which had been made by my grandmother which he had recorded during breaks in the filming without her knowledge. The director responded by threatening me.

Through filming my grandmother with astonishing lack of objectivity, Syberberg had reinforced the myth concerning her role during the Nazi period. His editing and commentary did nothing to improve this, as they were governed by the visual presence of my grandmother in the film. As an 'actress' she was both convincing and demagogic, as proven by the reaction of the audience. Instead of toning this down artistically, Syberberg's direction added to the message. As a result, those who didn't want to repress the Third Reich viewed the film as a piece of Nazi propaganda.

When I got back to Bayreuth I was deluged with criticism from all sides, as people identified me with the film. I was attacked in the press by the psychoanalyst Eberhard Pöhner, whose father, Konrad, had played an important part in the post-war rebirth of the Bayreuth Festival, and whose Jewish wife had been persecuted by the Nazis during the war. Unfortunately, he didn't give me a chance to defend myself, and so I missed an opportunity to build an important friendship. Jewish Wagnerians suspected me of being a Nazi sympathiser, while right-wing Wagnerians dubbed me a 'nest-fouler', and the liberal left publicly disowned me, claiming that I had crossed over to my grandmother's point of view. The Bayreuth Society Of Friends and the representatives of Bayreuth also decided to distance themselves, because they believed that the film had damaged the city's image. Even my intentions in writing my doctoral thesis were doubted.

Amidst all of this confusion, I was particularly annoyed by the opportunism of the Bayreuth newspaper the *Nordbayerischer Kurier* and its editor-in-chief, Erich Rappl, who regularly introduced the festival and was also a critic. Even as a teenager I had nicknamed this paper the *Festspielhügel Express*. Now, in response to Syberberg's film, the *Nordbayerischer Kurier* now carried the headline "Monument To Personal Courage", dedicated to my grandmother. There was no better way make her fascist past seem innocuous. Rappl's article itself was sublimely non-committal – his introductory talks at the festival were in no danger.

In July 1975, an international press conference was held in the *Festspielhaus* restaurant, with only one subject on the agenda: Winifred and Wolf. My father asked me to stay away, and announced to the media that my grandmother had acknowledged that her remarks were made "without due consideration" and had consequently withdrawn them. He also said that, for the time being, he had forbidden her to enter the *Festspielhaus*. He remained silent regarding his own role in the Syberberg affair, however, and, although he had been well aware of the conditions I had laid down before collaborating with Syberberg, and had initially approved them, he remarked that I had "collaborated in the film with youthful impetuosity" and was "horrified by the result". I later protested over such a public declaration of incompetence, but it did nothing to help my cause.

Afterwards, I went to confront my grandmother. When I opened the door I saw with horror that on her desk, next to the picture of my father, was Hitler's photo, inscribed with the dedication "From Wolf to his Winnie". When I asked her why she had felt the need to take out the photo she retorted furiously: "Wolf[gang] is treating me the same way Wieland did, with all of his talk about me still believing in the Final Victory. He, who was there at all of the negotiations with Syberberg! Now he's being celebrated as a left-wing resistance fighter." When I asked her about the relationship between Hitler, Wieland and my father, she said bitterly: "They understood one another perfectly, even though he is now pretending they never had anything to do with him. In 1945 I sacrificed myself for the two of them."

At the end of the 1975 festival season I sent Hans Mayer everything that I had collected on this subject in the last few years to be included in our collaborative work, *Richard Wagner In Bayreuth*. It was a mountain of documents and pictures. Mayer had already been grappling with the subject Wagner and the Bayreuth Festival for a long time, and he knew what it was all about, and was quite willing to include the compilation of the documents and photos, also managing to work in some text excerpts from the Syberberg film. It hardly needs saying that Syberberg foamed at the mouth when he got word of this; he had wanted to market my grandmother exclusively, in all media, including a book. In a telephone call to my father's lawyer, he announced that he no longer considered himself bound by the agreements he had made in June, and requested that I didn't make it public that I had withdrawn my support for the film. If I did, he threatened to issue damaging statements about me to the press.

The German premiere of the Syberberg film took place in November 1975. My father asked Ewald Hilger to be present, the chairman of the Bayreuth Society Of Friends, and it was he who later wrote to me, telling me what had happened. On 25 November he wrote that he had no objections to Winifred's remarks, that the film was an honest and fascinating account of a life, and that this was also the way it was viewed by the public – if people hadn't wanted to hear about it, then they needn't have asked her about it. He considered the media circus surrounding the film to be unfounded, although he admitted that he had some reservations concerning plans that were drafted to publish the interview in book form, because he believed that this would create a completely different impression. There was a difference, he said, between hearing Frau Winifred's "explosive statements" being spoken and reading them in printed form.

It was farcical. Hilger assumed the standard position for people of his turn of mind. He unquestioningly accepted that Grandmother continued to consider Hitler as a person, as though Auschwitz had never been, or even *Mein Kampf*, in which Hitler had already described his annihilation plans long before he had put them into effect. What could be honourable about Winifred Wagner doggedly refusing to recognise the mass murderer in her "Wolf", even thirty years after the war?

However, this was by no means the end of Syberberg affair. During our last Christmas holidays together in Arosa, in 1975, Father read me a reply from Ernst Bloch, in which the Tübingen philosopher refused my father's request for a contribution to the accompanying jubilee programme for the centenary celebrations of the festival. Bloch wrote that, as a Jew and anti-fascist, he was incapable of doing this: the old association between Wagner's music and the Nazis had re-emerged, through Syberberg and Winifred Wagner, and any de-Nazification by Wieland and Wolfgang Wagner had already been undermined.

I regretted Bloch's refusal. Then, as now, I disagreed with him over the role of my father and Wieland; there can be no question that the Nazi heritage of Bayreuth has been consistently diluted. Father tried to change Bloch's mind – visiting him in secret, as my mother informed me – but he didn't succeed.

Syberberg later showed his true political colours after 1990, when he became a right-wing chauvinist believing in the "new great Germany". I felt that this was always the truth behind the left-wing mask he wore in the 1970s.

CHAPTER NINE

THE FESTIVAL CENTENARY

I worked only one stint as assistant director in Bayreuth while my father was intendant. It was during the centenary production of the Ring in 1976, which was directed by Patrice Chéreau, with François Regnault as dramaturg. I should have been happy when I was told that I was to be part of the team, at the beginning of 1976, because it had been one of my childhood dreams to work on the *Festspielhügel*. However, my parents' imminent divorce was weighing on my mind, especially the circumstances. I was soon to learn that Dietrich Mack's wife was the co-respondent, which solved the riddle of Dietrich's sudden departure from the *Festspielhügel* in 1974.

My relationship with my father plumbed new depths, especially as he no longer wanted me in the *Ring* team, in view of the changes in his private life – in other words he wanted me out of the way. However, I was neither prepared to give up working with Chéreau and Boulez or to leave my mother in the lurch. Also, the book project with Hans Mayer couldn't proceed without Father's support and consent, as he was the source of some additional material I wanted to provide for Mayer.

The meeting with the new *Ring* team in the *Festspielhaus* on 21 February 1976 made a great impression on me. Despite later marketing statements issued to the contrary, after the production had been hailed as a success by the media, at the time Father didn't agree with Chéreau's and Regnault's vision of the opera at all. The atmosphere at that meeting was extremely tense, and the project nearly came to grief thanks to my father's patriarchal attitude. The tussles between Father and Regnault continued until June 1976. In a letter to Regnault, on 11 June of that year, Father wrote of the man's concept of the production, entitled "Richard Wagner's Theatrical Mission", and wrote that the theories presented by the writer were so misleading, half-baked and plainly false that, in the final analysis, it was obvious that he hadn't the faintest idea what the *Ring* was about.

I of course was aware of this disparaging letter: Regnault, very upset, had given it to me, asking for my opinion. I was fascinated by the brilliant analysis of key scenes – for example, the prelude of *Das Rheingold* – and of the characters of the leading figures, especially Wotan, and by his extensive knowledge of different cultures and mythologies. I also found his interpretation of German theatrical traditions from the Classical and Romantic periods particularly convincing. In a letter dated 20 June 1976, Regnault replied to Father's damning judgment, signing off with the observation that, in Bayreuth, it seemed that one had to capitulate before the power of the "all-knowing genius".

This meant that the hour had come for a new house dramaturg, in the form of Oswald Bauer, who later became head of the press department and close adviser to my father until 1986. Bauer shared Father's opinion on Regnault's contribution in every detail. He also watched my every step in the *Festspielhaus*, faithfully reporting everything back to his esteemed boss – no detail was omitted, however ludicrous. For example, he reported that I had photocopied some documents in preparation for an interview with the *Nürnberger Nachrichten*, and from then on Father forbade me to use the photocopier, because he suspected that I would use the interview to evil ends.

However, another incident hit me much harder. I had collected material to give Hans Mayer for inclusion in *Richard Wagner In Bayreuth*, and then discovered at roughly the same time that the music historian Michael Karbaum had been collecting similar documents on the same subject as part of his own work, under the aegis of the Thyssen Foundation. As my father already had copyright privileges, because of his family connections and because of his position as director of the festival, Karbaum was obliged to submit his material to him before using it. However, my father passed on this material to me, to supplement the material I had collected myself, informing me that this was material he had originally made available to Karbaum from family documents, and assumed that I would pass it on to Mayer.

Consequently, Karbaum filed proceedings against Belser Verlag, Mayer's publisher, for using material from Karbaum's book without permission. Karbaum lost his case.

Looking back on it today, I would like to believe that Father had wanted to help me, although it would still have been better if he had told me the whole truth on handing over the material appropriated from Karbaum. The incident subsequently earned me a reputation of being untrustworthy among German academic circles, and I was even accused of stealing intellectual property. It even caused problems for me when I applied for a research grant for my studies from the DFG (The German Society For The Advancement Of Scientific Research) in 1977 – my application was finally rejected after more than a year. I also experienced how much public opinion had been whipped up against me in February 1976, when Dietrich Mack stopped in the foyer of the Stuttgart Opera House to ask, sneering, whether the Karbaum affair wouldn't soon be blowing up in my face.

It was only now that I learned that his wife, Gudrun, was the reason for my parents' imminent divorce. The news had disturbed me terribly, and I responded to Dietrich's allusion to the "Karbaum affair", writing to him at the end of March 1976 to protest against such an attack on my reputation. In June, Mack wrote me a fawning letter in which he tried to make amends, which I rebuffed in writing.

It later emerged that Karbaum's historical interpretation differed considerably from Mayer's, as Karbaum emphasised the significance of National Socialism in the history of the Bayreuth Festival. Of course, today I know that my father's misleading statements were intended to foil any discussion on the subject of Bayreuth, Hitler and the Wagner family, which he knew that Karbaum was so thoroughly investigating.

In April 1976, Beatrix and I had moved to Martinsreuth, near Bayreuth, in order to distance ourselves further from my father and the Siegfried Wagner House. In the following month I began working as assistant director, under Chéreau. I tried to support him wherever possible, as he faced a lot of resistance in the *Festspielhaus*. My father frequently urged me to give up the assistant directorship, in view of the tense family situation. From that time on, he wanted as little as possible to do with his first wife and their children. He even locked my sister out of the office, after nine years of working with her, which was tantamount to giving her notice. As I had no intention of leaving the team, he started harassing me. In a whole flood of unpleasant letters issued threats, and even gave notice of legal proceedings against me when I tried to help my mother re-establish her life. After that, working on the *Festspielhügel* became a nightmare. For instance, even when the official group photo of the *Ring* team was taken in front of the *Königsbau* of the *Festspielhaus*, my father insisted I leave, on the grounds that I did not belong to the team, while the rest of the group maintained an embarrassed silence. The photographer, Siegfried Lauterwasser, who had been a friend of my father's since they were young and who for decades had been very fond of me, was horrified, and pointedly photographed me separately with my musical mentor, Maximilian Kojetinsky. Despite the strain of working in this environment, I carried on rehearsing the alternative cast for the production. Like Boulez, Chéreau fully understood my situation, and neither followed the majority of staff in the *Festspielhaus* in ignoring me.

Even today I look back with horror on the centenary celebrations, which took place on 23 July 1976. "Richard Wagner and the Germans" – so many lies about the composer and his heirs! The high point was a 'people's party' after the performance of the third act of my father's staging of *Die Meistersinger* (Festival Meadow), under the baton of Karl Böhm. The celebrations were consequently suffocated by Upper Franconian provincialism, in a sorry spectacle masterminded by Oswald Bauer.

Arriving at my father's reception in the *Festspielhaus* after the ceremony, without an admission ticket and, like my colleagues, in casual dress, I suddenly found myself in the hands of the police again. I shouted at the plain clothes officer: "I demand to speak to my lawyer. These are police state methods." One of the onlookers explained to the policeman that I was "the son of the boss of the festival" and at the word "boss" a bell rang in his brain, and he let me go. Deferentially, he said: "But why didn't you say who you were? Please go and get your invitation." As I hadn't received one, I couldn't very well do that and knowing every nook and cranny of the *Festspielhügel* since my childhood, I decided to try to get into the hall by one of my secret routes. I had almost reached my goal when I was caught by two security officers who started to lead me off. This scene was noticed by the publisher Klaus Piper, who was sitting at Martin Gregor-Dellin's table. He hurried to help me, took the policemen to task and invited me to his table. I looked around at the piqued faces of the guests from the cream of West German affluent society, especially those of the Friends Of Bayreuth, and discovered my father surrounded by his chorus of yes men. No, I could not stay here. I left the room as quickly as I could. I could easily have left Bayreuth altogether right then, but I had promised Chéreau and Boulez that I would continue rehearsing with the second *Ring* cast.

At the end of July I learned from the newspaper *Bild* that my father had married Gudrun, the former Frau Mack. Although I had had nothing to do with the matter, the tabloid press now plagued me as well. My parents' divorce during the 1976 centenary celebrations, after 33 years of marriage, came as such a shock to my mother that she never fully recovered. In an attempt to redefine her identity she absorbed herself in writing her autobiography, working through the copious entries in her diaries and her correspondences with Father after their engagement in 1942, complementing them with countless revealing comments which often called into question the official Bayreuth historiography. The conflict with national socialism and the role played by the Wagner family became one of her central themes, and one which she passionately addressed.

It wasn't until 1978, after she had moved from Bayreuth to her native city of Wiesbaden, that my mother actually began constructing a life for herself. This painful process made me look more closely not only at the consequences of the Wagners' Nazi past but also at our own relationship. Because of her total immersion with the Bayreuth Festival and Father, as had been expected of her, she had scarcely had the opportunity to adequately perform her role as mother, which she often regretted. However, since Father's first production of the *Ring*, in Bayreuth in 1960, she had looked more and more to me for advice and support, as Father became totally tied up with the directorship and competing with Wieland. The consequent discord between the two branches of the family worsened the situation even more. After Wieland's death in 1966, and with the subsequent social duties which went with her position as wife of the head of the festival, she found life on the *Festspielhügel* increasingly difficult as Father, Grandmother and Eva offered her no support.

My family's pursuit of the will to power in the years from 1966 to 1975 isolated my mother more and more from the outside world. Naturally she was aware of this, and tried to do something about it, but failed – she was no match for the concerted might of the other family members. Not surprisingly, it was during these years that my mother began to wonder what would have happened if she hadn't given up her successful career as a ballerina (at the Oper Unter Den Linden, in Berlin) in 1942, and even started questioning her career in the theatre, regretting that she hadn't instead been a nurse. After her divorce at the age of 57, however, she was forced to realise that it was too late to embark on a new career, and concentrated instead – almost by way of compensation – on looking into National Socialism and Jewish history.

A number of sensation-hungry journalists (especially those from *Bild*) took advantage Mother's lack of experience and engaged in the usual Wagner scandalmongering. In fact, they distorted her statements so outrageously that I was forced to take legal action. With her gradual liberation from her Bayreuth past, helped by her brother and his family, Mother's interest in the Italian side of our family grew, and she became especially fond of her grandson Eugenio. I was very happy about this: it showed that she shared my belief in harmony and peace, and the search for a meaning to life. A picture of her as four-year-old child, playing the part of the child Sorrow in a 1922 performance of Giacomo Puccini's *Madama Butterfly* in Wiesbaden, is on my desk as I write. Her beautiful, delicate, child-like smile still shines through today, revealing what was always the real love of her life: the world of the theatre.

CHAPTER TEN

IN SEARCH OF MYSELF

At the end of July 1976, at an international press conference, my father presented the newly-published Cosima Wagner diaries, which had been edited by Martin Gregor-Dellin and Dietrich Mack. I packed my bags shortly afterwards. The only thing that made my departure difficult was leaving Gunda, who had been my foster aunt since my childhood. She broke down, bursting into tears.

Beatrix and I first went to the Chiemsee, to see her parents. From there, we decided to continue on to Ireland, to recover from the lunacy of Bayreuth. During a stopover, we visited Charles and Germaine Spencer in London. They received us warmly, and Charles encouraged me to lead a life free of Bayreuth. In Ireland we were overwhelmed by the beauty of the countryside, although I found that I couldn't really enjoy it: I was still too deeply distressed by my experiences.

Fortunately there were at least some glimmers of hope on a professional level. I was negotiating with the theatre in Bonn to produce a staging of Beethoven's *Fidelio* in the spring of 1977. I also received a generous offer from Lys Symonette, in New York, to work in the Kurt Weill archives on the publication of Weill's written works.

Dieter Rexroth, head of the Hindemith Institute in Frankfurt am Main and notable for his brilliant conceptual ideas on the works of Beethoven, had discreetly contacted the Bonn Theatre in

1975. I also requested that Roland Aeschlimann be involved in the production. Dieter and I kept our negotiations secret, as I feared that my father and his cronies would obstruct any engagements for me. The influence of Bayreuth in the opera world should never be underestimated: the intendant of the Bonn Opera House, Joachim Heyse, informed me of the way in which the organisation had attempted to manipulate public opinion. During a meeting of intendants, on hearing that the contract had been already signed, my father said to Heyse: "You've landed yourself in a real mess there. *Fidelio*, in Bonn, in the year of Beethoven's centenary, as his first production – can he really pull that off?" My own father's doubts about my ability spread like wildfire among agents, theatre administrations and the media, many of whom were already closely connected with Bayreuth. For agents and intendants it was more important to keep in with the *Festspielhügel* than to find engagements for me. It was now known in opera circles that my father looked unfavourably on those who gave me work.

Since the autumn of 1976 I had been living in the same apartment in Munich that I had lived in before, on the Wartburgplatz. At that time I was concerned primarily with two things: securing my mother's livelihood and preparing myself for the *Rigorosum*, the final oral examination after the acceptance of my doctoral thesis in May 1976, scheduled to be held in Vienna.

Meanwhile, Father had cut off my monthly allowance. Fortunately, one of my guardian angels at the time, the hotel owner Peter Kremslehner, knew of my precarious situation and generously took me in as a guest in his Regina Hotel in Vienna.

In December 1976 I passed my oral examinations in Musicology, German Literature and Philosophy, but only my mother, Beatrix and a few Viennese friends came to the graduation party. Wummi called up later and told me that he had informed Father of my success, whose sole comment was: "He copied it all anyway!"

In April 1977 I started my work in Bonn. Dieter Rexroth had combined the first and third versions of *Fidelio* to produce a revolutionary interpretation. Now his concept had to be translated onto the stage. This exercise was explained in an extensive programme, including texts by Ursula Krechel, August Stramm, Ernst Toller, Kurt Schwitters, Peter-Paul Zahl, Rainer Kunze, Paul Celan, Marie Luise Kaschnitz and Norbert Friedrich.

At the curtain call I experienced my first clash with a predominantly conservative public, although the younger members of the audience applauded my updated production.

The reaction of the press was mixed. The German media adopted the tone set by Josef Herbort in *Die Zeit* on 3 June 1977, under the headline: "No Competition From Junior."

> "Wagner's great-grandson, Gottfried, makes his debut as director with *Fidelio*." His negative criticism was pertinent and only mildly irritating, but I deeply resented his further assertions: "When Wolfgang Wagner was asked a year ago about whether he would soon hand over festival production or even the running of the Bayreuth Festival to a younger member of the family, the shrewd Franconian answered diplomatically that he still didn't yet see a suitable contender among the next generation. Now that Wieland's son Wolf-Siegfried has dabbled with *Tristan* and *Die Meistersinger*, reducing Wagner to the one dimensional, and Wolfgang's son Gottfried has staged his non-dramatic vision of Beethoven's opera, the boss of the Bayreuth Festival can once again sleep peacefully. In fact, he faces no competition from either of the Master's great-grandsons, and if the rumour going around at the *Fidelio* premiere in Bonn is true – that Wolfgang Wagner warned his fellow intendants against his son – one may make what one will of the family quarrel between the guardians of the Nibelung gold. Fundamentally, however, the father is right."[23]

Herbort's piece had the desired effect. It was a long time before I found further employment in a German opera house, and even today reviews of my productions still contain Herbort's prejudice and insinuation.

The Bonn critic Hans G Schürmann was the only one who didn't share his German colleagues' opinion. In fact, reviews of my work became more favourable further away from Bayreuth. For example, the respected critic Roy Koch wrote in the *New York Times* at the end of May:

> "Bonn...here, in Beethoven's birthplace, where every note of the Master's scores is regarded as sacred, a starkly contemporary production of his only opera, *Fidelio*, is bound to raise controversy – all the more so when the producer is making his professional debut, and especially when that producer is the great-grandson of Richard Wagner.
>
> "Though visibly shaken by the few loud boos mixed with the enthusiastic applause at the end of the premiere on Thursday night, 30-year-old Gottfried Wagner stuck out the unmistakable Wagner chin, and his blue eyes flashed defiance at his detractors as he left the stage after several curtain calls.
>
> "'I hadn't realised I would be so affected by the violent reaction,' he said after the performance, 'but the booing as well as the applause convinced me that we have achieved a genuine dialogue with our audience – and that's what we set out to do.' ...Gottfried Wagner is regarded by many observers here as a force among the new generation of opera producer."[24]

Even then I could see that I would be better able to develop my career outside Germany.

Meeting Bettina Fehr again in Bonn was also comforting. We had been introduced for the first time only the year before, in Bayreuth, but she helped me through this and later crises, and soon became my second mother. Since then she has taken an active interest in all of the major events which have taken place in my life, both professional and personal. Her selfless involvement in matters of public concern has for decades been an example to me. For example, she worked for a long time as honorary manager of the Bonn Society For Christian-Jewish Co-operation, of which she has been a member since 1954. This involvement also has a lot to do with our common interest in German-Jewish relations, which she supports for reasons of family solidarity with her Jewish maternal grandfather, a distant relation of Heinrich Heine. The daughter of the respectable middle-class Christian doctor Arthur Lankes and classified in the ridiculous system of the Nuremberg race laws of 1935 as "half caste, second grade", she was forbidden to study and instead was forced to become a bookseller, one of the only professions the Nazis allowed her to pursue. Through her marriage to Götz Fehr, the long-time director of Inter Nationes, after the war she was able to rally people all over the world to her cause. One of our topics of conversation – apart from the German-Jewish question – is the subject of Bayreuth and my relationship with my father, whom she knows. It should come as no surprise that Bettina – despite the work she performs every day for people in need, and despite her large family – has also been active since 1992 in the Olga Havel Foundation For The Handicapped. Advising her to take it easy is a waste of breath!

Fortunately, in this difficult time Lotte Lenya and Lys Symonette renewed their offer of allowing me to join the Kurt Weill Foundation Of Music. Before I travelled to New York in the autumn, however, I had a difficult errand to perform in Bayreuth. Mother was determined to stay there, and for some reason had moved in with Grandmother, of all people. Beatrix and I turned up at Grandmother's 80th birthday celebrations, where ourselves and Mother were all shunned by the high-society guests. I had never heard so many compliments paid to my grandmother. If anything, the Syberberg film had strengthened her position with her right-wing admirers. The old-guard members of the Wagner societies, and of the Bayreuth Society Of Friends, toasted Hitler's Winnie while Grandmother gushed about Arno Breker, the Führer's favourite sculptor, who had just finished a bust of her. While she and her cronies wallowed in reminiscences about some golden era, my efforts to extricate Mother from this nest of Nazi vipers came to nothing.

Before my journey to New York there was an episode as short

as it was curious. In August, Wummi, Nike and I were interviewed by Klaus Figge for a programme called *Aspekte*, on the German TV channel ZDF. The media immediately reported that the fourth generation of Wagners was standing at the gates of Bayreuth, ready to wrest power from the old guard – this, even despite the fact that I had already made it perfectly clear that I wanted to make my own way outside Bayreuth and wanted nothing to do with the festival. Even so, Father wasn't at all happy with this. The interviewer had realised that he had already written off the whole of this fourth generation as incompetent, although he had been unable to give any specific reasons. In order to add weight to his opinion, in a letter to Dieter Stolte at the end of August 1977 – who was then head of programming and is now intendant of ZDF – Father described the interviewer's research as inaccurate, and warned against any repetition of such procedures, as this would ultimately also affect the interests of the ZDF. It did indeed have an effect on the interests of the ZDF: the channel was later frequently allowed to televise Bayreuth productions.

In September I returned to Bonn to oversee rehearsals for further performances of my production of *Fidelio*. The damning judgment of the German press had had a negative effect on the morale of the team and the theatre as a whole, but despite my misgivings the revival was a success with the section of the public that I wanted to reach at that time: young people, who traditionally never went to the opera.

I frequently met the neurologist and psychiatrist Johannes Meyer-Lindenberg, who lived in Bonn and whom I had first met at the premiere party for my production of Beethoven's *Fidelio*, through Bettina Fehr. She had told him about my difficult family situation, and he offered to stand by my mother, who was in a particularly bad state at the time, an offer which Eva and I gratefully accepted. Mostly, however, we talked about the conflict with Father. Through his own experiences, Johannes had developed a great sensitivity for discord among relatives. His father was of Jewish stock and his aristocratic mother came from a Christian background, and were forced to travel to Colombia to flee the Nazis, and it was here that Johannes was born, in 1938.

After the Second World War, his father was assigned as a West German ambassador in Rome and Madrid, and Johannes only ever came to Bonn as a student.

He immediately understood that my rebellion stemmed from my ideological incompatibility with my family's Nazi past, and that my ethical and politico-cultural positions were incompatible with those of my father. Observing how much I was affected by the situation, he offered to mediate between my father and myself. From the autumn of 1977 until his painfully early death in 1991, at the age of only 53, Johannes did all he could, through meetings and numerous telephone calls, to convince Father of the need to talk with me.

In Bonn, Bettina Fehr once again kindly looked after me. Once she even invited me to accompany her to a reception at the Israeli embassy, where she not only introduced me to the ambassador but also to Heinrich Böll, who said: "So you're the Wagner who got up people's noses here in the sacred city of Bonn with your *Fidelio*."

"People have been annoyed at me for that. Just look at what was said in *Die Zeit* at the end of May," I answered, rather despondently. I told him what Herbort had written.

He laughed. "Gottfried Wagner, what you dared to do there was perfectly right. Don't be upset by people like Herbort, who swim with the tide. You have to learn to free yourself internally from the opinion of opportunists, otherwise you'll go to the dogs in the German cultural jungle. Just stop believing that *Die Zeit* has a monopoly on truth and honesty."

I told Böll about the first time I had read his book *Wanderer, Kommst Du Nach Spa*, and how my father didn't appreciate his work. He wasn't surprised. "Your father certainly won't change now, not matter how far he goes to convince the press that he has." He was right about that, too.

I also used my time in Bonn to apply for a grant from the DFG (German Society For The Advancement Of Scientific Research) for a grant. After months of delays, I learned that objections to my proposals had been raised members of the board who held political grudges against my father. Now, with no money, no enthusiasm and no energy to spend battling an endless and expensive lawsuit, it was time for me to leave Germany and try my luck in America.

CHAPTER ELEVEN

ON THE TRAIL OF KURT WEILL

In November Beatrix and I finally flew to New York. The leaden fatigue I'd felt in Germany soon lifted when we landed in murky yellow smog at John F Kennedy airport. The border officials had a style of their own. Coming from Germany, it was a refreshing change for me to be greeted by a friendly Afro-American official with: "What do you want here, Gottfried?" I didn't exactly know myself. Rather embarrassed I replied: "I'm here for fun!" The official grinned, slammed his stamp in my passport and said: "So have fun, Gottfried!" In a terribly hot, crowded and stinking bus we drove to Manhattan. We went first to Beatrix's Aunt Gabriele, whose house was in Riverdale on the Hudson River, opposite the Toscanini house. Later, Francis de Vegvar and his wife Kitty, who were also Beatrix's relations, invited us to their beautiful penthouse. They were to be among my most faithful friends in the USA, in what proved to be difficult times.

The penthouse overlooked Central Park and the seemingly endless Fifth Avenue up- and downtown, a view which made me almost forget my bitter experiences in Germany. But I quickly witnessed a stark contrast with Beatrix's relatives' lifestyle of luxury: only a few blocks further uptown I witnessed the indescribable squalor of Harlem.

During this time, I presented Lenya with the book of my doctoral thesis, for which she had written an introduction. When she accepted the book, she said emotionally: "At last, Weill's name is in first place, and then Brecht's! It was always the other way round – you're the first one to recognise that Weill is the equal of Brecht." I answered, no less moved, "Weill's music makes the joint works with Brecht immortal, because what will remain of Brecht will certainly not be his ideology but, rather, his accurate knowledge of human contradictions and his wonderfully clear and poetic language!" Lenya shared my opinion. With great enthusiasm, she started talking of her work with Brecht between 1927 and 1933. "Brecht always said to me: 'You are epic theatre!'" she said to me, laughing.

Of course, I wanted to know more about Weill. The Jewish seminarian of 1927 – as her "serious little Kurt" was called in those days – was certainly not looking for the intellectual, emancipated woman in Lenya, but rather the seductive Lulu with whom he enjoyed all of the attractions of the Venusberg. I listened attentively to Lenya's stories of the nights in Berlin, up until March 1933. Often the names of people and cities were invented during a drinking binge, when Brecht would wildly spin a globe and Weill would stop it with his finger. At one time, his finger landed on a place called Benares, hence 'The Benares Song'. "It's absurd what all of these pseudo-intellectuals cobble together nowadays about the origins of works by Weill and Brecht," said Lenya heatedly, "and what ideological nonsense they pile onto Kurt."

From one moment to the next, she would swing between talking about her past and to wanting to know everything about me. "There's not so much to tell," I answered, "and you can imagine why I wrote my doctoral thesis on Weill and Brecht.

"Did you run into a lot of difficulties?" she asked anxiously.

"Certainly far fewer than yourself and Weill," I replied.

We fell silent, looking at one another solemnly. Then she suddenly burst out laughing, and told one of her Wagner stories from the time she worked as a stage extra in Zurich. "In the third act of *Parsifal*, as a servant of the Grail I and three others had to carry the coffin with the dead Titurel a long way from the centre rear of the stage, right down to the footlights. We were marching very solemnly, and I had to unveil the wax head of the dead Titurel, which was covered by a velvet cloth, even more solemnly. But unfortunately for me I pulled the cloth too hard, and Titurel's head flew off and rolled down into the orchestra pit. The audience roared with laughter, the curtain came down and I was sacked."

Lenya became more and more cheerful. She still had a girlish charm, and I saw clearly how easily one could have fallen in love with this woman forty years ago. The evening ended with our singing excerpts from *Lohengrin*: she sang Elsa's dream, in her rather smoky, brittle voice, but with clean intonation and exact rhythm. She knew every note and every word by heart, although she couldn't read music. I parodied the swan knight from the Grail Redemption Company. We were helpless with laughter, and lost ourselves completely.

In the next few weeks I was to learn to my horror how indiscriminate Lenya was in her choice of friends, many of whom exploited her shamelessly. Lys was no match for Lenya's false friends. On my second meeting with Lenya I didn't manage to clear up all the questions connected with my work, so I started looking for another job.

During various meetings with theatre agents, I was once again sharply reminded of my origins and of Bayreuth. The agents were well informed about my rebellions against family tradition – the long arm of the *Festspielhügel* had made sure of that.

Living in Riverdale complicated my life even further. Everything important happened in Manhattan, and to get there I had to take the bus, which went through Harlem. I shall never forget the faces of these neglected young black people, distorted by hatred. As soon as they saw the bus coming they would run towards it, swearing at the passengers, sometimes even banging on the sides. The polite drivers – who were mostly black – tried to get through Harlem without stopping, and were accused of being 'whities' friends' for simply doing their job. If a traffic light turned to red, the driver would open his window to try to repel the onslaughts of black kids with choice words, but they just answered with obscenities. I thought at such times that this was no melting pot. Many of these mostly unemployed young people hated us just because we came from the rich Jewish area of Riverdale, a social division which triggered off an explosion of class and race hatred. I increasingly doubted whether New York was really so wonderful, and the clean, beautiful Riverdale neighbourhood came to appear more and more like an ivory tower.

During this period I also met Gert von Gontard in the Metropolitan Club. He was one of the most influential sponsors of New York operas and the Bayreuth Festival, and an eager and knowledgeable proponent of art, theatre and music. I only ever heard good things about him. A member of the Budweiser brewery dynasty – which offered him ample means to pursue his love of opera – he was by no means a snob; rather, as the offspring of a bourgeois family, he obeyed the aristocratic mores of *noblesse oblige*. He had once supported Max Reinhardt when the great director had fled to New York to escape the Nazis. I described to him my unpromising professional prospects, and explained my opinion of the festival, of which he also had no good opinion. Although he could be described more as a conservative, he supported my criticism of the German cultural establishment – especially of Bayreuth – with paternal sympathy.

I was pleasantly surprised when my sister asked me to be a witness to her wedding in southern France. With fewer illusions about a professional future in New York, I flew to Munich in December 1977, and travelled on from there. Despite spending such a short (and only partially successful) time in New York being short, I now felt ill at ease on my return to Germany. The weeks I spent in America had had a salutary effect on me, and I began to view things in Germany with greater detachment. Job or no, I determined to return to America as soon as possible. What Everding – who was becoming more and more powerful in the German theatre scene – or any other theatre bigwigs might say was now immaterial to me. Even the fact that the German media ignored my book on Weill and Brecht didn't bother me much. America became for me the big challenge. I wanted to seek my fortune there, and build up a life of my own.

How I enjoyed the vastness and beauty of southern France after the confinement of Germany and the wildness of the New York jungle. Although it soon became clear to me that Eva was only being affectionate because Father had rejected her, the friendly and open nature of my brother-in-law, Yves Pasquier, worked wonders. In the end, Eva and I tried to talk honestly to one another, without the constant feeling of distrust that festered between us, or rivalry for the post of festival chief. "The brutal way our father has frozen us out of Bayreuth can still turn out to have its advantages," I said to her. "Let's use them!"

This proposal was ultimately to prove highly illusory, but in those days in southern France the divisive shadow of Bayreuth could not come between us. The wedding and the Christmas festivities that followed were so cheerful and warm that I became painfully aware of what we had never had as children: the feeling of belonging to a family, of security. Out of politeness, my new relations didn't ask about Bayreuth, and so the atmosphere was scarcely clouded at all.

In January 1978, Beatrix and I flew back to New York, making a stopover in London at the Spencers'. I began to systematically occupy myself those works which Weill produced after his escape from Nazi Germany, and worked out some initial suggestions on how they could be promoted in Germany. I also received a first lesson in how to behave to get a job from Betty Smith, a well-known New York media agent. She presented me with 20 questions which agents, theatre directors and publishers typically asked in job interviews. I answered them all wrongly, because I spoke the truth. Betty was horrified. When she asked me how I viewed the Bayreuth family tradition, I answered: "Why do you think I'm here? Because I don't want to have anything to do with the whole Bayreuth business!" Laughing at first, then seriously, Betty said: "Do you want to get a job or not? Being a Wagner is also an advantage. Use it wisely!"

She was right, of course. I had to learn how to handle my past and to present the relationship with my family in Bayreuth without doing myself a disservice, or losing my identity. I painstakingly began to de-Germanise myself, with the aim of becoming a liberal American. I began to frequent the doors of literary agents, which is how I met Eliot Ravetz, who worked for the influential Scott Meredith Literary Agency on Third Street. I soon enjoyed a warm friendship with Eliot, although it ended as abruptly as it had begun. The agency wanted to make my revolt against the family heritage the focus of advertising for my book. I, on the other hand, had no intention of being portrayed as an uncouth, hot-headed revolutionary. Eliot had to obey his boss, and we parted company without coming to words. I was sorry, as I found that I could talk to Eliot openly about Germans and Jews of our generation, and he helped me overcome my superficial philosemitism. I shall never forget Eliot's simple words on one of our drives from Manhattan to Riverdale: "Here in New York, where there are more Jews than in Israel, you'll meet a lot of unpleasant Jews who'll make you feel really antisemitic. Stop thinking that Jews are better than other people, especially here in New York. We aren't."

On one visit to the Met, I met Milcom and Yveta Graff, who were sponsors of the opera house. They had attached a condition to their terms of sponsorship: that the money be invested in Czech music, since Yveta came from Prague. The Graffs lived in one of the luxurious apartments on Park Avenue. As had been predicted, the 'entry ticket' to the Graffs' home – and consequently to New York society – was my name. However, people were extremely curious about everything concerning Wagner and Bayreuth. Talk was by no means confined to Richard Wagner and his works; I was also quizzed about my father's style of management and my relationship with him. Again and again I was asked whether I would follow him as head of the festival. Despite the charm and generosity of my hosts, I found this kind of conversation unpleasant. Most of the very conservative questioners were interested more in the private world of the Wagner family than in my views on culture and art. But with Betty Smith's advice in mind – "Do you wanna get a job or not?" – I endeavoured to answer politely and noncommittally. However, when I was asked why I had written my doctoral dissertation on Weill and Brecht, of all people, I decided that I'd had enough of evasions. I spoke bluntly about Hitler, Bayreuth and the Jews, and passionately confessed that the book was the consequence of a disastrous marriage between politics and culture in Bayreuth. Mrs Graff, who as a child had gone through the horrors of the German occupation with her family, showed sympathy for my commitment, but she remained an exception: the majority of the art sponsors present – some of whom were members of the arch-conservative Wagner Circle and Bayreuth pilgrims – maintained a polite silence. This was their way of saying that they were more than sceptical regarding what I then (together with Alexander and Margarete Mitscherlich) described as "mourning work". Their motto was: "What you can't alter is no longer a worthwhile topic of conversation." My impression wasn't improved when some of them assured me privately how they found my attitude courageous.

After a few moments of silence, those present broached the subject of whether Wagner had been a Jew. If there were any truth in this assertion it would have been tantamount to a vindication, in view of my great-grandfather's well-known antisemitic attacks and the traditional family line, culminating in Winifred Wagner. I was familiar with those speculations made by Ernest Newman in his biography of Richard Wagner. In Bayreuth, support for and denial of such theories changed as frequently as the weather, according to which seemed most appropriate at the time. I pointed out that it was by no means clear whether Ludwig Heinrich Christian Geyer had been a Jew or that he was Richard's biological father. All that was provable was that Geyer was Richard Wagner's adoptive father. I had no proof for my denial of the claim and could only promise to search for the answer.

A few weeks later, I finally succeeded. The Leo Baeck Institute had kindly looked out for me genealogical documents on Ludwig Heinrich Christian Geyer, which proved that he was not a Jew. Several weeks after that I met Milcom and Yveta Graff once again in the Met, at a performance of Debussy's *Pelléas Et Mélisande*, and told them of the results of my research. Yveta was a little surprised, and commented that for her only Wagner's music mattered, and not his ideology – an opinion which, with my knowledge of Bayreuth's history, I couldn't share.

That evening will always remain in my memory, although for quite another reason. After seeing the moth-eaten production, for which I had dressed up as an invited guest, I missed the last bus back to Riverdale. To make matters worse, there was a fierce snowstorm that day in New York. As a taxi would have been too expensive, I decided to go home by subway. I somehow took the wrong line and ended up in Harlem. I only noticed my mistake when I was standing in the middle of a snowstorm on 154th Street, with black faces peering at me from all sides. A black guy sitting next to me on the subway had warned me to avoid the area: "Hey, mister, what are you doing here? Take care you get out of here! And take a yellow cab. The other taxis can be dangerous." Looking around, I saw people standing silently, clothed in dirty rags, warming themselves around fires they had made in oil drums. Seeing such an elegantly dressed white man, their faces twisted in scorn and suspicion. My heart raced, and I frantically looked for a yellow cab. It wasn't until over an hour later, and after a number of dubious offers, that I finally found one. Before asking for any address, the somewhat surprised driver wanted to know if I had any money. When I told him that I came from Riverdale, he growled: "That's the rich Jews' district, and we've got a snowstorm. So you can pay double." I offered him 20 dollars, but he demanded 40, "or you can walk there in the snow". The thought of walking twelve kilometres to Riverdale through the district in the snow overcame my resistance, and I agreed.

Thus began a second adventure. The driver raced like a madman through short cuts and over enormous potholes. I was flung from one side of the cab to the other, and several times my head collided with the windows. I implored him to drive more slowly, but that just made him even more daring, and he started skidding his Buick over the uneven, snow-covered streets. The weather was so bad that I couldn't recognise where we were, and had visions of myself as a corpse in the Hudson River. Suddenly the driver slammed on the brakes and demanded his 40 dollars. White as a sheet, I had hardly handed them over when he got out and tore my door open. With a broad smile that stood out particularly in the snowstorm, he shouted: "Hey, man, you better learn something about Harlem!" I got out, he slammed his door and disappeared like a phantom. I took heed of this experience on all subsequent journeys into New York and, indeed, everywhere else. It was another illustration of the obscene gulf between the rich and the poor in that city. On that night I doubted whether my high-society life in elegant Riverdale really had that much meaning.

But I had little time for social conscience. My financial situation was becoming critical, and Lenya was further delaying the promised contract. She had a fear of being poor, which made it difficult for her to commit to paying wages, although she was otherwise very generous. This fear was probably also the reason that Lys and I had to take our own lunches on our visits to the beautiful Weill House on the river in New City, New Jersey, although it didn't stop Lenya inviting us to a restaurant afterwards. None of this bothered me much: I was happy to be in the Weill House.

The composer had financed the house with the money he had received for his work in Hollywood. I was particularly impressed by his attic work room, with its spartan furnishings: a desk and chair. Here he had written some of his major works, such as *Lost In The Stars*.

ON THE TRAIL OF KURT WEILL

Lenya suggested that I write a biography of Weill, as it looked as though David Drew would never finish his book. Unfortunately, she didn't tell me that the journalist Ronald Sander was already working on a similar project, and with her approval.

Another month passed before I explained to Lenya that I would have to return to Germany if she couldn't give me a contract, and she realised I was serious. Lys had also told her that I was already busy with Weill's work in America and had developed ideas on how best to promote his work. Furthermore, an interview with me was about to appear in the *New York Times*, which would help publicise the Weill Foundation. This time it worked. By March I had a contract in my hand, which ensured a modest living. At least it meant that I wouldn't have to depend on the loan that Gert von Gontard had generously offered me.

It was through Gert that I met John White, an unusual witness of Austrian-Jewish history, at a splendid lunch in the New York Metropolitan Club. As a Viennese Jew, he had fled the Nazis to the USA and, after an adventurous life, had become the successful managing director of the New York City Opera. With great empathy, he immediately grasped my situation: "The great-grandson of the Wagner, an antisemite, is working on Weill, a left-wing Jew. That won't make you very popular in Germany. And I won't even ask you about your family – you follow your Aunt Friedelind's anti-Nazi attitude!" He had got straight to the heart of the matter, and I replied: "You're right. I respect my aunt's attitude to National Socialism, but I don't share her uncritical attitude toward Richard Wagner's antisemitism. I can see an ideological line running directly from his article 'The Jews In Music' to Hitler." When he noticed how important a conversation with him about National Socialism was for me, he invited me to his office, where he made some interesting points relevant to my work on Weill, and gave me the results from contemporary research into National Socialism. He also recommended some standard works, such as Eugen Kogon's *The SS State: The System Of The German Concentration Camps*. White had made a lot of enemies as a businessman, but I owe him a great deal.

My meeting with Eric Werner a few days later – which was

important in the search for my own identity – went quite differently. After several phone calls, I finally met up with the distinguished music historian, with whose important writings on Mendelssohn I was familiar. He politely (but warily) enquired why I was occupying myself so intensively with Weill. Although Werner thought the composer interesting, he did not consider him important. Scarcely had I revealed my interest in German-Jewish history than he started to deliver a lecture on Wagner's antisemitism, that was as knowledgeable as it was filled with strong aversion. Nor did he just refer to Wagner's 'The Jews In Music', but also commented in detail on Cosima's numerous antisemitic remarks in her diaries, which had just been published in New York. I understood his horror at the antisemitic cult in Bayreuth, and wasn't offended when he expressed loathing for Wagner and the Bayreuth "cretinism", as Nietzsche put it.

However, it was more difficult to accept his condemnation of Germans in general – which, of course, included myself and the rest of my generation. In fact, he considered me to be part of the antisemitic tradition of my family, which I was quick to refute. I described to him those decisive moments in my life as I confronted National Socialism, and he finally understood why I had written my doctoral thesis on Weill. But his fundamental opinion remained unaltered, and the meeting left me feeling like an ugly little German, a Nazi Wagner, who could do no better than change his name as quickly as possible. I was greatly affected by Werner's bitterness and hatred, and I felt quite distraught when I left, dismayed by such a disinterest in even talking to those who, like me, were suffering under the burden of their parents' Nazi past. I later discovered that, as a Jew, he had undergone a particularly harrowing trauma, although he never spoke of it in detail.

At the end of February 1978, I gave my first large interview in the US. It took place thanks to Betty Smith, who had negotiated a discussion for me with Donal Henahan of the *New York Times*. As I had no experience at all of the American media, Betty prepared me for it with practised patience. We covered my life in a game of questions and answers. As usual, I answered her 20 questions on Bayreuth extremely critically, and had nothing good to say of Wagner and the German cultural scene. She, of course, was horrified: "You haven't learned a thing since our last talk. Just realise how important a successful interview with the *New York Times* could be for you!" So we went through the questions again, and worked out a more diplomatic – but still tenable – set of answers.

Betty's advice was spot on. Donal Henahan asked the questions she had expected, and my answers aroused his rather reserved but objective interest. In May 1978, the paper published an accurate account of what I had said regarding my production of Beethoven's *Fidelio*, music theatre in the 20th century and Kurt Weill. Finally, I was able to read an article on me and my work that contained scarcely one word on the Wagner family and Bayreuth. This interview was the first of several with other important American newspapers, although none of it helped to improve my precarious financial situation.

On one day I went to visit Lys in her apartment on West 73rd Street. By chance I noticed downstairs on the list by the doorbells, a name written in English ornamental lettering which triggered a quite particular memory. It said: "Dr Wolf, Kapellmeister." Kapellmeister Wolf was the alias that Hitler had jokingly given himself. Until 1935, whenever he travelled between Berlin and Munich, Hitler would always make a stopover at the Hotel Bube in Bad Berneck, just outside Bayreuth, where he would ring up "his Winnie". He would announce himself as "Kapellmeister Wolf", whereupon Grandmother would dash by car to pick up her Führer and take him back to Villa Wahnfried.

So who was this Kapellmeister Wolf on 73rd Street? I was cheeky enough simply to ring the bell. The door opened and a distinguished, friendly-looking gentleman appeared, who asked with a strong German accent: "What can I do for you?" I didn't dare present him with the Hitler story out of the blue, so instead asked in German, not very originally: "Are you Kapellmeister Wolf?" He smiled and said that he was. He opened his door wide and I spied a beautiful old Steinway grand that almost filled the small room. When I looked more closely, I saw there were a lot of yellowing photos standing on it. I don't know why, but to Kapellmeister Wolf's amusement I started looking at the photos and discovered to my excitement a photo from 1927 showing some people on the steps of the Baden-Baden Kurkonzertsaal. On the photograph was written: "18 July 1927, Baden-Baden." I couldn't believe my eyes.

"That was the day of the premiere of *Mahagonny!*" I blurted.

Wolf was amused: "Yes, just look closely."

I recognised Kurt Weill, Bertolt Brecht, Lotte Lenya, Otto Klemperer and Paul Hindemith.

"That's me on the left," said Wolf with modest pride.

"What? You were at the premiere?" I asked.

"Yes, but you seem very interested in Weill. Are you a descendant of his?"

In all the excitement I had forgotten to introduce myself. I laughed and said: "Excuse me. My name is Wagner."

"As in Richard?"

I nodded, and he started to study my profile. Then he beamed: "A Wagner in my home!" and we shook hands with mock solemnity.

We continued our discussion, during which I learned that he had not only been the repetiteur on *Mahagonny*, but also on the musical *The Eternal Road*, which was based on the novel by Franz Werfel, with music by Kurt Weill. It had had its unsuccessful premiere in New York, under the direction of Max Reinhardt. We talked about the many good conductors of the Weimar years, and I named my favourites, Otto Klemperer and Bruno Walter. "Walter was my uncle," said Wolf, and we roared with laughter. But the light-hearted mood came to an end when he told me his life story, which included persecution by the Nazis and emigration. Thanks to his lively and many-faceted stories, for a while I was able to journey back to the Berlin of the Twenties, as though in a time machine. We parted like old friends.

It was only during our second meeting in his apartment a short time later that I hesitantly told Kapellmeister Wolf the association with his nameplate. He found my story bizarre, and said: "There are two sides to everything. Hitler brought us together here." I shall never forget Kapellmeister Wolf. He helped me to see myself not as a lousy German and, even worse, a lousy Wagner in New York – an attitude adopted by so many German Jews, who weren't prepared to talk to the children of Nazi delinquents, by any means.

Lys Symonette had a demanding job at the Curtis Institute in

Philadelphia, one of America's leading conservatories, and gave up a lot of time to help Lenya, who left her all of Weill's mail to sort through. On top of that, she also looked after her husband and son – "like a true Jewish mamma," I teased her. Despite all of her commitments, we met regularly in her the stimulating atmosphere of her one-room apartment, which was littered with music scores and photographs from Germany and the USA. When Lys started introducing me step by step to Weill's work, in the period after his collaborations with Brecht, the room was transformed into a glittering music theatre. As soon as she started playing Weill, she was transformed, released from the cares of her taxing everyday life.

Lys helped and encouraged me, although she was of only modest means. We often despaired at the state of the Weill archive, and were hindered in our work by the fact that Lenya couldn't decide whether to transform the bequest into a professional centre for research into the composer. However, these concerns evaporated when she told me about her time with Weill on Broadway, sitting down at her Steinway grand and introducing me to American syncopation, jazz and the entire collection of Weill's scores. It became clear to me how many prejudices there still were against Weill and his work, even in North America. During one of our meetings – "with love for our Kurt" – I noticed a black-and-white photograph of a conservatively-dressed gentleman with a fine face, melancholy eyes framed by round spectacles. "He looks like your son Victor," I blurted. Lys smiled and answered: "That's my father." She then started to tell me about her dramatic flight from the Nazis via Italy to New York.

There was also a connection between the Wagner family and a cousin of her father, Emil Holzinger, who was a well-known member of the Jewish community in Bayreuth. After the First World War, when the general financial crisis even reached the festival, my grandfather asked Holzinger to urge the rich Jews of Bayreuth to support the festival financially. He advised Holzinger not to take Richard Wagner's antisemitism too seriously, which – in view of his antisemitic writings and their effects even within the Wagner family – wasn't very convincing.

I maintained an embarrassed silence throughout Lys' tale. Her parents, who came from a Jewish family in Mainz, had left the Jewish community, and so Lys hadn't been brought up in the Jewish faith. In time, all of the members of the family managed to emigrate from Nazi Germany.

Incidentally, Lys is also a distant relation of the liberal German-Jewish playwright Carl Zuckmayer (1896-1977), a fact of which she is justifiably proud.

How paltry my problems seemed in comparison with the fate of so many others! And my father's lamentations: always bemoaning the "sacrifices" he had had to make in the difficult years during and after the war.. What did he know? And what did the one-time Hitler protégé want to know, anyway, about the suffering of the Jewish victims? The same suffering about which Lys never complained. When she noticed in her fine, sensitive way that her life story was moving me, she smiled and said: "I must confess to you that, when I heard that you, a Wagner from that Bayreuth family, had written your doctoral thesis on Weill, I thought you must be *meshugge*. Other than your Aunt Friedelind, all of the other Wagner generations before you had probably been Nazis and antisemites."

This conversation strengthened our friendship. In the knowledge that we had become spiritually elective relations, we had a lot of fun when, as "free-thinking atheists" eating kosher chicken soup and garlic bagels, we blended the 'September Song' and the prelude from *Tristan Und Isolde*, or parodied the 'Waltz Of The Flower Maidens' from *Parsifal*, and Lys attacked the piano with gusto to create what she called "the Hollywood Wagner orchestra sound". She confessed to me, with mock bashfulness, her lively eyes twinkling: "My family and I are Wagnerians! Can you forgive me? In spite of everything?" I blessed her solemnly, and pronounced: "In the name of the Richard, the Kurt and the Holy Ghost, may you and your family be forgiven for the mortal sin of being Wagnerians."

Lys is always there when I need her. That's something I can say of many friends, when I think of all the traps I've fallen into in my life and how I only emerged thanks to people like Lys.

Finally, my itinerary was ready to follow the trail of Weill in North America and I flew to Los Angeles. After three cold months in the New York jungle, Beverly Hills seemed quite unreal, with its summery weather, its palm trees, the sterile cleanliness of its ostentatious mansions and its snobs, with their permanent impersonal smiles. This American artifice became more bearable when I was able to spend a few days with the widow of Ernst Josef Aufricht in North Canyon Drive. Aufricht had been the distinguished director of the Theater Am Schiffbauerdamm in Berlin during the Weimar period, and until 1933 had staged the premieres of works by Brecht and Weill, Ernst Toller, Robert Musil, Paul Kornfeld, Georg Kaiser, Ödön von Horvath, Jean Cocteau, Karl Kraus and Marieluise Fleisser. I had read Ernst Josef Aufricht's 1966 autobiography, *Erzähle, Damit Du Dein Recht Erweist*, in New York in preparation for the meeting with Margot Aufricht and Paul Vambery, who had been Aufricht's dramaturg in Berlin. I found the book interesting, not only for its description of how Brecht and Weill collaborated on *Die Dreigroschenoper*, but also for the shocking account of Aufricht's flight from the Nazis to North America.

My passionate interest in her husband's work pleased Margot Aufricht, and she knew a lot about it. She spoke German to me, demonstrating that she didn't view all Germans – certainly not my generation – in the same light, and answered my questions quickly, accurately and with great kindness. She described Brecht's family – their craving for money and power – in terms which reminded me of Bayreuth, which I pointed out to her, to her amusement. Her words made Weill, whose gentle and modest character I had already learned of through Lys and Lenya, more and more likable and easier for me to understand. During these talks, I thought again and again how much generosity it must take for her to talk in an unprejudiced way with the grandson of Winifred Wagner, whose friend Adolf Hitler had driven the Aufricht family out of Germany. When we were talking of Nazi and New Bayreuth, she said: "Your family, with its view of German history, has bequeathed a legacy to you which you will carry for your entire life."

During one of my visits, I was surprised to find a beautifully-decorated candlelit table, laden with coffee and cake. It was 13 April: my 31st birthday. She gave me one of the last copies of her husband's book with an affectionate dedication; it is one of my most treasured possessions. I was so moved that I couldn't hold back my tears: the gesture was made all the more meaningful by the fact that I hadn't had any kind of birthday greetings from my family. At such moments, I identified strongly with the German Jews of my grandparents' and parents' generation, and my anger against my family had grown to such a degree that, after the four days I spent in Margot Aufricht's house, I toyed with the idea of becoming an American citizen and changing my name.

In mid April I visited the lyricist Ira Gershwin, the brother of George. He had suffered a stroke only a few weeks before, but nevertheless agreed to see me in his luxury mansion in Beverly Hills. His staff, however, were obviously not enthusiastic about my visit. Ira sat immobile in a wheelchair, and had great difficulty in articulating his speech. We spoke briefly of his screenplay for the Hollywood film *Lady In The Dark*, which critically examines the psychoanalysis of a woman. The little that he was able to tell me was revealing. When I asked him about Kurt Weill, he said: "You Europeans will never understand that the *volksoper* was the model for the American musical, as George and I showed in *Porgy And Bess* and Kurt and I tried to do in the two works we did together. Kurt was a fine, soft-hearted gentleman. Lenya never understood his character, but she felt the greatness of his work." When I told Ira how much I liked *Porgy And Bess*, he wheeled himself laboriously to his desk and pulled out an LP double album, with all of his well-known lyrics, and gave it to me. At the end of my visit, he said: "Richard Wagner was a bastard but a great composer!" He then let one of his minders know that it was time for me to go.

In the previous year, at Bettina Fehr's home in Bonn, I had met Cornelius Schnauber, the executor of Fritz Lang's estate and an expert on literature of Jews in exile. On meeting him again, he invited me to his home. Among the guests were Ronald Schoenberg and his wife, and Martha Feuchtwanger, whose Bavarian origins were evident every time she opened her mouth, even when she was speaking English. In spite of her great age, she had a very lively mind when she was talking about the work of her husband, Lion, and about her life with him. She said: "Your work on Weill is a pleasure for us emigrants. In this way, we shan't be entirely forgotten either." What melancholy there was in her eyes when she said these words!

I had a very different encounter with Judge Ronald Schoenberg

(Arnold Schoenberg's son from his second marriage) and his wife, the daughter of the Austrian composer and pupil of Schoenberg Eric Zelsi. I wanted to know everything about his father and his Jewishness, and Ronald – a Wagnerian – wanted to hear everything about Richard Wagner but nothing about his antisemitism. We talked very pleasantly, albeit at cross purposes. He enthused about Bayreuth, and was quite amazed that I had a different opinion. Although he is ten years older than me, I identified with the role of the parents' generation of Jewish emigrants, whose American-born children don't want to hear any more of their parent's stories from the Nazi period, and in defiant reaction sometimes act almost pro-German. All attempts at finding a common subject for discussion came to nothing. When we said goodbye, we promised to try afresh if we ever met again. "But please, not Wagner!" I said, to which Ronald retorted: "And please, not Schoenberg!"

During one of my meetings with Paul Vambery, who passed on fascinating impressions of his time with Weill and in the Theater Am Schiffbauerdamm, I came to know Joseph Joachim, a close childhood friend of Weill's. Joachim has never come to terms with his flight from Germany; he even assumed an English name – Jackson – in an attempt to sever all ties with Germany. However, he was completely unaware of how German his manners were. Outbursts of hatred against everything German were followed without pause by wild enthusiasm at the beauty of the German language. There we sat on Paul Vambery's veranda, overlooking the city of Los Angeles, and still we couldn't get away from Germany. Vambery and Jackson agreed that Weill was ruined by being kicked out by the Nazis.

The two men asked me about my grandmother and the rest of the family. It was difficult for me to answer their questions without opening old wounds, and I wanted to convey a discriminating picture of the generation of the children of the perpetrators, so I spoke reservedly about Bayreuth and the Germans. In doing so, I gradually realised that I had become an outsider: I only liked being with Germans who had de-Germanised themselves abroad and tried to become cosmopolitan. Again and again, Hitler occupied centre stage in these discussions, which were often interrupted by tearful silences.

How many uprooted people I met, with broken off lives! Not all emigrants were as successful as Weill. I learned a great deal about Germany from Vambery and Jackson, and it's wonderful for me to read Paul's letters today.

On 20 April, I flew via Chicago to Bloomington, Indiana – the last stage rather hazardously, in a single-propellered plane. In Bloomington, I hoped to meet another witness in time: Hans Busch, who has since died. He was the son of Fritz Busch, who conducted *Die Meistersinger* in Bayreuth in 1924 and had to leave Nazi Germany because of his liberal views. He later became one of the founders of the Glyndebourne Festival in England, which is a sort of anti-Bayreuth. He had worked together with Weill in 1926, and conducted the premiere of Weill's *Der Protagonist* in Dresden.

Hans invited me to the dress rehearsal of John Eaton's opera *Danton And Robespierre*, which, after dedicated and thorough preparation, was premiered in Bloomington. While the dress rehearsal was in progress that evening, I briefly left the darkened auditorium. Pushing my way through one of the two swing doors, I was about to let the door go when I noticed a small figure behind me who called out to me with an unmistakable German accent: "Attention, please!" I held the swing door back, and a little lady, whom in the darkness I couldn't really recognise, thanked me.

"My pleasure," I answered, and introduced myself.

"Like Richard Wagner?" the lady in the dark asked curiously.

"Yes, but with mixed feelings. May I know who I'm talking to here in the dark?" I answered, amused.

"You may. My name is Busoni," said a friendly, laughing voice.

"Like Ferruccio?" I asked, just as curiously.

"Yes," she said, and suggested that we should continue our conversation in the light of the foyer. Thus began one of my most important friendships, with Hannah Busoni, who in the summer of 1978 took me into her apartment in her "Hansel and Gretel house" behind Carnegie Hall, and which was to remain my New York base until 1994. When I was up to my neck in trouble, Hannah helped me, discreetly but generously.

She told me a lot about Ferruccio Busoni, Weill, her husband, the painter Raffaele Busoni, Lotte Lenya, the premiere of *Die Dreigroschenoper* (which she had attended as a girl in Berlin), and about her flight from Nazi Germany. Her maiden name was Apfel, and she was the daughter of a very respected Jewish lawyer in the Weimar Republic, who had fled to France in 1933. As Hannah's parents were divorced, she escaped with her mother to England.

Hannah had an extremely lively mind, a dry sense of humour and spoke such excellent German that her style of expression reminded me of my favourite German authors of the 1920s. She was gratefully affectionate towards New York, where she had survived by performing a wide range of jobs, until the Federal Republic finally awarded her the pension of a German judge as restitution. (The Nazis had prevented her from finishing her apprenticeship in law.) Committed and selfless, she was now assisting young musicians and musicologists interested in her father-in-law, Ferruccio. It was through Hannah that, for the first time, I saw in America the other, better, intellectual legacy of my family: that of Liszt, of whom Busoni had thought highly. Anyone staying with Hannah might have thought that she was living in the Berlin of the Weimar Republic. Many of her friends had a similar German-Jewish history, and all of them welcomed me – the grandson of Winifred Wagner – like a grandson of their own.

It was also at Hannah's house that I met Paul Falkenberg. Until 1933, he had lived in Berlin as a prominent sound editor. He thought it exciting and plausible when I told him that Weill had also appropriated Jewish sacred music in his songs with Brecht. One day, when I was asking Hannah about her identity, she answered: "It's good to be Jewish," by which she meant the fated community of the persecuted German Jews, not the religious community.

Time stood still for us. Our goodbyes were always quick, as we assumed that I would soon enough come puffing and sweating up the steep stairs to her room on the second floor. With my suitcases standing in front of her door, we would hug and she would set to cooking for her greedy guest. I put a stop to it in the end by taking her out for meals, but I will never forget Hannah's shining eyes when she opened her door. She died in 1994.

After my trip to Bloomington, I stayed in Chicago for a few days with Peter Jonas, who was at that time artistic administrator of the Chicago Symphony Orchestra and before that personal assistant to the famous conductor Sir Georg Solti, whom I also met. He offered to help me in America, and wrote a letter of recommendation.

I returned to New York at the end of April, where I moved into new lodgings – in the Lincoln Tower in West End Avenue – that Lys had fixed up for me. I started writing a synopsis for a biography of Weill, and together with Lys studied all of those works which he had written in America. Even though the rather sparsely-furnished apartment was on the 13th floor, I felt as though I was living in the middle of the street; cars and trucks thundered to and from uptown and downtown all through the day and night.

It was during this time that I first heard that Lenya had also made material for a Weill biography available to the journalist Ronald Sander. Eliot Ravetz, my agent at the time, wanted to sue her for this, as I had been assured exclusivity in my contract. However, I had no desire to take legal proceedings against Lenya: I was very fond of her, despite her weaknesses. Once Sander's biography of Weill was announced, my business relations with Eliot Ravetz and his agency deteriorated, and contacts with publishers also became more difficult. I learned what it means to try to do business in the jungle of New York publishers and literary agents. As always, Lys Symonette and Hannah Busoni stood by me with advice and practical help.

In this, I noticed that I was still far from becoming an American. I couldn't come to enjoy an existence in which all of my energies were devoted solely toward survival.

Amidst this crisis of identity and work, by chance I met one of my closest childhood friends, Eckart Grebner, in Greenwich Village. Eckart's mother had worked for many years in the *Festspielhaus*, so he knew what had been happening to me, even after we had lost contact with one another. If we spoke of the past in Bayreuth, we did so with the awareness of two Germans who in no way wanted to be typically German.

When I talked with him, I realised how much I still had in common with Germans, and I found these reminiscences of the German language and culture as a great palliative to my homelessness. Like myself, Eckart was fascinated by everything that was different from himself, and loved every kind of cultural stimulus. He lived an alternative life in every respect, and with such charm that I loved listening to him, even though he couldn't always convince me of his "really new art or ecological trends"; he unwittingly made me feel like an old man. He never spared a thought for a moment of his financial security or insurance for his old age; he never moaned, even when he fell flat on his face. He registered every essential change in my development with curious sympathy, and never made me feel that I had to justify myself for the drastic changes of direction my life proceeded to take – in his eyes, nothing should stay as it is. Without self-denial or false politeness, he proceeded to live with me in my new world, beyond traditional morals. Out of interest – and out of aversion to conventional Christianity – he immersed himself in Eastern cultures and meditative techniques, and also looked into Judaism. In Eckart's inner indefatigable search for new facets of one's own identity, I also recognised something of myself.

When Hannah Busoni went on her annual summer trip to a German health resort, she invited Beatrix and I to move into her apartment near Carnegie Hall. We gratefully accepted the offer to stay in a rent-free location, and the apartment was much better and quieter than our current location. We took every opportunity to go to concerts, operas and productions on Broadway. I went mainly to the less well-known and more lively venues, which had sprung up in a reaction against the New York establishment. The more avant-garde the production, the more curious I was.

At the end of June, we saw the first signs of summer in New York. Our clothes stuck to our bodies as if we were in a sauna. The only salvation was provided by the omnipresent whirring air conditioning.

An invitation from Schuyler Chapin and his wife Betty came like a bolt out of the blue. I had known Schuyler since his time as Leonard Bernstein's permanent adviser. He had been chief administrator of the Metropolitan Opera for some years, and at the same time dean of performing arts at Columbia University in New York. He is one of the least typical representatives of the New York establishment: always modest, discreetly helpful and unselfish in his advice. With a warm-hearted spontaneity that ignores all social boundaries, he is a real liberal gentleman. Betty came from the famous piano-manufacturing family Steinway, and was just as modest as her husband. We celebrated Independence Day in their country home at Long Pond, on Cape Cod, with its own lake surrounded by beautiful forests. In such a beautiful environment, I soon forgot about my struggles with theatre and literary agents.

In Schuyler's beautiful apartment, on the corner of 66th Street and Lexington Avenue, I met Leonard Bernstein. I had first met him 1977, during a rehearsal for my production of Beethoven's *Fidelio* in Bonn, and we had become friends. Lenny was always interested in learning about the Wagner family's stories, so seeing him in New York reminded me of Bayreuth. He enthused about Wieland, and fulminated against my father, whom he held to be a closet Nazi in spite of all of his liberal-left airs. When I asked him how he had reached this opinion, he told me about a meeting he had had with my father to discuss him conducting *Tristan* – an assignment which eventually came to nothing. "As long as he is festival boss in Bayreuth, I won't conduct on the *Festspielhügel*," he declared angrily.

On the other hand, like many Jewish artists, Bernstein had a lot of sympathy for Aunt Friedelind. "You seem to be continuing the tradition of your aunt with your work on Weill," he told me.

"Friedelind still believes in Richard Wagner's innocence where antisemitism is concerned," I answered. "I don't."

It was obvious that this subject moved Bernstein. He became thoughtful, and pondered aloud: "How is it that a Jew like me loves the music of this repulsive antisemite? Especially *Tristan?*"

"I have no right, as a great-grandson of Wagner, to say anything to you," I replied, "but I can't see any antisemitism in *Tristan*, despite my aversion to the man. And you should record it one day."

Later, he did record *Tristan*, in Munich, and produced a video on the dilemma he found in conducting Wagner. In 1990 he provided me with the still-incomplete film, and asked for my opinion. I didn't think it very well done, and told him so at our last meeting in April. Amused by my answer, he asked me to work with him on it. He died shortly afterwards, having helped me with my lecture tour on Wagner in Israel, in opposition to the machinations of Bayreuth.

CHAPTER TWELVE

THE LONG ARM OF BAYREUTH

At the end of July 1978, Beatrix and I travelled back to Germany; my mother was moving house, and I needed to secure some professional contacts. My flying visit was clouded by the deterioration of my mother's health. She agreed to leave Bayreuth, however, and so Eva, Beatrix and myself planned to set up a home for her in Wiesbaden.

I was worried about my professional future, and so tried to pick up some commissions in Germany, in theatres or in the media, but my efforts were all in vain. I had one unpleasant meeting at the end of September, in Mannheim, where I applied for the job of dramaturg with Friedrich Meyer-Oertel, who was head of opera production there.

After the initial meeting with Meyer-Oertel, I had strong doubts as to whether I had a future in the German theatre scene, with its uptight, intellectual proceedings. It was a curious situation. I wrote about Lotte Lenya's 80th birthday for the *Neue Zürcher Zeitung* and the Viennese paper *Die Presse*, and couldn't wait to pack my bags again and get out of Germany.

This desire grew even stronger when I collected my mother in Bayreuth, where she had been living with Grandma Winifred. Grandma was once again the politician she had once been. Although she had initially made out that she would support her former daughter-in-law and her grandchildren, she had now swung completely the other way, to my father's side. When I asked her for an advance of 4,500 marks against my inheritance, shortly before we left, she answered with a cold smile: "You can get money from your rich New York Jews, or the Kurt Weill archive." She was now very enthusiastic about my father's second wife, Gudrun, although back in 1976 she hadn't had a good word to say about her. It was no wonder that I felt less comfortable at home than ever before. By the middle of October 1978, I flew back to New York on a cheap Pan Am ticket.

Immediately upon my return, I attended to the final details of plans that I had made with Betty Smith concerning a concert of Weill's music in honour of Lotte Lenya, which was to be held in the Avery Fisher Hall. I had started to plan the concert months before my visit to Germany with David Gilbert, whom I had met in Bayreuth in 1976, when he was Boulez's assistant. He had since become given the role of permanent conductor of the Greenwich Philharmonia Orchestra.

We staged a trial run of the Weill concert on 12 November, in the Avery Fisher Hall in Greenwich, New York State. Lenya was there, coiffured, made up and dressed like an ageing Hollywood star. However, our timing was unfortunate, as far as the media were concerned: the press in New York were on strike on the day of the premiere, and in America, if it doesn't happen in the media, it hasn't happened. Consequently, there was no improvement in my job prospects.

I was now working even harder on the structure of my biography of Weill, while my new literary agent, Elsie Stern, looked for a publisher. The theatre agent Germinal Hilbert had also promised me the job of directing a production of *Don Giovanni* in Marseille. With the money from this, I would have been able to live carefree for several months.

Beatrix and I moved twice during this hectic period, ending up as lodgers of Marion McLaughlin in two small rooms in a house on the corner of 71st Street and Lexington Avenue. The house was oppressive: our landlady liked to discuss her personal problems with me, even at night, and some of the neighbours didn't like us being there. I was frequently rung up after midnight and sworn at in German by a quavering male voice: "Dirty German swine, get out of our house! We don't want any Nazis here. Clear out, or we'll bump you off!" It literally took my breath away; I had never encountered such naked aggression before. I inhaled deeply, and replied: "We should get to know one another personally. I am German, yes, but I'm not a Nazi. And anyway, I was born in 1947." On that, I heard a furious snorting, and the nervous caller slammed down the receiver. This malicious game was to be repeated several times. It wore me down, not least because I couldn't get a good night's sleep. I later noticed that silence fell whenever I got into the lift, from which I had heard German being spoken only moments before. I now suspected the kind of circle the caller came from; people with a German-Jewish history were obviously living here. Now, I'm a man who finds all forms of hatred offensive, and I tried my best (unsuccessfully, as it happened) to dismiss these incidents quickly.

By mid June 1978, I had met the man who wielded influence over the entire world opera market: Ronald Wilford. As an agent, he commanded the highest fees for himself and his artists, although such exorbitant demands were jeopardising the whole opera world, and the opera repertoire in particular. Anyone looking for a career in opera took care not to criticise his business methods – no one wanted to land up on Wilford's black list. He seemed interested during our hour-long discussion, and was distantly polite, like many other powerful people in the opera business. Most of all, he wanted to know how things stood between Father and me, and whether I would be the successor, in spite of all the tensions of which Eva had apparently informed him. I understood: he was already networking for future business. When I answered him evasively, he cut short our conversation absuptly. But I hadn't come to exchange civilities with him anyway, so I presented him with my CV, showed him interviews I had given, and supplemented all of this with other material which an agent might find useful. He concentrated on the interview in the *New York Times*, and declared that he would give it to his best agent, Matthew Epstein, and ask him to see me. He then asked me to pass on his regards to my father. And so, after an hour, I was no wiser than before.

After eight months of many humiliating attempts at finding

employment, I was finally able to make an appointment with Epstein, in mid February 1979. The words of a highly dramatic American singer, who shortly before had not been exactly encouraging, still rang in my ears: "Don't expect anything! You're neither gay nor Jewish, and everybody knows that your father is against you!"

We met in his New York office, and I quickly realised that he was making it hard for me to find any kind of basis for discussion with him. The man was hysterical, and, from the first moment of our hour-long conversation – constantly interrupted by telephone calls – to the last, he made it quite clear that he was the boss and I was a little nobody whose career now lay in his hands and who should be honoured to be received by him.

I felt as if I were being interrogated about my views on opera. When I spoke of Bertolt Brecht, Konstantin Stanislavsky, Vsevolod Meyerhold, Erwin Piscator and other writers and directors, he said at once: "Unmarketable! You are only marketable as a Wagner who produces Wagner, and who is the future director of the festival. If you want to get into the business here in the USA – and this applies for Europe, too – then you'll have to give up your left-wing ideas because you won't get anywhere with them. Drop Weill, too! You're entering an area there which is no concern of yours."

I interrupted his monologue, and asked: "Why shouldn't I work on Weill? I've written a book on him, after all, which earned me my doctorate at the University of Vienna and a job with the Weill Foundation."

"For a grandson of Winifred Wagner there's no place here for anything to do with Weill," he answered with a disparaging smile.

I had to hold myself back from telling Epstein that this was racism under a different name, and instead answered guardedly: "I am a convinced liberal, even in the American sense of the word. Out of all the Jewish intellectuals I have met here in the USA, I have never heard anyone say that I'm unwelcome because of my work on Weill and because of my origins."

Epstein became rather embarrassed, and bit his nails even more. "I know," he said irritably. "Things have changed. We're also doing business with Bayreuth, although we know everything about

Wagner and Hitler. But that doesn't mean that we've forgotten that you come from the Nazi Wagner family."

I became more confident, and retorted with some energy: "All forms of discrimination and ideological fanaticism are repulsive! It's part of my identity to have a wide variety of opinions in art and life, and that has nothing to do with the character of my family in Bayreuth!"

Epstein was cool. "You'll never make a career for yourself like that. Your only chance is that Wagner makes Wagner, in line with Bayreuth and your father."

I remained silent, on the verge of leaving. Epstein noticed this, and said: "I'll write you a letter of recommendation. No one knows you here in the USA; I'll introduce you as a Wagner who produces Wagner, and is following in his father's tradition."

"No thanks. I'll try to make my way in life without going against my convictions," I said, albeit unwisely.

Epstein was thunderstruck. "You'll never find a job here or anywhere else if you don't follow my advice. I only want to help you."

Disgusted, I left the office and hoped that I would never be dependent on people like him. Sadly, this was to prove one of the many illusions I had with regard to agents.

Meanwhile, Germinal Hilbert, who had offices in Paris and Munich and who collaborated closely with my father, was now talking not only about Marseille but also about Buenos Aires, where he offered me the prospect of working on a production of *Lohengrin*. Preliminary contracts already existed, apparently. I worked out detailed plans for both productions, and asked Hilbert to conclude the contracts. However, he had totally misled me: it transpired that he couldn't even produce documentation supporting that negotiations had taken place. When I told the conductor Karl Böhm about this, and mentioned the fact that I considered bringing an action against him, Böhm said: "If you cross swords with Hilbert you'll never set foot in any of the bigger opera houses in Europe again. Come to terms with Hilbert and your father, and there'll be no lack of work."

But I had no intention of coming to terms with them, although I didn't want to risk legal proceedings either, given my desperate financial situation. Eventually, with the help of a lawyer, a compromise was reached.

CHAPTER THIRTEEN

RETURN TO GERMANY

Unable to earn enough money in the USA, in February 1979 I flew back to Germany, where I started to look for work without an agent. I wrote to every theatre in Germany, and rushed around like a mad thing. In mid March, I received an offer from the Kammeroper in Vienna that seemed to be firm, and began working with my friend Johannes Dreher on Johann Nepomuk Nestroy's parody of *Tannhäuser*. In the Sixties, Johannes had been a set painter and artist for my uncle and my father, but he remained a friend – one of the few from my Bayreuth past who did not swim with the tide.

Johannes had led a colourful life. As a pupil of the painter Otto Dix, he had been on the Nazis' black list. They had persecuted him, and the torture to which he had been subjected had left him with a permanent limp, but he had refused to conform. He was a painter, and his set paintings were in demand in all of the important opera houses all over the world. He was always up to the latest developments in stage and lighting techniques, and the Bayreuth and Salzburg Festivals owe him a great deal. His modesty was endearing, but didn't do him much good in the hostile environment of opera, which continued to exploit him, much to my anger. I could talk about everything with him, and he followed my ideas for expunging corruption from the theatre, the opera business and the world in general, with amused approval.

When we worked together, he was sometimes as enthusiastic as a young man. Both sanguine people, we raged and screamed at one another if things didn't go as we had planned, afterwards hugging one another affectionately. We were equally glad when things on the stage finally worked out as we had imagined.

I owe a great deal to Johannes, not only for essential advice on how to succeed in the theatre but also for a valuable warning: never forget those for whom one makes theatre.

I wrote a new prologue for Nestroy's *Tannhäuser* parody, and read it aloud to the writer Hilde Spiel. She liked it, and so in April we started rehearsing. However, after only two days, Hans Gabor, the director of the Kammeroper, stopped the rehearsals without giving any reasons, and refused to discuss his actions. I was both upset and confused, and became even more so when the Kammeroper gave guest performances of the work in August 1980, in the Bayreuth Margravian Opera House. Someone in Bayreuth had evidently once again been pulling strings.

At the beginning of May 1979, my mother's and sister's lawyer informed me that I could collect my furniture and other items from Bayreuth. I wanted to get the disagreeable business over quickly, so at the end of the month I hired a small van and drove there with Beatrix's brother for moral support. As my father refused to see me, I turned to the caretaker, the successor to the kindly Grandpa Lodes, who had always been a faithful servant of my father. Despite having known me for many years, he treated me like a stranger and in great haste unlocked a shed that had been named *Rüdelsheim* after one of the Bayreuth chorus masters. It was cold and dirty inside. The caretaker pointed into the corner where my things were stored, then stayed close by me to check every single piece I loaded into the van. I lost my temper and shouted at him to clear off. This was precisely the language that he understood, and he deferentially apologised, pleading that he was only following Father's orders and had nothing at all against me personally. "Father has always surrounded himself with people like you," I growled angrily.

The caretaker finally got off my back and stood between the door and the spot where my things were piled, and I set to sorting through everything. When I looked more closely, I found that the furniture with which I had lived for many years was missing, and that Father had left a few shabby old wardrobes in its place. I didn't want them, and gave the caretaker the job of telling my father so. Amongst the dirty pile, I discovered my puppet theatre and the sets I had made as an eight-year-old boy, with the help of the set painter Otto Wiesner. Everything was falling to pieces and useless, but the puppets were in an old Bavarian chest and by some miracle had survived storage. Not so my diaries, unfortunately, which I had been keeping since the beginning of the Sixties; they were mouldy and dirty, the pages stuck together and unreadable. I only had one thought: to get out of here, where they let memories of one's past disintegrate.

On leaving the shed, all I took with me were the puppets and a chair by the famous Viennese furniture makers Thonet. The chair had been used in Wieland's production of *Parsifal* to carry Amfortas into the Temple of the Grail. When I recognised the *Parsifal* chair I decided to exact my own compensation, and saved it from the pile of junk.

How many memories came flooding back at the sight of that stage prop from Wieland's time! Thoughts of George London and Thomas Stewart, singers who played Amfortas, and of the guest appearances of the Bayreuth Festival in Franco's Barcelona. Before I drove off, I told the caretaker that he was welcome to tell my father about the 'theft'. Then, in the almost empty van, we tore along the Siegfried-Wagner-Allee, past Breker's heroic bust of the composer in the *Festspielpark*, and then past Wahnfried on the Richard-Wagner-Strasse, without visiting my grandmother. I wanted only one thing: to get away as quickly as possible. Later, I gave up my claim to the furniture – it would have been nothing more than a constant reminder of Bayreuth.

Although I didn't want to give up America as the big alternative, I was reluctant to give up the illusion that I was able to build an existence for myself in the world of German theatre and opera, especially as my finances were at a very low ebb, and so in summer 1979 I accepted a job as assistant director at the Salzburg Festival, working on Dieter Dorn's production the Richard Strauss' opera *Ariadne Auf Naxos*. In his personal relations outside the theatre, Dieter is a witty, sensitive man, with brilliant ideas, and I greatly admire his directorial work; but as soon as he entered the Salzburg *Festspieltheater*, he transformed into one of the most stereotypical of theatrocrats.

The Salzburg Festival, like its Bayreuth counterpart, is a collection of (allegedly) prominent figures, who regard nothing to be more important than themselves – indeed, the acme of high society. They were only interested in me in as long as I was the subject of Bayreuth gossip. They asked about the family quarrel, and whether I would follow my father as head of the festival. It became clear to me that a Wagner without Bayreuth connections would be unable to find a foothold in Salzburg.

In Salzburg, they were also celebrating Karl Böhm's 85th birthday. Leonard Bernstein's Jewish melody was performed by Christa Ludwig as 'Piccola Serenata', and the great Herbert von Karajan congratulated his friend Karl, who was greatly moved. In fact, everyone was moved, the public no less than so than the icons of classical music. The biographical grey areas of the musical heroes of the Nazi period remained unmentioned; they had all been long forgotten.

In September 1979, after spending a few weeks in Salzburg, I flew to Ankara to direct a production of Carl Orff's *Carmina Burana*. When I arrived at our quarters with Johannes Dreher – who had negotiated this contract for me – after a tiring flight and a wild drive, in what was at the time a rather unattractive Ankara, we both felt quite ill. The sanitary installations weren't functioning, however, so we went out for a walk. The city resembled a besieged fort – the ruling military junta apparently feared armed resistance.

During the first night, we heard a number of shots followed by a bloodcurdling scream. I dashed to the window, and witnessed two soldiers in the twilight beating a man to death with their rifle butts, after they had shot and wounded him. It was the first time I had seen someone being murdered. Angry, but paralysed by fear, my instinct was to fly back to Munich immediately. When I told the directors of the opera house the next morning of my traumatic experience, they retreated into an aloof silence, which made me even more uneasy and strengthened my urge to get out.

I decided to stay on until the dress rehearsal after meeting with the chorus of the opera house, and with the ballet master, Attila, and his group. Most of the chorus members were young, open-minded conservatoire graduates who were eager to learn. They agreed with the way I wanted to stage the work, which was to play *Carmina Burana* in the Ankara of 1979. I disregarded Orff's mythological *kitsch*, which was incomprehensible to them. They amused me in particular by giggling with embarrassment as we worked on the many erotic scenes, but prudishness soon disappeared and together we examined the political statements contained in *Carmina Burana*, which – like those in *Der Ring Des Nibelungen* – portray a struggle between love and power.

However, for some friends of the military junta, the staging was unacceptable. For some unknown reason, the stage equipment wouldn't work and rehearsals were often boycotted for days. Even so, after the dress rehearsal, as I said goodbye to all those who had gone through the last weeks with Johannes and myself, we were inundated with presents and invitations to visit.

What was particularly important for me in those days in Ankara was the beginning of my friendship with Pulat Tacar and his wife, Selda. Pulat came from one of the few families who had considerable influence in Turkey. He had been general consul in Munich, and had enjoyed great esteem among the Turkish population there, earning the honorary title of 'workers' consul' because of his efforts on behalf of their interests. When we met in Ankara at the beginning of my rehearsals, he had our quarters transformed into a place fit for human habitation within a few hours, before disappearing off on diplomatic affairs. When he turned up at the end of rehearsals, he opened my eyes to his country, its culture and its people, with which he felt inextricably connected. He is extraordinarily cultured, speaks eight languages and is passionate about art, world religions and philosophy, in particular the Chinese philosopher Lao-tse. It also came as no surprise that he was also highly knowledgeable in Richard Wagner's works. His wife, Selda, was equally unusual; an Austrian herself, she hadn't found it easy integrating into the Turkish diplomatic corps. Both were superb hosts.

In October 1979, Johannes and I left before the premiere of *Carmina Burana*, protesting against they way our work had been obstructed. It was difficult to say goodbye to Pulat and Selda, and we brooded on the plane to Munich. I later proudly told my son the story of the Turkish carpet, which is now lying at the side of his bed, and which Pulat had acquired for me at an incredibly cheap price at a bazaar in Ankara. It represents my director's fee for *Carmina Burana*.

On 1 November, I began working at the Frankfurt Opera House as evening director, a position that had been won for me by the journalist Wolf Rosenberg. At that time, the director of the opera house was the conductor and composer Michael Gielen. I only saw him once, for a brief and formal conversation during which he asked me if I really did need the job quite so urgently, because it wouldn't bring anything other than the salary. I was surprised by this comment; I thought highly of Gielen as conductor, and it was because of him that I had accepted the job in Frankfurt. The deputy director, Christof Bitter, told me which parts of the repertoire needed freshening up. He also managed the evening performance, and gave me the directorship of *Carmen*, an old production by Jean-Pierre Ponnelle, along with an old warhorse: a production of Johann Strauss' *Die Fledermaus* from the Sixties.

The conditions under which I worked were pathetic: there was no piano score for *Carmen*, just a rather useless video recording. The opera house officials were totally indifferent to this miserable state of affairs, and it was made clear to me yet again that a Wagner who has crossed swords with Bayreuth finds no allies on the administrative floor of German opera houses. Even in Frankfurt, people acted in what, in 1968, was viewed as a left-wing and progressive manner, but were were in fact authoritarian in the way they treated people.

As the least influential people in the opera house, my colleagues and I had a bad deal in the day-to-day tussle. Many people depended on their jobs, although they found often found them pointless. To quote one of the intellectual super-cynics on the administrative floor of the Frankfurt Opera House, we were "alienated wage-earners". People indulged themselves in unworldly ideas for saving the workers, and indeed all the world's oppressed, and understood theatre as an instrument for overcoming social contradictions or as a platform for promulgating doctrines of salvation. This masturbatory theatre comprised incompatible elements: the production of absurdly luxuriant programmes, which dripped with pseudo-left jargon; always keeping one eye on the media and sponsors; being continually deferent to political power; and exhibiting contempt for the public. And the whole time, their gaze was directed at the next free chair in Everding's intendants' merry-go-round.

When I saw the ambassador from Bayreuth, Dorothea Glatt-Behr, creeping around in the ugly underground shafts of the opera house, with its linoleum flooring and washable bright green walls, I resolved yet again to have nothing to do with these theatre managers, who confuse the microcosm of the stage with reality.

Once my work at Frankfurt was completed at the end of January 1980, I began work at Trier. I had chosen Busoni's *Turandot* as a parody of opera, and his *Arlecchino* as a caustic settling of accounts, with moralising ideologies of every kind. As the performances were taking place in the right-wing stronghold of Trier, I had incorporated harsh anticlerical allusions which were taken up with great enthusiasm by the chorus, the ensemble and the excellent extras. Our popularity among our colleagues grew, to the great annoyance of the administration, when I started battling against the despotism of the administration in the interests of chorus and soloists – the intendant tolerated the chorus master not even turning up for the dress rehearsal! I therefore brought in the media to draw attention to the unbelievable working conditions in the Trier theatre. The premiere was a success despite all of these obstacles, and the intendant endured our working methods, although Mützel later blackened my name at a meeting of other German intendants.

After my experiences in Trier, I accepted an offer to work as dramaturg and director at the opera house in Wuppertal. I discovered only later that opera director Friedrich Meyer-Oertel and general intendant Hellmuth Matiasek were only interested in working with me because of my name, and because of the possibility that I could still play a role in Bayreuth, albeit in the distant future. Moreover, when Richard Wagner's first opera, *Die Feen*, was performed in Wuppertal in February 1981, they thought it appropriate to pass me around the media like a museum piece. Meyer-Oertel also voiced his approval when I collected 60,000 marks for the Wuppertal Opera House from Wagner societies and a private sponsor.

However, the mood changed when the media showed more interest in my work on *Die Feen* than in the opera director's conventional staging of the opera. In fact, it triggered off a number of melodramatic scenes and petty jealousies. In a crowded canteen, Meyer-Oertel made it clear to me – in a particularly loud voice – that he was the opera director and I was only his employee. The intendant regarded Wuppertal merely as a stepping stone in the path of his career, and that he was the boss in Matiasek's absence. Tensions were therefore inevitable.

However, I did forge some new friendships, including one with the set designer, Hanna Jordan. Our conversation revolved around matters which we believed important: German-Jewish history, and national socialism and its effects on Germany's cultural and political climate.

Hanna and her family had been victims of the Nuremberg race laws, and she reacted violently to any form of intolerance or discrimination. She is a true left-winger, a person who has suffered a lot and by no means feels at ease in Germany and its undigested past. We're therefore bound together in a special way. The fact that I am a Wagner amuses her, in particular because, when we met, she was living in the Wotanstrasse in Wuppertal-Elberfeld, of all places. "Hanna of the Wotanstrasse" – we still make jokes about, it as we do about Wagner, whom we both consider to be important as a "theatre animal". When we met again years later, in Wuppertal in 1992, at my lecture on "The Case Of Wagner In Israel And Germany", it was as though we had seen each other only yesterday.

On 5 March 1980, my grandmother died in hospital in Überlingen. I had seen her for the last time three weeks earlier, a visit which will always remain in my memory because of the way she spoke with such disconcerting clarity about her approaching death. Aunt Friedelind displayed the only genuine grief. The funeral, held on 10 March in Bayreuth, was an embarrassment from beginning to end. My father had worked out a seating plan, separating the family into the pro- and anti-*Festspielhügel* contingents, while a string quartet provided the only relief from interminable speeches, in which my grandmother was acknowledged as the saviour of Bayreuth. Not a word was said about the intimate friendship between Winnie and Wolf, and even Mayor Hans Walter Wild distinguished himself by maintaining total silence on her national socialist past.

The media circus was adroitly handled by the festival's PR department. Among the onlookers were delegates of the NPD and other old friends of my grandmother's from the Nazi period. I took some pains to avoid their condolences. Free of his mother's presence, my father now became the omnipresent festival boss, apparently not considering it necessary to receive his own family or the guests. Whilst the family feigned mourning to the outside world, they privately rejoiced that the domineering shadow had finally lifted and got down to business: dividing up the inheritance.

Far more traumatic than the death of my grandmother was the breakup of my marriage to Beatrix. Over Christmas in 1980, Beatrix and I faced up to the fact that our weekend marriage between Munich and Wuppertal was ultimately unsustainable: among other things we disagreed about having children and the paths our careers should take – especially mine, since I had no intention of returning to Bayreuth. She didn't want to move to Wuppertal, as the prospects for her career as a lawyer were better in Munich, and though I hoped to dissuade her from separation by offering to give up my job in Wuppertal she wouldn't agree to that either. As divorce proceedings began, so did one of the most difficult periods of my life. I took refuge in my work, and it soon became like a drug to me.

After four years of trying, Johannes Meyer-Lindenberg finally succeeded in persuading Father to meet with me face to face, and so, in February 1981, we drove through a snowstorm to Bayreuth. The only place we could find to stay was the Hotel Goldener Anker, on the first floor, right next to room number 23, the same room in which Hitler had stayed in 1923 when he had met my grandmother for the first time. I thought that this boded ill, but Johannes quickly told me not be so suspicious.

Father received us in the *Festspielhaus* out of consideration for his wife and my half-sister, Katherina, whom I didn't meet. The conversation began with platitudes and with commentary on the weather. It was obvious that Father found the meeting awkward: he kept repeating that he had very little time and that he had a lot of other important things to do, but neither of us allowed ourselves to get irritated. Johannes' tactical skills amazed me – he told Father to stop his public attacks and derogatory remarks and to meet me regularly to air our views. However, when Johannes tried to arrange the next meeting, Father was reluctant to commit himself. Annoyed, Johannes insisted that we meet in Wuppertal.

What we had achieved, in fact, was an agreement in principle to have regular conversations and for Father to no longer make negative remarks about me in public. Satisfied, Johannes left my father's office on the second floor of the *Festspielhaus*. As we parted, I tried to look Father in the eye, but he avoided it and something told me that he wouldn't hold to the agreement.

In March 1981, my father and his second wife, Gudrun, attended a production of mine for the first and last time: Mozart's *Bastien Und Bastienne*. For the administrative staff of the Wuppertal Opera House, the appearance of Wolfgang Wagner was a great coup. The performance took place in a school in Wuppertal-Ronsdorf under extremely modest conditions. There had been no publicity, and the hall was half empty. Father's wife commented: "In Bayreuth we are swamped with audiences. You seem to have quite the opposite problem." An embarrassed silence followed.

I met again with Johannes Meyer-Lindenberg in April, and asked him to help me cope with my divorce. With some reluctance I took the sedatives he prescribed, and then the treatment began and I started talking. After I had talked for half an hour, Johannes declared with a kind smile: "You don't need psychoanalysis. You need your own family and the right professional environment, which you certainly don't have in Wuppertal with career-conscious types like Meyer-Oertel and Matiasek." The very next day I stopped taking the tablets and, to the amazement of my boss, stopped living for the theatre. After the premiere of my production of Berlioz's *Béatrice Et Bénédict* – which was attended, to my great joy, by Aunt Friedelind – I flew to Paris to attend a Jewish wedding. I had a brief and refreshing flirtation with an enchanting Parisienne, and slowly began to recover. In this new, positive frame of mind, I became aware of the pointlessness of my former existence. Things had to change.

CHAPTER FOURTEEN

TERESINA

My new appetite for life was unimpaired by the appearance of my father, along with his new wife; at this point I believed that things could only get better. I began the task of extricating myself from my self-imposed isolation, and enjoying the generous company of my landlady, Dodo Koch, who accepted me into her household like a son, spoiling me rotten. Dodo took a warm-hearted interest in both my professional experiences and private escapades. I lived in a small annex, which, like the main house, was situated at the beginning of a forest path leading to the Gelpe valley in a beautiful countryside setting.

In the first week of July, Dodo took to preparing for her seventieth birthday with all of the skill and attention to detail typical of a perfect hostess. Being a member of Wuppertal high society, she enjoyed great popularity, and so had invited a large number of guests, and planned the seating arrangements meticulously. As she knew about my divorce from Beatrix, she asked me in her direct way: "And who should I invite as your lady partner at the table?"

"Better not have anybody!" I said defensively.

Dodo wouldn't give up, however. "Teresina Rossetti would be a charming partner," she said, jokingly.

The comment slightly annoyed me. "Her of all people. I had such an awful row with her a year ago over the Pope and his reactionary views. You can't do that to me."

"How silly you are not to see Teresina's human qualities, just because of your views on the Pope!" Dodo replied, irritated. She had a great deal of respect for Teresina, who had been a regular visitor since 1973, first as an au pair, and later as a friend.

A few days before the birthday party, Dodo and I were sitting in her drawing room talking about the party arrangements when the telephone rang. Dodo picked it up, listened, and answered: "Teresinchen, how nice that you've arrived! Get straight into a taxi and come here. No, wait: Dr Wagner will pick you up at the station." I could hear Teresina's comments quite clearly, as I was sitting next to Dodo: "I'd rather take a taxi," she said firmly. Dodo was firmly against this, however, and that she allowed me to pick her up.

On the drive to the station I debated whether I should direct the conversation immediately to the Pope or to the emancipation of women. Then, when I saw her waiting in front of the station with her suitcase, tired from the long train journey from Milan, I refrained from all the little digs and greeted her with a friendly *"Ciao, come sta?"* [How are you?]

Surprised at my friendliness, she answered with an irresistible smile: *"Bene. Grazie per essere venuto a prendermi."* [Very well. Thank you for coming to collect me.]

From that moment on, I preferred to talk with her Italian. When we were sitting smiling in the car, I couldn't resist asking her why she had insisted on not being picked up by me. With disarming hilarity, she answered: "I didn't want to start fighting with you about the Pope straightaway, as I can hardly imagine that you've altered your opinions since our argument a year ago."

"A lot has happened in my life since then," I admitted. "I've changed a lot, and I'm more capable of listening to you now."

From that moment on until the time she left we met up whenever we could, telling one another the stories of our lives with an openness of which only old friends are capable – or people who have just fallen in love. We made it clear to one another from the first moment what we considered to be meaningful and what we didn't, based on our own bad experiences. And yet the hurdles before us were anything but insignificant: my divorce proceedings, my difficult professional situation, the incurable illness of Teresina's father, the geographical distance and our very different families. Amidst all of these plans we had for our future together, we completely forgot Wuppertal. With some satisfaction, Dodo immediately sensed that we had fallen in love. My change in behaviour didn't escape the other guests, either, and people whispered behind our backs: "How happy and open Gottfried Wagner has become! And how well this charming Italian woman suits him."

When I watched the train leave Cologne station, escorting Teresina back to Italy on the evening of 12 July 1981, I knew that I had a chance of leading a meaningful and fulfilled life with her. Problems that had seemed insoluble to me diminished in significance. I began to understand who I was. Through Teresina's love, I was becoming myself.

I made preparations to meet with my old teacher, Maximilian Kojetinsky, in Bayreuth to go over the various versions of *Tannhäuser* with a view to staging a production by Meyer-Oertel for the coming season. Beforehand, I had met the Israeli set designer Arno Adar, who was working with Meyer-Oertel on a production of Volker David Kirchner's opera *Die Trauung*. At that very first meeting we discussed how far art can influence politics. Arno was not against politically-committed art, but he doubted its political influence. At once we were thrown into discussion on the dependency of art in totalitarian states like Nazi Germany and the Soviet Union, and it was only after this that Arno started talking about his experiences as an Austrian-Jewish emigrant. I had finally found a new debating partner in Wuppertal, in a time which was otherwise not very stimulating.

Arno's scepticism towards my idealistic arguments impressed me, as did his reliability. He brought me closer to Erich Fromm, Hannah Arendt and Viktor Frankl, authors I knew only superficially. He also broadened my horizons, inspiring me to investigate the subject of art and politics more profoundly. When I asked him if he would like to go with me to Bayreuth, he said curtly: "With you, yes."

On the way there, Arno told me of his flight from Nazi Austria, speaking exhaustively about Israel, and his fascinating story aroused my own curiosity about that country. We stayed with my mother, who had moved back to Bayreuth, against my advice.

On one afternoon we wanted to attend the dress rehearsal of *Tristan*, under Ponnelle's conventional set design and directing. However, when I went to pick up the tickets for the dress rehearsal from my father's office, I wasn't allowed in. The porter, whom I had known for 30 years, clearly found the situation painful, and apologised: "The boss' wife said you're not allowed into the *Festspielhaus* any more. Frau Pitz will bring you the tickets." Arno was surprised: "But this is the son of the festival boss. Can't he go in?"

At that moment, Frau Pitz arrived. She wanted to avoid a lengthy and painful discussion and invited us into her office, which was crammed with flowers and presents – small tokens from those fortunate enough to attend dress rehearsals or performances. For the first time in my life I had to sign a receipt for the tickets for myself and my guest. When I introduced Arno as a friend from Israel, my father's colleague reacted with exaggerated friendliness. "Herr Barenboim is an Israeli too," she declared enthusiastically. Evidently, a new chapter in Bayreuth's tactical philosemitism had begun. When I asked her whether we could see my father, she answered that first she would have to discuss the matter with his wife, Gudrun. "I'll let you know at the beginning of the first interval."

Without asking for permission, I showed Arno the *Festspielhaus*. People either returned my greetings unenthusiastically or not at all – my presence was obviously undesirable. Arno quickly picked up on this, and I told him about my father. The story clearly moved him. After the interval at the end of the first act we went back into the auditorium, and I was peered at as if I were a half-wit. Behind my back I heard people muttering "he's back, he's made it up with his father". The curtain finally went up on Act Two, and in spite of myself I was enthralled yet again by Wagner's music to *Tristan Und Isolde*. I completely forgot my frigid reception.

Arno was thrilled by the acoustics and the stage, and during the second interval said: "Let's just go up and say hello to your father." Without announcing ourselves, I led Arno to my father's office. In front of his door, his secretary intercepted us and requested, with some agitation, that I should make an appointment. I answered drily: "I'm sure my father would receive Mr Adar from Israel." On hearing the magic word the secretary threw herself into a paroxysm of obsequiousness, and after a few minutes we were allowed in to see my father. On greeting him, Arno said almost provocatively: "I would never have dreamt it: me sitting in the Bayreuth *Festspielhaus*." My father misunderstood the remark, interpreted it as flattery and answered: "We have a great tradition of employing Jewish conductors here at

Bayreuth, and now Barenboim as well." I bit my tongue. After two minutes, the secretary burst in and reminded my father of an appointment, a familiar trick Father used when he wanted to get rid of troublesome guests. Generously, he allowed us to visit Barenboim in the interval.

I didn't particularly want to join the queue of fans waiting in front of Barenboim's room, but agreed to do so for Arno's sake. He spoke to Barenboim in modern Hebrew – quite new and unexpected sounds in the Grail temple. Arno introduced me to Barenboim as the son of the festival boss. I spoke of Aunt Friedelind, who had known him since he was eleven. The conductor remained diplomatically silent; he knew my aunt remained *persona non grata* with my father.

On the following day I met Meyer-Oertel and Maximilian Kojetinsky in the Siegfried Wagner House, as agreed, in order to discuss the Dresden and Paris versions of *Tannhäuser*. Afterwards, when showing Meyer-Oertel around the house, I noticed that several valuable family heirlooms had disappeared, although the final division of the inheritance had still not taken place. After visiting the 'Führer's room' we stopped off at my grandmother's bedroom, where we saw photos of my Uncle Wieland in a Nazi helmet and my father as the Führer's soldier, standing on the bedside table just as they had years ago. Meyer-Oertel understood my horror and my wish to leave the house immediately.

It was then that I understood why he had engaged me as his colleague: he had totally succumbed to a desire to be connected with Bayreuth. Thank God that Arno was nearby; he had closely observed what had happened, and we understood one another wordlessly.

After the dress rehearsal of my father's production of *Die Meistersinger*, I set off for Italy in order to meet Teresina's family for the first time. The initial separation from Teresina had seemed like an eternity to me, although it had only lasted eleven days. Arno smirked and said that he hoped I'd have a good time. "Remember," he said to me as I left, "Italian families are like Jewish families: matriarchal."

I will always remember 24 July 1981, as on that day a new chapter began in my life: my integration into Teresina's family, in Cerro Maggiore, near Milan. It was a procedure not without some friction; as I came from such a broken home, it was difficult for me to fit in with the Rossettis. Also, knowing Italy only as a tourist, I had to overcome a few prejudices. It made me realise just how questionable the social and cultural conditioning I had undergone in Bayreuth had been. Combined with this was the fact that I was still in the throes of divorce, and I didn't know how a Catholic family would react to this. Also, my professional prospects were pretty thin.

Teresina assured me that the fact that I was German didn't bother her family, but I was aware that the SS had established a base in Legnano, very near Cerro Maggiore, and had terrorised the local population. With my heart pounding we drove into Via Saffi, where Mamma Antonietta, Papa Antonio, Uncle Luigi, his wife Maria, Teresina's sister Francesca, her husband Enzo and their little daughter Silvia were waiting for us. I was scrutinised by curious, expectant eyes, focused totally on me. I was received as Teresina's fiancé. Teresina had advised me not to blurt out everything at once and not to mention my still pending divorce, as had been my original plan. I restrained myself, partly out of concern for her father's health.

The *fidanzato* [fiancé] *Goffredo* was automatically assigned a place in the home – the idea of having the future son-in-law stay in a hotel would have seemed absurd to Teresina's family. In the living room, the evening meal was waiting on a long, beautifully-decorated marble table. Mamma Antonietta provided us with undisputable proof of her culinary skills, which immediately won me over. I earned a few brownie points in her eyes as well when, much to the amusement of the whole table, I helped myself liberally to every dish. To my joy, I soon learned that food was a valuable item in the Italian culture. There was a relaxed, jolly atmosphere at the table, such as I had never known before, and I was equally amazed by the passionate discussions between family members. I also relished the fact that Richard Wagner wasn't the key topic of conversation: after a few well-considered remarks on Wagner's orchestration, Uncle Luigi – Mamma Antonietta's brother and one-time musician in the local band – changed the topic to his favourite composers, Verdi and Puccini. Wagner was, to my relief, only one of the many music subjects up for debate.

The family were at their most animated on the subject of mothers and children. In Italy, children are the centre of attention for female members of the family, and so the nine-month-old Silvia was the main topic of conversation. It almost made me a little jealous when Mamma

Antonietta, Francesca or Teresina said to Silvia: *"Fai un bel sorriso!"* [Give us a nice smile!]

In contrast, I began to perceive how unkindly my sister and I had been treated. Again and again – often quite reluctantly – I compared experiences from my past with my new family, and the gift of being given an opportunity to live in the here and now. Confused and happy, I started acclimatising myself in Cerro Maggiore. The introductions to relations, and the festivities which went along with each introduction almost by necessity, were endless – there was no question of any intimate time alone with Teresina. But when she looked at me with an understanding smile, I felt the warmth of the reception and gladly gave in to it.

Then, at a stroke, everything changed. At the beginning of August, Teresina's father was admitted to the hospital in Legnano, where we learned that the bone cancer from which he was suffering would not give him much more time. From that moment, I witnessed what it can mean when a family is united in grief. There was no longer a moment when Papa Antonio was not being cared for by Mamma Antonietta, Teresina, Francesca, his four still-living brothers Ernesto, Franco, Angelo and Luigi, or his sister Giannina, with their respective spouses, children and grandchildren. It was also the first time that I had been present at someone's death. The silence was only interrupted by prayers in Papa Antonio's sick room, by the shouts of the children in the corridor or by the nurses dashing to and fro in the corridor outside. On a number of occasions, one of the relations convulsively burst into tears.

Teresina's constant suffering moved me in a way that I had never known before. Mamma Antonietta, who sought comfort in prayer when her husband was sleeping, did her best to hold the family together. As always, she forgot herself and showed superhuman strength in supporting us. She silently showed us, with a great and calm dignity, how to overcome this sense of paralysing helplessness, pain, sadness and hopelessness.

Only when Papa Antonio had a rare moment free from pain could I talk to him. His concern was only for Teresina, who was suffering too much pain to talk to him, and needed all her energies to stop herself continually breaking down in tears. On one night, when I was alone with him, we spoke frankly about my marriage to his daughter. In view of his imminent death, I now felt responsible for Mamma Antonietta and Teresina. "Don't worry, Papa," I told him, "I'll be there for Teresina and Mamma."

At that moment I felt such a loss at my own fatherlessness: my own father had never been there for me, while Papa Antonio, who had accepted me as a son, now lay dying. In my despair I rang my father, intending to ask him to come. But his secretary answered: "Herr Wagner can't be contacted, he's in a meeting." I left my number with the secretary, along with a request for my father to ring back – which, of course, he never did.

That night, a notary from Legnano, who was on the same floor in the hospital as Papa Antonio, wandered around the corridor of the intensive care ward. I don't know how, but he had learned that I was a great-grandson of Richard Wagner. As he was a passionate Wagnerian, he sought to talk with me at all costs, and so, softly but quite audibly, sang in the corridor the story of the Grail out of *Lohengrin*, in Italian and with perfect intonation. Even Papa Antonio was amused, and said, smiling faintly, "*È matto, ma simpatico, il notaio!*" [He's mad, but nice, the notary!] Papa Antonio knew some of Wagner's most popular pieces; we had listened to Toscanini's 1954 recording before he went to the hospital. "Tell him he's got to stop singing Wagner in the middle of the night, or the others will get annoyed," he said.

I hurried out into the corridor and saw a scene on which Fellini couldn't have improved. The notary and Heldentenor *manqué* stood there in an operatic pose, with a transfigured gaze, waiting for an miracle. "Bravo! Bravo!" I applauded, shaking his hand with melodramatic gratitude.

"How does the great-grandson of the great composer experience mankind?" the self-styled Lohengrin replied.

"I'll tell you if you promise me to let people sleep now," I answered. "It's three in the morning."

He sighed. "*Che bello. A domani, maestro!*" But I didn't have the time then – and even less the inner calm – to talk about Wagner. The notary understood and showed a delicate sympathy.

Papa Antonio died only three nights later. I shall never forget

Teresina's horror and shock when the coffin was sealed. His death touched me, too; for the first time, I became painfully aware that our lives must one day end. I began to appreciate just being alive.

Despair had triggered a crisis in faith with Teresina. Who was this God who had let her father die in terrible pain at the age of 59? In this mood we went to a place that was to become a refuge for us: Cannero, and the Order Of Augustinian Fathers Of The Assumption, who lived over on a rock at Lago Maggiore, which commanded a splendid view of the lake. Over these difficult days, one of the priests, Father Giuliano, helped us immeasurably, and becoming a great friend. No subject was excluded: Teresina's religious crisis; my indiscriminate aversion to Christianity, in particular to the Catholic Church; and my divorce. I also had to acknowledge shamefully the stupid prejudices I had held against priests.

Father Giuliano was a warm-hearted, modest debating partner, with a lively vision of the Bible and Christianity and a wide-ranging knowledge of culture. I began to realise that the Catholic Church consists not merely of a repressive hierarchy but lives in worldwide spiritual dialogue with other monotheistic religions and even with atheists. Teresina's crisis of faith and the discussions with Father Giuliano inspired in me the need to once again seek out the answers to my questions concerning religion. I saw that I had made it too easy for myself when I criticised from outside instead of introducing a little of the lesson of the sermon on the mount in my own world.

On my return to Wuppertal, I made contact with a Franciscan monk, Father Ising, who was anything but conventional. In a district of 128 different communities of faith and sects, he had turned his Catholic community into a particularly lively and well-attended spiritual centre. He raged against the Pope, the ecclesiastical hierarchy and corrupt priests, and considered his brother Leonardo Boff, the Brazilian liberation theologian Hans Küng and other rebels in the Catholic Church to be true Christians. He spoke with such sensuality about men and women, marriage and bringing up children, that I couldn't believe my ears. On 31 October – Reformation Day, of all days – I decided to enter the Catholic Church.

Mamma Antonietta went on her first flight to attend the event, and Bettina Fehr also came as witness. After the ceremony, Father Ising – who later converted to Protestantism, married and became a father –

said to me: "The Christian Church is a heterogeneous universe. You'll never subject yourself unconditionally to the Church and its hierarchical ideology, but the Church needs heretics like you, or it would soon die, just as it did in the Nazi period! Just don't give up your dialogue with the Jews – that's part of your life."

He was to be proved right.

CHAPTER FIFTEEN

THE MONASTERY AND THE BANK

In the weeks immediately after my return from Italy, and during conversations with Father Ising, my preoccupation with my life as dramaturg and director in the Wuppertal Opera House seemed pointless. By the time Meyer-Oertel scrapped a production of *Mahagonny* that I had planned with Arno Adar, and which had been announced as my production for the coming season, in my mind I had already served notice. I was simply waiting for the right moment to leave Wuppertal. I needed another job, and one came up quite by chance.

I had met the former director of the Deutsche Bank, Hans H Asmus, at a premiere in Wuppertal. Asmus is a keen friend of the arts and thinks highly of my theatre work, and despite my objections he saw me as the future boss of the Bayreuth branch, and opined: "What you need is training and ordeal by fire in the Deutsche Bank. The German intendants have no idea about balancing the books. If you can read balance sheets and music scores, the world is your oyster."

He had no sooner made the suggestion than the deed was done, and on 16 December 1981 I stood in front of Adolf Sievers, one of the three personnel directors of the Deutsche Bank in Frankfurt Am Main, dressed as a junior banker. The meeting, however, had nothing to do with banking. Mr Sievers was of a cheerful amiability and sensitive refinement and steered our one-hour talk in a direction that almost made me forget why I had made the appointment with him. Like myself, he loved Mozart and understood interpretation to a degree which surprised even a professional of the classical music scene like myself. For him, appreciation of Otto Klemperer or Bruno Walter was a question of conscience. When I finally reminded him of the reason why I had come, he asked laughing: "What do you understand of the banking business?"

"Nothing," I answered, "and I never want to be a banker, only to learn how to handle money. And I need a job because, for various reasons, the Wuppertal theatre doesn't interest me any more."

Sievers harrumphed. "Seeing that an exotic bird such as yourself will first have to prove yourself in our cage, I'll give you a half-year trial period. Where do you want to go?"

With my imminent divorce in mind, and a desire to live as close to Cerro Maggiore as possible, I suggested Munich.

The Christmas of 1981 was the first that I spent with my adoptive family. It was also their first Christmas without Papa Antonio, and the house brooded under a melancholic atmosphere, which was relieved only by my one-year-old niece, Silvia. As they did each year, on Christmas Eve the family went to midnight mass in the overcrowded church in Cerro Maggiore, and over the next two days they all met in Enzo and Francesca's house. Despite the loss of their father, the family danced and sang, determined to give little Silvia a merry Christmas. This air of merriment – even if forced, out of love and respect for the children – made me wistful, reminding me of the quarrelsome Christmases in my family, in which children were assigned the role of decorative extras.

It occurred to me that this was perhaps the fundamental difference between Italian Catholic and the German Protestant families: the former being matriarchal and the latter patriarchal. In the Italian family, mother and child form an inviolable unit – the cult of Maria. Mamma Antonietta explained to me that respect for the child is a fundamental value that she had passed on to her daughters.

It was also clear that, after the death of my father-in-law, I was expected to support the family with all my strength. It was taken for granted that, as Teresina's future husband, I would be completely integrated into the family. What objection could anyone have to joining a family such as this, which stuck together in good times and bad and which accepted me as I was? Until that moment it was something which I had never experienced.

Before long I had the opportunity of proving my loyalty to my new family when I learned that Teresina and her mother would soon have to leave their home. It was the last thing we needed after the death of Papa Antonio; I was not yet divorced, a probationary trainee of the Deutsche Bank, and still hadn't yet officially completed business in Wuppertal. Nonetheless, we began to search for an apartment. Supported by my courageous fiancée, I signed a purchase contract on an apartment, despite my lack of assets. I was relying on the fact that Father would pay me my inheritance, which for the moment was doing nothing but lining the lawyers' pockets.

1982 began dramatically in every way. With the help of Father Ising, I had found a room in the Franciscan monastery in the Annagasse, in Munich. Unfortunately, my furniture wouldn't fit into the room, so I had to store it in Dodo Koch's garage in Wuppertal, and it later ended up in a furniture warehouse in Bonn. In mid January, I ended my contract with the Wuppertal theatre, to the horror of Aunt Friedelind and many friends. My last task in Wuppertal was to organise a matinée. With no little detachment, I observed what Meyer-Oertel had thought up for himself, as director of *Tannhäuser*.

It was with some relief, rather than regret, that I left the German stage at the end of January and travelled to Munich. After I had unloaded my car, Prelate Guardian invited me into his room, looked at me somewhat sceptically and declared: "Brother Ising has told me that you were working in Wuppertal as director and dramaturg. Now you want to work in the Deutsche Bank and live with us. Theatre, church, bank: that sounds like a novel. But it's a monastery here. Please respect that!"

In return for a nominal rent, I was given a relatively large room on the first floor of the monastery, which looked down into the garden. It wasn't easy for me to share a bath and telephone with high-school children and students; they looked on me as a rather strange old man. I knew, however, that the coming months would be only a transitionary phase in my life.

Firstly, I had to visit the personnel office of the Deutsche Bank Bayern, in the Ungererstrasse. One of the heads of personnel explained to me that I was now employee number 42,411 of the Deutsche Bank, and as such had to give up my former identity. When I mentioned my Munich address, it caused roars of laughter.

On 1 February 1982, I began working as trainee of the branch in the Schwanthalerstrasse. The director welcomed me warmly and made no attempt to hide his amazement at my former life. He assigned me a narrow place between the many desks behind the counter, and I was immediately let loose on humankind. As I hadn't even the slightest idea what I was supposed to be doing, I copied my new colleagues and played the part of the experienced banker to the customers. When I didn't know what to do – as was frequently the case, at first – I would smile and say, "Excuse me, but my colleague is more experienced in this matter," and turn to one of my colleagues for help, who with some amusement helped me out of often embarrassing situations.

At noon, on walking from the branch to the bank's main canteen on the Promenadenplatz, three things along Schwanthalerstrasse struck me: banks, brothels and dubious export and import shops. The owners and employees of the latter enterprises formed the core of the clients I had to deal with in the first stage of my rather awkward training. They had no sympathy for my lack of knowledge, and reminded me of it with a rudeness I had never before experienced. I put up with it, however, reminding myself of Brecht's *Dreigroschenoper*, but found that the reality had nothing to do with the world of theatre. After working their night shifts on the streets, the ladies of the horizontal trade would come into the bank and sullenly tip their earnings out of their cleavages, growling at me when I didn't know immediately what I was supposed to do. It took some effort not to respond in kind.

When it finally got too much for me, I complained to my superior. In reply, the deputy branch manager gave me a lecture: "The fact that your name is Wagner, that you've studied musicology and philosophy and worked in the theatre, is totally irrelevant. Here only one thing counts: that you stop costing us money and finally close some deals. With whom, why and how doesn't interest us. And if you don't like it, there's the door. There's a long line of people outside it who would do your work without complaining."

I said nothing, simply giving him a withering look, for which he paid me back whenever he got the opportunity. He was a typical functionary, kowtowing to his superiors and trampling those beneath him. As such, he was no different to most little bosses I've met. I soon worked out how I could avoid their petty attacks, however – I pretended that I was on personal terms with their superiors. As well as that, my academic title impressed them. In the end, they believed that I was on the threshold of a long career and held back.

The branch manager was, in his Bavarian stolidity, rather predictable. He taught me how to arrange credit loans, and then expected immediate results. Every morning, before the bank opened, he asked his employees for their "racing lists" – their signed agreements. I didn't fulfil his expectations, initially, and saw with some horror how my colleagues targeted foreigners in particular, talking them into taking out risky overdrafts and shamelessly exploiting their difficulties with the language.

I refused to adopt these methods, and soon got used to being reproached on a daily basis for not having concluded any deals. As scarcely any of my colleagues spoke foreign languages, I was often called in as interpreter for Turks, Italians, Yugoslavs, French people and Americans. I warned poor clients against signing long-term policies with the branch, especially if it were clear that they would be incapable of repaying the debt. Word of this got around among Turkish, Yugoslav and Italian workers, and to the annoyance of my boss they came to me in droves. I had to see to them in a side room – foreigners without fat wallets were not welcome.

It so happened that these groups brought me presents out of gratitude, and invited me for meals after work. When this reached the ears of the deputy branch manager, he bellowed through the bank – to the amusement of clients and employees alike – "we are not a charity, Wagner!" and shunted me off to the cellar to sort through the savings leaflets. My protests were to no avail, and my only comfort was that my time in the Schwanthalerstrasse branch would soon be over.

When I left the Schwanthalerstrasse branch of the Deutsche Bank at the end of April 1982, I felt like I had been living on a completely different planet. Working in the heart of bank administration on the Ungererstrasse from May, I was initiated into the secrets of banking. As I was only tolerated as an observer, and even then mostly reluctantly, people preferred it if I didn't disturb them with questions, which meant that I could finally pursue my own interests. To the amazement of my colleagues, I spent my time under the desk, reading the Old Testament of the Bible with growing enthusiasm, along with the works of Shalom Ben Chorin, whose *Brother Jesus: The Nazarene From The Jewish Viewpoint* impressed me in particular, as did Pinchas Lapides' books on Bible translations.

Back in the monastery, after my boring day at work, I would continue reading the German translations of the Jewish Bible, transcribed by Moses Mendelssohn and Martin Buber, and would compare them with the New Testament. It made my isolation in Germany bearable, and my later integration in Italy easier. It became clearer and clearer to me how inconceivable Christianity was without Judaism, and I distanced myself more and more from Bayreuth, which remained immersed in its Wagnerian pseudo-religion.

In May I visited my sister, who was living with her husband in the elegant Schönbergstrasse in Munich. Both were working for Leo Kirch, the future media tycoon, who was already powerful. Eva didn't understand the direction of my life, either professionally or privately, but unfortunately it never came to an open and frank discussion. The gulf between Eva's world of opera and film and my spiritual development, coupled with my adoption in my new family, proved to be unbridgeable.

After working in the administration department of the Deutsche Bank, I finally moved to the Bavarian headquarters on the Promenadenplatz. For two months I worked my way through the foreign department. There was no evidence of the oft-quoted principle of trainees learning on the job, however; I was allowed to observe what the others did, and only showed interest because I hoped to get a place in a branch in Milan, or failing that a job with an Italian bank.

The monotony of the work, squabbles with lawyers over the divorce settlement and the struggle for my inheritance were all left far behind, however, when I drove to see Teresina in Cerro Maggiore for the weekend or when I met up with friends in Munich. Unlike my colleagues at the bank, I had no desire to join the jet set, with their parties and BMWs, in much the same way that I didn't want to immerse myself in the opera world. I felt that it was more important at that time to improve my Italian, in readiness for my future with Teresina, and attend marketing courses that might perhaps one day help me.

I continued to feign interest in the banking business, determined to prove that, despite the predictions of friends and relations, I would stick it out in the Deutsche Bank. The first positive evaluations of my work amused me: Adolf Sievers was the only colleague with which I didn't need to pretend, and he was constantly encouraging me to keep going.

At the beginning of June, I happened to be passing my sister's home and dropped in to find out how she was, as in May she had given birth to a son, Antoine, in America. My brother-in-law proudly showed me the baby's American passport, made out under the name of Antoine Wagner-Pasquier.

In August and September 1982, I was initiated into the deeper mysteries of capitalism in the property department of the Deutsche Bank, and I also visited the Munich stock exchange. The stockbrokers screamed hysterically and rushed around like hungry wolves. The scene reminded me of Brecht's work: he saw no moral difference between bank robbery and bank business. To be fair, however, in the Munich branch of the Deutsche Bank, the great commitment demonstrated by superiors and colleagues alike provided me with an essential insight into the banking business. I am still in contact with them today; they understood that my professional life would not end in a bank, and found me – the exotic bird – to be a welcome change in their day-to-day lives.

I found myself bored to death in the property administration department, as well. My only comfort was the monthly cheque. In my free time I once again studied Wagner's concept of religion in *Parsifal* – it now seemed to be so dishonest.

I wanted to work in the theatre again at all costs, so I went to see Alberto Zedda, who was commanded some influence in Pesaro and in the Italian left-wing cultural scene. I also consulted the conductor Claudio Abbado. Both assured me that they were convinced of my professional competence, but didn't help me in my search for a job.

Meanwhile, the dispute over my inheritance entered a new phase. My father was demanding that I hand back the rolls of film that had been shot during the Nazi period. They were still being stored with Beatrix's parents, but in January 1983 he had his lawyer's chauffeur collect the originals from me. I sent the copies to my sister, making it clear to her exactly how explosive the material that she was now guarding was. As I had no projector, I had to inspect the films by holding them up to the light: they showed Hitler with the Wagner family in the Wahnfried garden and in the *Festspielhaus*, and Father as a stalwart member of the Hitler Youth on the Bayreuth Sternplatz, his arm held aloft. What unfortunate intimacy and foolish merriment! There followed images of the Nazi rallies at Nuremberg, with my grandmother and other family members being cheered by fanatical crowds.

Meanwhile, the divorce hearing took place before a Munich court and was remarkably unpleasant. Beatrix and I left the court building like two strangers – after a relationship of almost eleven years.

But now, of course, there was no turning back for Teresina and me. As I hadn't had a church wedding the first time around, there was nothing to prevent us from having a classic Italian wedding. In the months up to 3 July 1983, the big day, I became aware of just how important the ceremony was to my new family. After undergoing an atheist upbringing, and suffering from spiritual and ethical neglect in Bayreuth, the Catholic rites seemed very strange to me, as did all of their feast days and holidays. I envied Teresina and her family (especially Mamma Antonietta) their deeply-rooted piety, which had nothing to do with bigotry or dependence on the Church. In time I learned to understand that what my new family possessed was a much more realistic philosophy of life than that of my idealistic, pseudo-Protestant German world view, in which the idea has nothing to do with human nature, with all of its corresponding inconsistencies. Irrespective of all dogma and the omnipresence of the Catholic Church, I realised that a strong sense of individualism prevailed in my new family, which made any form of state and ecclesiastical tutelage impossible.

Fascinated, I discovered new family's capacity for living life in the here and now, with all the sensuality of Mediterranean culture, and the way in which this reflected not only Christianity but also pre-Christian rites and myths. Many of my beliefs began to waver. I embarked on what was to prove just one of many often painful self-discoveries.

In February 1983, before the wedding, I had agreed in Munich to a disadvantageous settlement of my inheritance, mainly because I had to make a downpayment on our future home together in Cerro Maggiore. Bad though the settlement was for me, it nonetheless meant a further step in the direction of Italy.

Also in February, the celebrations began for the centenary of Richard Wagner's death. Although I lay low in the bank, my past in Bayreuth still came back to haunt me. I rejected ridiculous offers from the media to make an appearance, as his great-grandson. However, the Munich publication *Abendzeitung* offered me a deal that seemed to be of a somewhat higher calibre: I was asked my opinion on Wagner's work and his influence in the music world, and I believed that I could answer that with a clear conscience. But, of course, it was only the gossip about who would succeed my father as head of the festival that was printed.

The bookshop windows were crammed with literature about Wagner, although the only significant title that I could find was the new edition of Hartmut Zelinsky's *Richard Wagner: Ein Deutsches Thema*. On the other hand, I found the commentaries in Dieter Borchmeyer's ten-volume series about Wagner to be very superficial; in particular, he tried to gain status in Bayreuth with his remarks about Wagner's article 'The Jews In Music'. There was once again a Wagner boom in the book market, but I didn't want anything to do with it.

Meanwhile I had advanced in the bank from being the lowest of the low to potential management material, and I was under increasing pressure to perform. In February I was allowed to speak in the Bayerischer Hof Hotel in Munich before Dr Siegfried Gropper (known as 'God the Father'), director of the Deutsche Bank in Munich, and his humble retinue from affiliated Bavarian branches, on the topic of strike insurance from a left-wing viewpoint. A few days earlier, I had assisted Peter Glotz of the Bavarian SPD as electoral assistant in Haselberg, Munich's working-class district. Contrary to expectation, my talk was calmly received.

Later there was a dinner, to which trainees had also been invited. Many of them wanted to seize the opportunity to play up to the boss, in a display of deference and obsequeiousness. It reminded me of Heinrich Mann's novel *Man Of Straw*. I was under no pressure to gain status and so chatted amiably with Gropper, even daring to contradict him when he entered what was for him the uncertain territory of art and music and when he tried to coach me privately on Wagner. My trainee friends enjoyed the spectacle, while the others just stood agog, amazed at such lack of respect.

The meeting had one distinct advantage: I could present myself as a specialist on Italy without even hinting at the true reason behind my interest. Lo and behold, after I had finished my basic training in the credit department in Munich, my request for a transfer was granted. The Munich bankers were glad to see me go, and found me a new job at the bank in Milan. I could now plan my move to Cerro Maggiore.

CHAPTER SIXTEEN

MY ITALIAN WEDDING

Most of my friends from Germany had already arrived for the polterabend [pre-wedding party] on 2 July 1983, the evening before my marriage. My new family, however, weren't familiar with this tradition. We celebrated in glorious weather in Antonio Lazzati's little summerhouse, with its huge garden, until far into the next day. In the morning, at the ceremony, it was mainly the Italian friends and relations who came into Mamma Antonietta's home. I was allowed to talk to Teresina only through a locked door, as the groom could only see the bride in the church, standing in front of the altar. Even though these rituals seemed strange at the time, I kept to them during the course of the day, with the help of Uncle Luigi, who discreetly whispered instructions to me.

The wedding guests gathered on the piazza in front of the church. The family exuded such a merry atmosphere that I couldn't feel any regret that my father had declined his invitation. My mother did come, however, and accompanied me to the altar, with Teresina following shortly after, escorted by her father's eldest brother. She and Mamma Antonietta were visibly upset that Papa Antonio wasn't there, but as she walked down the aisle, to the wedding march from *Lohengrin* (which the Cerro Maggiore choir performed for us in Italian), past pews bedecked with roses, the months since July 1981 flashed again through my mind. My witnesses, my sister Eva and my friend Louis Landuyt, a singer and music teacher from Luxembourg, sat to my right in front of the altar. I chose my sister to be a witness in the hope that we could start our relationship afresh. Behind us, in the nave, sat my mother and my cousin Christa, representatives of Mother's side of the family, and behind them sat Bettina Fehr and my friends who had helped me in the difficult transition from theatre to bank: Eckard, Rosi, Dieter, Ulf, Dodo, Walter, Maureen, Florian and their partners. On the left side of the church sat my brother-in-law Enzo and sister-in-law Francesca, and behind them Teresina's relations, including Mamma Antonietta and her brother Luigi and Ernesto, Papa Antonio's third brother, all of whom are still particularly close to me. They knew from the beginning that it would be difficult for me, a foreigner, to be fully integrated into Italian society.

The marriage ceremony was performed in German and Italian by our friend Father Giuliano. Teresina and I had chosen the text from I Corinthians 13 XIII, on the love that overcomes all obstacles. I was caught totally unprepared when I was asked perform a reading for our German guests, however; the words were printed so small that I could barely decipher them. Because of this – as well as being profoundly moved by the occasion – I improvised, much to the amusement those of our guests who were better acquainted with the Bible than myself. When Francesca sang the Bach/Gounod 'Ave Maria', quite unexpectedly but with incredible tenderness and perfect intonation while accompanied on the organ by Ars Nova choir leader Franco Pasquali, there wasn't a dry eye in the church.

In those moments of burgeoning hope, a new chapter began in my life. Behind me lay nothing but crisis; I had even toyed with the idea of taking on Teresina's family name, to make a visible break with my Bayreuth past, but she convinced me that this would be a pointless denial of my identity and that I should soon continue my career. When I came out of the church with my new wife, to the accompaniment of Mendelssohn's wedding march (which I had selected in preference to my great-grandfather's wedding music), I felt like a completely different Wagner.

The exalted mood was abruptly broken by loud cries from the Italian guests and curious onlookers – "*Evviva gli sposi!*" [Here's to the newlyweds!] – and we were deluged in a hail of rice, and all of a sudden the congregation erupted in merriment. Before driving off to attend the reception, we laid roses from the church decorations on

Papa Antonio's grave and on those of other deceased relations. Again, this was such a contrast to my family's indifference toward their dead, who were only remembered on official occasions, and always with a view to media coverage.

We spent out honeymoon in a magical place on Crete, the cradle of European and Mediterranean culture. Over the next few days we completely forgot the rest of the world and our worries, as we were surrounded by sweet-smelling, lush, flowering woodland and the chirping of crickets. In August 1983, however, we travelled to Bayreuth, along with Mamma Antonietta and some of our Italian friends. As Father refused to receive us in his house, Aunt Friedelind invited us to dinner in the chic Schloss Tiergarten Hotel. On hearing that we had no tickets for a festival performance of *Tristan Und Isolde*, she rang up Father, deaf to our protests, and demanded tickets.

I took Teresina and Mamma Antonietta on a guided tour of Bayreuth, through Wahnfried Park, Villa Wahnfried and the *Festspielpark*, where I heard people whispering behind my back. The lackeys of the festival court were there, and as soon as they were sure that no one was watching them they greeted us with insincere friendliness.

In the *Festspielhaus* we encountered Father's coterie of yes men. When I asked to see him, so that I could to introduce him to Teresina and Mamma Antonietta, I was told that he could see only Teresina and myself, and then only briefly. Outraged, I threw the tickets on the desk and stormed out of the room, shouting: "Either my father receives myself, my wife and my mother-in-law or I leave the *Festspielhügel* immediately. Who does he think he is? My mother-in-law is not going to be discriminated against here!" The guests waiting in the corridors pointedly turned their backs on us.

However, when I asked Mamma Antonietta to leave the *Festspielhaus* with us, she pulled me back firmly. "Calm down. You're going with Teresina to your father; she certainly won't have the the opportunity to meet her father-in-law again. Think of her. Don't think of me." My loving foster aunt Gunda, who thankfully was on duty that afternoon, pulled Mamma Antonietta down beside her next to her desk in the telephone exchange and urged Teresina and myself up the stairs to the first floor, in the direction of my father's office. When Teresina and I arrived there, Gudrun greeted us with a gracious smile and offered me her hand to kiss. I shook it.

We met Father shortly afterwards. He shook our hands without looking at us, then started talking non-stop in a strong Upper Franconian accent, which Teresina of course couldn't understand, and tactlessly compared his second marriage with mine. I replied calmly, but firmly: "Everyone has to make his own decisions." He refrained from discussing this further. I also remained silent, for Teresina's sake, but shot meaningful glances at him, urging him to change the subject. Instead, he extolled the idea of a second marriage, praising it as a source of renewal for a man.

This torrent of words was only interrupted when one of his secretaries flung open the door to indicate to us that we should go. Turning to my father, she said in a thick local accent: "Herr Wagner, you're wanted on the stage!" Father said goodbye, bowing deeply and hastily so that he didn't have to look at us directly, and tore out of the room. As we left, I recognised the secretary: she was the daughter of one of my nannies. We had met many times previously, but she didn't seem to recognise me now.

Teresina and I collected Mamma Antonietta from Gunda's office and hurried to our seats, as the performance was about to begin. I briefly explained the plot of the first act of *Tristan Und Isolde* to Mamma Antonietta while we headed for the stuffy family box, where Gudrun had rather tactlessly seated me next to the lawyer who had drawn up the agreement for my inheritance settlement.

We went to the festival restaurant during the intervals. Most of those present there pointedly ignored us, with the exception of Philip Wults, who was writing a history of the Wagner family and appreciated my situation. I sat impatiently in the auditorium, eager for the performance to end; the brief visit to my Father had put me in a bad mood. I wanted to avoid Mamma Antonietta and Teresina taking home an even worse impression of Bayreuth than I had given them.

Mamma Antonietta liked both the music and Ponnelle's production. However, when I asked her how she found her stay in Bayreuth, after the performance, she was concerned: "The performance was beautiful, but I don't think you could be happy in Bayreuth." She said nothing about what she'd had to put up with in Bayreuth, but that first trip was also her last.

At the end of August 1983 I organised my transfer to Italy, which was paid for by the Deutsche Bank. They also paid for me to enroll at the expensive Bocconi School Of Economics in Milan, but more importantly they gave me an advantageous contract for a position in the credit department of the Deutsche Bank. Four weeks later I began my new life with Teresina.

I started work immediately and went to school every evening, pursuing both activities with the sole interest of earning money. The most valuable possession for anyone involved in the theatre scene at that time was a membership card for Bettino Craxi's Socialist Party, and of course I didn't have one. Corruption of this type disgusted me. Anyway, I was excluded from the opera and academic circles because I worked in a bank, and all of my attempts at denying this failed.

Right from the start, I had mixed impressions of my superiors in the credit department, although over time I developed a warm friendship with one: Eleonore Finsterbusch-Horn. My other boss, a man we called only 'Semmel' [bread roll], appeared awkward and stiff when I first met him, and I soon suspected that we wouldn't see eye to eye. In fact, it was through Semmel that I experienced first hand what it means to be a subordinate in a bank hierarchy, in which deviations from the prescribed norm is not tolerated. This system, which served no other purpose than to increase the bank's profit, stifled the development of any individuality below positions of management. There were two options: submit or get out.

As I fully intended handing in my notice once my course had finished, I could afford to stand up to Semmel. After I had caught him repeatedly talking disparagingly about "the Italians", I requested that he stopped such discrimination; my family was Italian, and he was insulting me, too. This was the opening volley to a series of squabbles, for which I was fortunately well prepared. News of our feud spread like wildfire. Eleonore took my side, and our Italian colleagues began to trust us. Pleased to be able to offer them help, I advised them to join a union, but most were frightened of losing their jobs and scarcely dared to demand change. Semmel took the coward's way out and complained to the director, a former Luftwaffe officer, who tried to intimidate me. I soon brought his efforts to a halt, however, by casually mentioning that as a sideline I worked as a journalist. He and Semmel then set to preparing a report about me to send to head office at Frankfurt.

Shortly afterwards, I noticed that Semmel no longer greeted me, and seemed relieved if I closed my door, which was directly opposite his. Any contact was via the internal mailing system, and minutes of meetings filled entire files. I collected these documents, and in the spring of 1985, when I had collated enough relevant material, I asked for a meeting at head office in Frankfurt Am Main. The ever-helpful Adolf Sievers saw only one way out, in the short term: transferring me to Berlin.

CHAPTER SEVENTEEN

BACK TO THE CULTURE JUNGLE

Amidst the guerrilla warfare that was currently taking place at the bank, Götz Friedrich, intendant of the Deutsche Oper in Berlin and the Theater Des Westens, made me a tempting offer: he wanted me to write a programme feature for a production of Weill's and Brecht's opera *Aufstieg Und Fall Der Stadt Mahagonny* in the Theater Des Westens in April 1985. I accepted the offer gratefully. I had unlimited resources to draw on; in fact, I had only to think of my experiences in the bank and Bayreuth. I called the article 'I Remember: The TV Memoirs Of Leokadja Von Begbick'. My story of *Mahagonny*, with its strong autobiographical allusions, was based on the idea that there is scarcely any difference between methods of procedure in banking and in opera, where ultimately everybody is trying to outdo everyone else. I played off the decadent, bourgeois world of Wagner against the progressive forces in the opera scene of the Weimar Republic, while also hinting that there wasn't that much difference between the past and the present. Götz Friedrich understood my allusions immediately, and commissioned another feature, this time for the programme for the premiere of his new production of *Götterdämmerung*, in autumn 1985.

Re-inserting myself in the cultural scene at this time, I was armed with new and valuable experience. My work in the bank had taught me a great deal about economic and political forces, including those in opera.

Shortly after the publication of the article, my sister sent me an interview that my cousin Wummi – from whom I'd heard nothing since moving to Italy – had given to Karsten Peters, editor of the German edition of *Harper's Bazaar*. Entitled 'I Always Have The Feeling Everything's Going To Happen Today', the interview contained statements I couldn't possibly endorse. Wummi didn't just restrict himself to his work as an opera director, and his ill-informed comments on my situation and attitude angered me. It proved once again that even Wummi and I had forgotten how to talk – really talk – with each other, which I suppose was a consequence of the distrustful and acrimonious atmosphere in which we had grown up. The interview certainly portrayed a reaction to long-endured humiliation.

However, I did agree with his criticism of my father's work as director. When Peters asked him about the identity of my father's successor as festival head in Bayreuth, Wummi answered: "Wolfgang Wagner wants to be the longest [sic] and last festival head from our family, and actually I don't find that a very responsible attitude." So far, so good.

PETERS: "Who other than Wolfgang Wagner could hinder you there?"
WUMMI: "Oh, Wolfgang can't hinder me there either, I think. It's just a matter of the circumstances under which it happens."
PETERS: "In that case, is there a practical possibility of you taking over the festival before your uncle's death?"
WUMMI: "He ought to bring me on board now, instead of waiting for the moment when catastrophe strikes or something else unexpected happens."
PETERS: "And he expressly rejects that?"
WUMMI: "Yes, he rejects it."
PETERS: "And does he give any reasons for that?"
WUMMI: "Yes. He says I should have worked my way up from the bottom after my father's death. But he forgets that he made that impossible for me. I also find that it's more beneficial to make your way outside a firm you belong to than inside."
PETERS: "Among the other 'Young Bayreuthers' – who aren't actually that young any more – are there no other candidates?"

WUMMI: "Oh yes, there's my cousin Eva, who's already heavily involved in arts administration, and there's my cousin Gottfried, although for the moment he's not concentrating on administration any more."

PETERS: "How is your relationship with them?"

WUMMI: "I have – amazingly, for our family – very good contact and we get on very well. And there's no reason at all why two or three people couldn't take it on together."

PETERS: "Wagner directs Wagner – one generation after the other. Isn't that a sort of artistic incest?"

WUMMI: "Of course it's incest. But I'm of the opinion that amazing things can come out of incest as well. And in my case that is so; I get most of my ideas while listening to this music."

The following passages of the interview gave me a great deal to consider.

PETERS: "What characteristics would particularly apply to you?"

WUMMI: "Fury and vindictiveness."

PETERS: "And whom do you hate at the moment?"

WUMMI: "Myself, most of all."

And then Peters returned to his favourite subject again: "Do you want to be the heir of Bayreuth? Here and now? Today?"

WUMMI: "Yes, rather the day before yesterday than yesterday. Wolfgang should stop dismissing the rest of the family as incapable…and if he were to look back on what he's done in the past, then I would say that my qualifications are certainly worth more than his were then."

PETERS: "What makes your uncle act like that?"

WUMMI: "He must still be reacting to a distorted relationship which – and I can only guess at this – goes back to that battle he had to fight as younger brother. I can't understand that, especially as my father has now been dead a long time. Wolfgang established himself a long time ago, and he's recognised. He doesn't have to fight for his reputation for ever."

PETERS: "Was the enmity between Wolfgang and his big brother Wieland really so great?"

WUMMI: "Yes. They were at daggers drawn."

PETERS: "Doesn't it also have something to do with the envy of the less gifted?"

WUMMI: "It must be, I suppose, or he wouldn't react the way he does."

PETERS: "What's his relationship with his own children, Eva and Gottfried?"

WUMMI: "That's the real tragedy of the whole story: he regards his own children exactly as he does his brother's children – they mean nothing to him. That's pretty alarming."[25]

To my mind, the historical basis for doubting my generation's claim to succession are further illustrated by an event which took place during the festival in the summer of 1984. Some friends told me of the exhibition *Wagner And The Jews* in Villa Wahnfried, and I received details about it in a exhibition catalogue a year later. I still believe that the exhibition and its catalogue were an historical misrepresentation, for the following reasons.

Firstly, Richard Wagner's antisemitic and inflammatory essay 'The Jews In Music' is presented totally without commentary and without a critical comparison of the three versions.

Secondly, this essay is only the beginning of Wagner's antisemitic writings up to 1881.

Thirdly, the historical development of antisemitism – from Richard to Cosima, and then on via Houston Stewart Chamberlain to Hitler, Winifred, Wieland and Wolfgang – was only partially demonstrated in text and pictures.

Fourthly, the biographies of the so-called Jewish friends of Richard Wagner – Hermann Levi, Samuel Lehr, Carl Tausig, Heinrich Porge, Angelo Neumann, Joseph Rubinstein, Joseph Joachim and Wagner's artistic Jewish paragons Felix Mendelssohn and Giacomo Meyerbeer – were presented falsely.

These four points constitute an attempt to trivialise Wagner's antisemitism, falsifying it almost to the opposite extreme.

Fifthly, an indispensable element of the exhibition should have been the inclusion of specialists on the historical connection between Wagner's antisemitism and the Holocaust.

Sixthly, in the exhibition nothing is said about the connection between the antisemitic content of Wagner's writings and stage works.

In its presentation of Wagner's antisemitism, I found the exhibitions contempt critical scholars of the composer such as Hartmut Zelinsky particularly unpleasant. Bayreuth was going in a direction that I now resisted. In a telephone call to Father, I asked him whether he was behind this. "It's high time to draw a line under this," he said and hung up.

Before I could continue my attacks against the *Festspielhügel*, however, I still had to overcome my own inner struggle, in which Teresina selflessly stood by me. After serving notice at the Deutsche Bank, and receiving a surprisingly positive reference, I tried to sustain us financially in whatever way I could. For a time I worked as an insurance agent in Milan, after which I sold shoes with some success at the Milan shoe fair for a friend in Cerro Maggiore, who made designer shoes, which allowed me a bit of leeway for my work on Liszt and Wagner. All of my efforts at finding a job in the cultural sector via Everding unsurprisingly came to nothing. I heard nothing from him, except for a few pious phrases laden with compliments. He was only interested in Bayreuth family gossip, and I soon tired of asking him for favours. The only person connected with the opera who didn't abandon me was Götz Friedrich.

Because of the official historiography in Bayreuth, and my desire to continue with my German-Jewish studies, I concentrated on the 19th and 20th centuries. I also continued studying Liszt, fascinated by his contradictory personality: he was Mephisto and saint, social lion and Christian socialist. He considered himself to be cosmopolitan, and had occasionally shown great courage in publicly standing by his convictions, but he was incapable of holding down a relationship and building a family.

As I studied, a new and exciting world opened up before me, a cultural concept that I felt more and more to be the antithesis of Wagner. The contrasts thrown up by Liszt's confrontation with the outside world seemed extreme; he had experienced reality as a direct contradiction to his artistic idea of the world. In vain, he sought to solve this conflict by retreating into artistic isolation. Through his work as composer, pianist, music theoretician, opera director, conductor, teacher and coordinator of the essential musical trends of the 19th century, his effect on the music of his and successive centuries is enormous.

I found myself confronting yet another giant from my own family, but Liszt seemed to be much more likeable than the one whose name I shall always bear like a millstone around my neck. While studying Liszt, I also realised that I still had to find my own identity – it wasn't enough to define myself by reading other people's literature and music scores.

In the course of my research, I drove to the European Liszt Centre in Eisenstadt, Austria, which turned out to be an insignificant little archive. However, in nearby Raiding, the composer's birthplace, I discovered that the long arm of Bayreuth had already reached the Liszt museum there. I felt that it was important not to leave the composer to the sanctimonious Lisztians and the all-powerful Wagnerians but to interpret his work independently.

After this disappointing trip, I contacted my Parisian cousin, Blandine Jeanson, herself a direct descendant of Liszt. Her mother, Daniela Jeanson, had looked after the artist's legacy, and Blandine continued in her mother's work. When I informed her of my studies, she gave me some valuable advice, and informed me of the coming international Liszt Congress at the Sorbonne in the autumn of 1986.

This was to be Teresina's first trip to Paris, and I enjoyed showing her around the museums, especially the Louvre. I was particularly looking forward to meeting Blandine, whom I hadn't seen for years. The sympathy and concern she demonstrated for my career in conversations about our families' destinies helped me to find a role in my family that had nothing to do with being a Wagner.

In addition to my studies on Liszt's ethics, as an antidote to Wagner, I was also working on an article for Götz Friedrich, concerning the final bars of *Götterdämmerung*. At that time, I still didn't recognise the antisemitic overtones of the work, even in Wagner's outline of the drama *Jesus Of Nazareth*, published in 1849, which had preceded *Der Ring*. However, I felt that, compared with the whole of *Der Ring Des Nibelungen*, the end of

Götterdämmerung was nothing more than a kind of artificial operatic epilogue, with a happy ending.

I then received an offer from Stephan Kohler, the head of the Richard Strauss Institute, to give a lecture on Strauss and Liszt. I had met Kohler in Salzburg in 1978, during rehearsals for *Ariadne Auf Naxos*. He is a man with a wide-ranging knowledge on many subjects, not just Strauss, and is very brave when it comes to tackling awkward subjects. As I had just been working on Wagner's vague final message in the *Ring*, of love as the redemption and salvation of mankind, I was interested in the transcendence and immanence of the unorthodox Christian Liszt's *Bergsymphonie*, and in the bourgeois and one-time Nietzschean Richard Strauss' *Alpine Symphony*. The point of departure of my theme ("Christ – antichrist or artist between transcendence and immanence?") was Kant's definition in his 'Critique Of Pure Reason', from 1781: "We want to name the principles, the applications of which are held completely within the limits of possible – not merely actual – experience, immanent, but those which should go beyond these limits, transcendent principles."[26]

In preparing for this lecture, I read the correspondences between Liszt and Nietzsche during the January and February of 1872. Nietzsche, who at the time was still strongly influenced by Wagner, misinterpreted Liszt as a dionysian – that is, a man who follows his own daemon and gives his passions full rein because he is strong enough to master them. Liszt's answer was full of respect, but he wrote that he was a Christian. Then I read in Nietzsche's essay 'The Case Of Wagner' (1888) of the development of Nietzsche's judgment of Liszt. I found the following lines in the epilogue, which became important for my exposition of the composer: "If Wagner was a Christian, then Liszt was perhaps a church father! The need for redemption, the quintessence of all Christian needs, has nothing to do with such buffoons: it is the most honest expression of decadence, it is the most convinced, most painful affirmation of decadence in the form of sublime symbols and practises. The Christian wants to be rid of himself. *Le moi est toujours haïssable.* [The ego is always hateful.]"[27]

I started to understand Liszt's thinking a little better when I read that the *wünderkind* had had a nervous breakdown at 16 and wanted to be a priest. His desire to escape from the world re-emerged two years later, after the tragic end of his first love affair. The composer's subsequent relationships also ended tragically, and he was a terrible father, which accounts for much in the character of Cosima, his daughter.

Liszt fought against the rigid musical forms of his time, but like Wagner he allowed discussion about music to peter out in vague interpretations. At that time I saw Liszt as the complete opposite of Wagner, which was very important for my further understanding. In October 1985, in a lecture to the choir of Cerro Maggiore, I declared myself totally in agreement with Liszt's ideas, against a dogmatic, intolerant exercise of religion and music. My audience was not enthusiastic, however, and in fact this expression of my views signified the start of my growing distance from the intellectual life of Cerro Maggiore.

In the middle of December, the conservative cultured classes of Munich heard my views on Strauss and Liszt in the presence of the Strauss sons, who were devoted to Bayreuth. Not only had I carried out my assignment but I also had some money in my chronically-low bank account.

However, it was only in the following year that I really discovered Liszt. In lectures and radio broadcasts in Switzerland, Italy, Belgium, France and the USA I was offered many opportunities to exchange views, and I gradually came to understand Liszt's attitude to the Jews. His book *The Gypsies And Their Music In Hungary* of 1859, with its crucial chapter 'The Israelites', had without doubt been prompted by Wagner's inflammatory and racist 1850 text 'The Jews In Music'. Liszt ends his book, not like Wagner with the "decline" and "suicide" of the Jews, whom he understood as a nation, but with the advice that they should re-conquer Palestine through their "own efforts".

At the end of October 1986, after attending the unsatisfactory Liszt Congress in Paris, Teresina and I went on to Luxembourg, where Louis Landuyt and his wife Cathérine had invited us to attend a Liszt evening. With the assistance of the Luxembourg Ministry of Culture, the German Embassy and (of all things) the Deutsche Bank, Louis had put together a well-balanced programme in the Théâtre des Capucins, comprising piano pieces, which were played by Cathérine, and songs, which Louis performed whilst accompanied by his wife.

I had given a lecture at the start of the evening, reading out mainly provocative quotations from Liszt's writings on all essential aspects in the life and creativity of the artist. An angry silence spread through the audience (which comprised mainly bankers) when I read out the following passages from Liszt's 1852 article 'Chopin's Virtuosity':

"Among the kings and princes of the financial world on the other hand...everything is paid for in cash, even the visit of a potentate like Charles V, to whom, should he condescend to be accommodated by his banker, is offered his own bill to light his fire. Hence poets and artists need not wait in vain for a fee, which protects their old age from care...The enriched bourgeoisie lets artists and poets founder in the voracity of materialism. Here women and men know of nothing better to do than to fatten themselves up, as a King Charles spaniel on the boudoir sofa is fattened, until, at the sight of their Japanese porcelain dish, they die of obesity...The parvenus, who do not hesitate to pay for their gratified vanity as they only feel great through the sums of money they have lavished [upon themselves], may hear and see with wide open ears and eyes, but they understand nothing of true poetry and art."[28]

Then, in the Catholic country of Luxembourg, when I read out Liszt's opinion of the Roman Catholic Church and his letter to the excommunicated social revolutionary the Abbé de Lamennais, a slight coughing became audible in the hall. The audience remained polite, however, and refrained from heckling, which I had been hoping for. Later, in the interval, I stood alone with Teresina, obviously being punished. Louis and Cathérine were amused by the audience's embarrassed silence. But then, like a *deus ex machina*, before the concert in the second half of the evening a representative of the Hungarian Ministry of Culture came up to me to inform me that, on the basis of my work on Liszt, I was to be awarded with the Liszt Medal for 1986 – the only German to ever receive it. Suddenly I was a member of the 'in crowd', and after the concert Teresina and I were paid court. People were amused by Liszt's 'jokes' in precisely the way in which he had intended: "with wide open ears and eyes". A director of the Deutsche Bank said: "Those are just the opinions of an artist who understands little of the banking world. For you, as for your great-grandfather, our world would certainly be quite alien."

I answered: "You're right, the banking world is alien to me, but I know it. I worked for three years in the Deutsche Bank." There was general amusement. I don't think anyone quite believed me.

In 1987 I was contracted by the Bonn Theatre to be the dramaturg for a production of *Die Meistersinger Von Nürnberg* in the 1987-8 season. The project required me to be in Germany, initially to carry out research in the Richard Wagner Museum in Bayreuth, but it was some time before I was permitted to visit. The archive administration knew its master's voice, and looked on my work with suspicion. A few ugly scenes occurred before I was able to read my own family's letters without submitting detailed reasons every time. Because of my resentment of bureaucracy, I began to look around a little more thoroughly in the archive, and started to probe into areas which, in Bayreuth, were taboo: antisemitism, Gobineau, Cosima Wagner, Houston Stewart Chamberlain, Winifred Wagner and Hitler.

My research was also useful for my introductory lecture at a Toscanini symposium in Parma, in the beginning of November 1987. Harvey Sachs, the internationally-acclaimed biographer of Toscanini, allowed me to choose my own subject, and I decided to talk on "Toscanini's Bayreuth Conducting Style". Going through the *Bayreuther Blätter* and the festival guides covering the period from 1878 to 1943, I felt so nauseated by the Nazi material that I had to break off several times and go for a walk in Wahnfried Park. So this was the cultural soil from which my own family grew! I copied all of the material I needed, knowing that there were (and still are) many sources in Bayreuth that are supposed to be withheld from public view, or which my father and his rewriters of history would like to keep under lock and key for ever.

Each visit to the Richard Wagner Museum and Bayreuth was like a nightmare: the repression, concealment and distortion of German

Back view of
Villa Wahnfried

Winifred Wagner saying goodbye to the
children as they leave Bayreuth station for
their holidays in the early 1930s. L-r:
Wolfgang, Verena, Friedelind, Wieland and
their nanny Emma (in the background)
who devoted fifty years to the family

Siegfried (left) with Arturo Toscanini in
June 1930 during the *Festspiele*

Siegfried and his wife Winifred in the grounds of Villa Wahnfried, 1924, the year the *Festspiele*
reopened after World War I, with their children. L-r: Wolfgang, Siegfried, Verena, Winifred,
Friedelind and Wieland

The racist writer, Joseph Arthur Graf Gobineau (1816-1882), in 1880: one of the many forbidden topics of conversation after 1945

Parsifal by Fidus, 1890. Despite being brilliantly innovative even Richard Wagner's early works were antisemitic including the *Ring*, *Parsifal* and *Meistersingers von Nürnberg*

Alexander von Spring and Heinz Tietjen (standing) with Wilhelm Furtwängler, Winifred and Arturo Toscanini. Taken in the garden of the *Festspielhaus* in 1930

Houston Stewart Chamberlain (1855-1927): the English racial theoretician and one of Adolph Hitler's mentors. He married Richard and Cosima Wagner's daughter, Eva

Festspiele artwork, 1908-1927

Winifred, Hitler and Wieland ahead of Wolfgang and Hitler's guards in the villa grounds. Adopting the role of father figure to Wieland and Wolfgang after Siegfried's death in 1930, Hitler felt very much at ease at Villa Wahnfried whether attending official functions or relaxing in a family atmosphere

Winifred greeting Hitler at the front entrance of the *Festspielhaus*

Hitler, Winifred and some of her guests in the Siegfried Wagner House. It was extended especially for the Führer

Bust of Richard Wagner by Hitler's favourite sculptor, Arno Breker. A similar bust was shown in the Nazi-occupied Paris in 1942, then put in the festival's park in 1955. A third copy in the *Festspielpark* in 1955 created some understandable protest

Lebrecht Collection

Winifred, Goebbels and Hitler, 3 August 1938

Crowd gathering outside the *Festspielhügel* to see the Führer at the window of the Wagner family box

Verena, Hitler and Friedelind

Wieland, Uncle Wolf and
Wolfgang, 1935, at Villa
Wahnfried

Wieland at the piano with Wolfgang

Below: Wolfgang in Nazi uniform, proud of his
active role for the fatherland. Hitler even
overcame a phobia to visit him in hospital when
he was injured and despatched his private
ambulance to bring Wolfgang back to Berlin.
Wolfgang has always held dear the memory of his
times with Uncle Wolf

1938: in the
uniform of
Arbeitsdienst

Taken in
September 1939,
the week the
Nazis invaded
Poland

Wieland and Wolfgang in Wahnfried Park,
1945

L-r: Wieland, Verena, Winifred, Heinz Tietjen (artistic director of the festival from 1930 until 1944. Wolfgang became his assistant in Berlin in the 1940s), Wolfgang and Friedelind

Margarethe Matzenauer (1881-1963): famous international Wagner singer who took a role in *Twilight Of The Gods* in Bayreuth, 1911

Hermann Weil (1876-1949): sang leading Wagner roles in Bayreuth from 1911-1925 as well as internationally

Henriette Gottlieb (1884-1943?), murdered in Auschwitz. Gottlieb also sang a role in *Twilight Of The Gods* in Bayreuth

Ottilie Metzger-Lattermann (1878-1943): famous Wagner singer of the twenties, also died in Auschwitz

Gottfried's mother Ellen (left) and her brother Gustav (right) at their confirmation in 1934 with their parents, Adolf and Thora Drexel. Gustav is now Gottfried's only surviving uncle

Ellen Drexel. She gave up a career in dance when she married Wolfgang, something she regretted after their divorce. This picture summed up for Gottfried her eternal innocence, something which made her a victim of Winifred's powerful personality

Wolfgang and Ellen in Wahnfried Park, April 1945

history had reached the the point at which skeletons lurked in every archive. Even my route from the archive in the Chamberlain House towards the city centre took me along the Richard-Wagner-Strasse, reminding me of my heritage yet again.

Before I left Germany, I met Father in the *Festspielhaus*. I wanted to write an article on the centenary of Nietzsche's 'The Case Of Wagner' in the following year. He answered shortly: "Send in your idea. Dr Bauer will look through it." I was surprised that Bauer still had any influence on my father, in spite of his new job as general secretary of the Bavarian Academy Of Fine Arts (which Father had strongly advocated). His answer was equivalent to a rejection.

"Is Dr Bauer the specialist for Nietzsche too now?" I asked, remembering how much Father despised Nietzsche. "When he was still working in the *Festspielhaus*, he already had his problems with Wagner." Father stalked off angrily.

I knew that Bauer was now looking forward to rejecting my proposal, but I wanted his and Father's opinions in writing. I received them in April: Father's comment was that the subject was still too emotionally charged and that he didn't consider such topics desirable in the programme, especially from a descendant of Wagner.

In August 1987, in Munich, I came to know Alfred Frankenstein, a Jewish Wagnerian from Tel Aviv. Mother had been in contact with him for years, and had often mentioned him. His love of Wagner's music had blinded him to my criticism of Wagner's antisemitic writings and the role of the Bayreuth Festival in German culture and politics. He refused to acknowledge that the ideology behind Wagner's racist writings and the Bayreuth Festival had contributed to the Holocaust. Unfortunately, he also didn't realise how shamelessly the festival were exploiting him in marketing the new philosemitic Bayreuth. As part of this calculated attention, he was overwhelmed with festival tickets.

Like many of my Jewish friends, to whom Wagner was like a drug, Frankenstein could never completely understand why I didn't identify with my great-grandfather. Like many other Jewish Wagnerians he wanted to repress the Nazi connection, while I didn't. However, we liked each other in spite of all these contradictions, and he voiced his appreciation of my work when he found out that I was

investigating German-Jewish history. We spoke about Kurt Weill, and
the question arose of whether or not I would give some lectures in
Israel. However, he pointed out that this idea would be difficult to
put into practice, alluding to Uri Toeplitz, who in a concert
programme in 1966 had written:

> "We speak of music to emphasise that we can only accept
> Wagner as a composer, not the ideologist of the 'total work of
> art', even less so the theoretician, the writer of inflammatory
> works on cultural or political subjects, the unprincipled,
> egoistic, ambiguous revolutionary, friend and exploiter of
> kings, friend of Jews and arch Jew-hater – in short, the man
> who acted out all of the contradictions of his complex
> personality. We do not want people to forget what the Nazis
> made of him, namely one of their spiritual ancestors, but we
> should also bear in mind that we can never know what Wagner
> himself would have said about it, because he had been long
> dead when National Socialism emerged."[29]

That attitude was typical of the majority of liberal German Jews in
Israel, opposed as they were at the time by the Israeli population's
radical rejection of all things Wagner, whom they equated with
Hitler. None of this discouraged me, though, as I had forged my
own path away from my family and its past, and I owe Frankenstein
and his wife Esther a great deal for their part in providing me with
my first contact with Israel.

In July 1987 I sat in on some dress rehearsals in the
Festspielhaus. Although Barenboim was conducting, I enjoyed
hearing *Tristan* there again, and I also sat in on the dress rehearsal
of my father's production of *Tannhäuser*. I had tried to correspond
with him about the production beforehand, but he hadn't even
answered my letters. During the dress rehearsal, I once again
realised that we were worlds apart, which was illustrated by our
ideas of the 'Venusberg'.

My interest now turned to an offer from the French town of
Orange. They have an open-air Roman theatre there, and they
wanted me to help – as dramaturg – to produce a video, organise

an exhibition and put together the programme for the summer of 1988, alongside a production of *Der Ring*. After a meeting with the director, Raymond Duffaut, I noticed that there were scarcely any differences between marketing methods in Bayreuth and in Orange, where the administrative department wanted to market my name above all else. The idea of the video attracted me, however, as I wasn't exactly inundated with offers at that time, so I thought of the fee and said yes.

Meanwhile, back in Cerro Maggiore, I was told over the phone that I had become one of the short-listed candidates for the directorship of the opera house in the northern Swedish town of Umea. Lennart Rabes, the pianist and well-known interpreter of Liszt, who was working in Umea as repetiteur, had nominated me as a candidate and, with no great hopes, I had sent my details to Umea. I flew to Stockholm for the first time at the end of August, and found myself enchanted by its lakes and architecture, untouched by the centuries. I was received very warmly by Bertil Hagman, who was then the dramaturg of the Royal Opera, along with the liberal politician Jan Eric Wikström and the prominent physician Marietta Kardos. Marietta and I soon became friends, and I later learned that, as a child, she and her mother had survived the concentration camps.

My new friends instructed me on what would be expected of me, and, once prepared, I flew on to Umea. I was impressed by the sight of the wild landscape of lakes and forests, and no sooner had I landed when I was met by the entire opera staff. I was completely frank with them, emphasising that it was a privilege to work with them, and that any form of work in the cultural sector should be based on the initiative and responsibilities of individuals.

The cadre of Party Socialists in the opera house didn't approve of my views, however; they believed that art should be fully organised, from the inception to exposition. Despite my opposition to such political nannying, I was elected as the new opera director by an overwhelming majority. There was great disappointment, however, when I decided, after discussing the matter with Teresina, that I would prefer to continue my life in Italy rather than do battle with party functionaries in beautiful Umea, and many of my friends and acquaintances were horrified that I hadn't seized such a unique opportunity to further my position in the world of opera. Even so, there was no question of my pursuing an uncertain future in a field that had become strange to me, at the expense of my private life. A friend in Bayreuth told me that the *Festspielhügel* sighed with relief.

I started preparing some radio broadcasts, covering the musical versions of Goethe's *Faust* written by Liszt, Berlioz and Wagner, and also the young Liszt's opera *Don Sanche*. I also soon had a lecture to prepare on 'The Cases Of Nietzsche And Wagner' for the Bayreuth young people's festival meeting.

CHAPTER EIGHTEEN

BONN AND ORANGE

After an absence of six years, it seemed to be a good time to establish new contacts in the opera business, during my preparations for Die Meistersinger in Bonn and Der Ring in Orange. This new beginning did have its downside, though: Jean-Claude Riber, the general intendant in Bonn, had brought me in solely because of my name, and in the course of our preliminary discussions on *Die Meistersinger* I noticed that, intellectually, we had nothing in common. He revelled in the absurdly large budget of his opera house in the federal capital, staked everything on the 'star circus', and anyone who didn't go along with it was frozen out. During one such discussion I saw the set model by Günther Schneider-Siemssen, whom André Heller had rightly called "Karajan's *basteltante* [handicraft auntie]". The design was appalling: it reminded me of Bayreuth's productions of *Die Meistersinger* staged in the Thirties and Forties. Schneider-Siemssen sensed my disapproval, and retaliated by criticising Wieland's *Die Meistersinger* of 1956. As this was one of my favourite productions, I could hold back no longer: "Where content and aesthetics are concerned, we don't seem to have anything in common. Wieland's *Die Meistersinger* of 1956 will make theatre history. This one won't." With that, all further contact with the set designer came to an end. I realised that, in the next year in Bonn, I would have to concentrate on finishing the programme.

Before that, however, was the Toscanini convention in Parma, where I was to deliver my lecture on "Toscanini's Bayreuth Conducting Style". The great Italian conductor's period of residency at the *Festspielhügel* was directly before the age of National Socialism, and I was interested in the political environment in which it occurred, in particular the role played by my grandmother, who from 1923 helped to win Hitler over to the German bourgeoisie. In preparation, I re-read Aunt Friedelind's 1948 autobiography, *The Royal Family Of Bayreuth*, in which she describes the unbridgeable gulf that lay between her and my father.

Shortly before I left for Bonn, at the beginning of March 1988, I met the poet Karl Lubomirski and his wife, the painter Enrica Lubomirski, at a reception in Milan given by the Austrian consul, Rudolf Novak. They made such a humane contrast to the seedy world of opera which awaited me in Bonn and Orange. From the beginning, our talk touched on many subjects, including the concept of taking an interest in the fate of others. I soon became familiar with Karl's colourful narrative style, with its nuances of subtly caustic humour and deep melancholy, alternating with explosive *joie de vivre*. I knew, after the first hours we spent together, that our paths were sure to cross again. I read a poem from his book *La Zolla Di Luce* [The Clod Of Light] to him, which his wife Enrica had translated with great sensitivity into Italian. Poems such as 'The Tree', with the line "The tree of my life bears doubts", won me over immediately to his work. He had also been persuaded to leave the narrow confines of his native Austria by the *italianità* of his wife.

Although Karl had left Innsbruck forever, much as I had left Bayreuth, whether we liked it or not we remained marked by and dependent on the German culture and language (Karl, as a poet, even more so than myself). Between us, a quiet solidarity arose in opposition to the friendly but ultimately impersonal attitude of Italian Catholicism. Although it was clearly better for us to live in Italy than anywhere else in Europe, nevertheless we felt like cosmopolitan outsiders and nomads. The similarity in our beliefs, when it came to decisive issues, became clear to me too when I read Karl's poem of 1990, 'Auschwitz', in which he manages to speak the unspeakable:

Here fell a great leaf
from the tree of death
greater still than Babylon
Jerusalem and elsewhere too
a leaf
that follows no winds
that lies and lies and lies
and when history itself is blown away
then only will perish
with its place.[30]

For me there is no doubt of his importance as a poet. He also became a trusty fighter for the establishment of a German-Jewish dialogue, following the controversy that raged in Bayreuth after my trip to Israel in 1990. What will always bind me to Karl is his incorruptibility in matters of humanitarianism. He was discriminated against by self-styled popes in a pseudo left-wing international cultural lobbying scene – this is something else that we have in common.

In March 1988, at the beginning of our friendship, I was able to go to Bonn without fear of Riber or the others. At first I stayed with my second mother, Bettina Fehr, and as always we talked at length about Father, Mother and Bayreuth. Bettina always counselled mediation and conciliation, but over time she had realised that there was little I could do about what was clearly an impasse.

Inspired by our conversations, Bettina gave me something to read in bed on 14 March which was to have a lasting influence on me: Ralph Giordano's *Die Zweite Schuld, Oder Von Der Last, Deutsche Zu Sein* [The Second Guilt, Or On The Burden Of Being German]. "This book will have a significant effect on you," she said, knowing me all too well. She was right. I didn't just read the 363 pages – I devoured them, for what I read in Giordano's book touched my soul. The clarity of its content, its linguistic beauty, his thorough historical, political and cultural analyses and his humanity overwhelmed me. Here, finally, was a German-speaking author who had something to say to me. His life of suffering made him unusually sympathetic as a human being; here was someone who stood up with the courage of his convictions, against German repression. He seemed to be able to put everything that was important to me into words.

On 15 March, I got up at seven o'clock, wide awake despite having hardly slept at all. I couldn't resist waking up Bettina (who isn't an early riser) by rattling around noisily during my morning ablutions. Still somewhat sleepy, she made coffee for me in the kitchen while I told her enthusiastically about the book she'd given me the night before. "Can't you ring Ralph Giordano?" I asked her impatiently. Bettina laughed: "Now? At half past seven in the morning? Let's wait 'til nine." At nine o'clock she rang him up and introduced me in her charming, irresistible way, not only as "the Weill Wagner" but also as someone who was very much hoping for a discussion of German-Jewish history with him.

Three days later, at Giordano's invitation, Bettina and I went to Cologne. We rang the doorbell and waited outside until the door opened, and peering inside we saw a beautifully-laid coffee table and a number of other pieces of tasteful period furniture. Instead of being greeted by Giordano, we walked in to the strains of the prelude to *Tristan Und Isolde*. Then Ralph Giordano approached us. He said to me, pensively: "This music is one of my favourite pieces by Wagner."

"It's impossible not to be fascinated by Wagner's *Tristan Und Isolde*, but unfortunately we have to live with the 'other Wagner' as well," I answered. He agreed and shook my hand.

I had intended asking Ralph Giordano about his life and work, but I didn't get around to it during the next three hours, as he had a great many questions about my life. And as we relaxed on the sofa, I noticed how his fine and melancholy features brightened while I was answering him. I found it so easy to open up to him, and talked to him as though he was an old friend. When I told him about Winnie and Wolf, he gripped my arm and interrupted me with a question that annoyed me: "Are you really Wolfgang Wagner's son?" I hardly reacted, as I thought I'd misheard, and carried on telling him about the correspondence between Hitler and my grandmother. With friendly obstinacy he repeated the question: "Are you really Wolfgang Wagner's son?"

He was evidently asking about my father, so I countered laughingly with the question: "Why do you want to know that?"

"I once interviewed your father in Bayreuth," he answered gravely. "I'm sorry, but I didn't believe a word he said. There's no humanity in that man."

"You don't have to apologise – you're only saying what I've known and felt since my I was a boy," I answered.

Giordano reached for a copy of his novel *The Bertinis* and inscribed in it: "For Gottfried Wagner, who I liked on sight." He then said emphatically: "Whether you want to or not, you must write the story of your life. You owe that to your own generation and those who follow."

I didn't like this idea at all. "You mean write an autobiography? About the conditions in Bayreuth? I'm 41 years old. Why? Who would be interested? Why should I isolate myself even more than I am now?"

"You have nothing to do with the Bayreuth of the Wagners," Giordano replied, "but you are a Wagner who is aware of his responsibility to humanity and history. Write your life story. Going over it will help you personally, and one day may help you to be re-integrated in Germany. I'll help you."

When Bettina and I left Ralph, I was deeply moved. I knew that the meeting would have great consequences in my life.

Day-to-day life in the opera house once again caught up with me. My initial fears that Riber would misuse his production of *Die Meistersinger* in Bonn to further his own career were proved right. In mid March I sat in on one of the rehearsals, which took place on the small main stage. The set, which was already partly assembled, was even more tasteless than the model had looked. In accordance to the idea that anything expensive must be good, Riber had brought in all the stars of the international Wagner market, René Kollo and Bernd Weikl among them. These stars stood around in the rehearsals, bored and feigning interest in Riber's arrangements, which they then supplemented with ideas and experiences from other productions at other opera houses. At first Riber even made video recordings of these embarrassing scenes in order to preserve them for posterity. When I tried to point out to him some mistakes in the way he was directing the blocking he was terribly insulted. He was accustomed to those around him paying him compliments and praising his artistry, not criticising his work.

My work on the large programme booklet for *Die Meistersinger* was going well, and to distract my critical eye from his rehearsals as quickly as possible he immediately agreed to all of my suggestions for the programme and then changed them back when I wasn't there. He viewed me as a rival, and did everything he could to trip me up. Every step I took, every call I made, was watched over by his staff. The dramaturg, Monika Rottmaier, who like me didn't take these repressive measures lying down, was given notice – although this was certainly not because she lacked expert knowledge. Riber and his cronies destroyed a respected opera repertory house through the implementation of a soulless, interchangeable star programme. And what was I supposed to think about singers who ridiculed Riber in the canteen but then went back into rehearsals feigning admiration for his direction? Underpinning this hypocrisy was the box office; I hoped that this system – which was so inimical to art, and which was prevalent not just in Bonn – would soon end. In fact, such inflated mediocrity was to explode in the 1990s.

One of Riber's last attempted coups against me occurred when he and his staff tried to delete my name from my the programme. A visit to the lawyer soon clarified the situation, but that wasn't enough for Riber and he then made every effort to squeeze me out of the production of *Der Ring* in Orange, which he was also directing. He asserted that I hadn't contributed anything to his "brilliant" production, even though the public and the media had reacted positively to the programme booklet. Later Riber had to retract his calumnies in court.

The premiere, held on 17 April 1988, was just as one would have expected from the rehearsals. In Bonn, as elsewhere, the media and the public were taken in by the glamour of famous names. The 1980s were obviously the culmination of a politico-cultural dictatorship of mediocrity, based on political and economic lobbies who only allowed to succeed what they wanted to succeed.

I had only one opportunity to protest against this state of affairs in Bonn, and that was in the programme. I quoted from Wagner's writings and the opera, and wrote commentary which, if read carefully, contradicted what was happening on the stage. I unmasked Riber via the revolutionary Richard Wagner and his avant-garde ideas about music theatre, while Riber tried to present the composer as a *petit bourgeois* garden gnome. Not even the contrary Wagner and his ambiguous works deserved that accusation!

I quoted Wagner's letter of 14 October 1868 to Ludwig II, in which he complained about the production of *Die Meistersinger*: "The utter wretchedness and deep decline into which the German theatre has sunk is something I shall discover to an even fuller extent by what happens to this very work of mine."[31] This was precisely how I felt about the Bonn production.

During a conversation with the Bonn music critic Hans G Schürmann, I added further fuel to the fire. The resulting interview appeared in the Bonn newspaper *General-Anzeiger* under the title "The Other Wagner: Against The Flow Towards His Own Goal" over the weekend of the premiere. I used the interview as a vehicle to criticise the 'opera jungle', and advocated "achieving opera as a constructive group experience on the basis of individual responsibility, motivation, initiative and the permanent evolution of professional competence and creativity".

Instead of provoking open discussion, however, my attack prompted a deluge of effusive compliments, the generally non-committal nature of which reminded me of exactly where I was: Germany, the home of repression, in which silence – especially in the case of Wagner and his opera *Die Meistersinger Von Nuremberg* – has well-known, well-founded reasons.

Riber's scheming against me in Orange was successful: without warning, Duffaut, the festival director, suddenly wanted me off the set, and offered to settle with me for half my fee. We quarrelled so fiercely that we could be heard over half the town. I demanded that I should be allowed to fulfil my contract as dramaturg, and Duffaut realised that, legally speaking, I had a strong case. I gave him the programme I'd prepared, re-asserted that any alteration had to be discussed with me beforehand, and then left.

My next task was to prepare a video production of *Der Ring*, and

I set to collating copious amounts of material. After the débâcle in Bonn, I chose the subtitle "The Consequences Of The Misuse Of Power" for the project. In my précis of the plot of the work, Wotan and Alberich appeared as two crooks locked in a struggle for world domination. My narrative was addressed at a public that understood both opera and the way in which Wagner used it: as a stage for the self-presentation of high society. I was particularly inspired by the pictures of the famous photographer August Sander. In a crazy melange of pictures, from Botticelli to Roy Lichtenstein and Coca-Cola, I show the decline of a degenerate society, from Red Square to Wall Street, culminating with the launch of an atom bomb. Thierry Bénizeau saw to the technical assembly of my meticulously-worked-out material.

The next battle took place at the end of July 1988. Duffaut and Riber eventually changed the programme without consulting me, thus breaking the contract. My lawyer advised me to leave Orange, and informed the media of this decision. It caused quite a stir – a few days earlier the production of *Der Ring* had won first prize at the Biarritz video festival. The subsequent legal action against the administration in Orange dragged on for four years and ended in an out-of-court settlement, as I couldn't afford to continue the proceedings.

I then began to prepare a multimedia lecture for Bayreuth. In it I wanted to continue what I had begun in Bonn and Orange: an open attack on the Wagner money-making machine.

At that time I was living in Bad Kissingen and was in poor health. I was being treated by a friend, the distinguished cardiologist Peter Deeg, whom I had known since 1960 – the year in which my father had directed his first production of *Der Ring* at the *Festspielhügel*. Like myself, he had to contend with a strong father, who had written a book in the Nazi period on the "court Jews" and had forged a second brilliant career as a lawyer, after Germany's miraculous economic upturn.

Throughout the first years of our friendship, Peter and I avoided talking about our fathers' Nazi pasts as a point of principle. Peter's father had brought him up to be a conservative, but I knew that behind this apparently impenetrable façade there were other qualities, and indeed these emerged when he married Jadwiga, who came from Gdansk. Jadwiga, with her radiant openness, altered Peter so much that, to my amusement, the effect of his years-long bachelorhood was completely undone. Their four lively children grew up in a stimulating environment, rich in German-Polish culture. Jadwiga's cosmopolitan father, Stefan Angielski, had survived Poland's Nazi occupation, and been detained in a Stalinist labour camp in Siberia.

At about this time, July 1988, I found myself in a conversation with his father. Initially, he had helped my father to draw up the Bayreuth Festival's foundation statutes, until he discovered that they didn't lead to a settlement of the succession within the family. That grated with him, himself a strongly family-orientated man, as did the shoddy way my father treated my mother during the divorce, who from 1976 onwards Peter's father and his wife continued to help. During this conversation, he surprised me by talking about National Socialism and the Jews. He acknowledged the Holocaust as being a terrible crime in German history – I had never heard this kind of admission from my father. This admission had an effect on my friendship with his son, to the effect that we gradually began to talk about our fathers' pasts and openly discussed the antisemitism of the Third Reich and our responsibilities towards future generations.

In the middle of August 1988, within the framework of the International Young People's Festival Meeting in Bayreuth, I delivered my talk on "The Cases Of Nietzsche And Wagner". My collection of quotations from Nietzsche's "The Case Of Wagner" and "Nietzsche Versus Wagner" created an icy atmosphere, and Nietzsche's marvellous analysis of the Wagnerians was received with silent fury. I then described the reasons for the breakup of the friendship between Wagner and Nietzsche in 1878, which occurred because Nietzsche could no longer stand Wagner's woolly, late-Romantic conception of life, with all of its ideological dynamite.

I then turned to Nietzsche's description of the antisemitic "Wagner neurosis", the danger of which he recognised very early on. In summing up Nietzsche's convincing criticism of Wagner – his passionate attack on the contemporary and future opera-going public, along with his gloomy diagnosis of "Bayreuth cretinism" (which was already exhibiting totalitarian tendencies) – the people in the the auditorium clearly understood: I was getting even with the public adherents of the dishonest New Bayreuth era. I garnished this speech with provocative collages of Wagner's music and caricatures by Marc Sautet and Patrick Boussignac.

As I brought the lecture to a close with Nietzsche's eulogy of Bizet's *Carmen* and a resounding soundtrack of the end of that opera, the atmosphere in the auditorium was edgy and aggressive, just as I had expected. Some of the *Festspielhügel* faithful managed to twist the facts in such a way that there was no possibility of discussing my lecture with the audience. The Bayreuth Society Of Friends, whom I had invited, preferred not to have their view of the world shattered.

After the lecture, Teresina and I stood with a few friends and acquaintances in the otherwise empty auditorium. It was impossible to discuss Wagner, Nietzsche and the Jews openly in Bayreuth. As we left, a man came up to me with a friendly smile and said: "My name is Janos Solyom. Don't be discouraged by the reaction of the audience. I agree with your talk, which was bound to be unpopular here: you're not only questioning absolutely everything but you're also denying the repression of the past, and the truth hurts. Nothing has changed here, and I'm afraid that makes you quite unwelcome." He shook my hand warmly, and we arranged to meet up during one of the intervals of the opera, *Die Meistersinger*, which was about to begin.

Janos was Hungarian by birth but became a Swedish citizen after escaping Hitler. When we met, he told us of his international career as a pianist, and of his wife Camilla Lundberg's work as a journalist. The friendship between the four of us developed almost as a reaction to the dishonesty which was so prevalent in Bayreuth. We talked about Liszt and the way in which his life and works had been misused by Bayreuth, and made plans for the future together. One of our joint projects was our much-admired Theresienstadt evening in Stockholm in 1994, in which Janos played piano works by Pavel Haas, Gideon Klein and Viktor Ullmann in a uniquely intense way. His tolerance, along with his artistic and cultural richness, made the hours we spent with him seem timeless. It was only in Stockholm that I learned that Janos is related to Kurt Weill, and that the Nazis had murdered his father in Russia.

On one day, after meeting Janos, my video production of *Der Ring* was screened at the Bayreuth Young People's Festival Meeting. The negativity which followed my lectures persisted, but because I was the son of the festival boss things fortunately didn't come to a head. As I played my video several times over, a large section of the audience indignantly left the hall. However, such conservatism among these young people didn't surprise me – it was a reflection of the *zeitgeist*, in which there was no vision and no protest, simply the quiet laying down of career plans. Discussions with younger participants of the Young People's Festival revolved mainly around aesthetic details instead of the politico-cultural phenomenon of Wagner in Bayreuth. Older members of the audience were just as shocked by the video, but to my amusement I realised that they hoped that this meant that I had disqualified myself as my father's successor.

The only positive outcome of my visit to Bayreuth was the offer which I received from the *Neue Zürcher Zeitung*, who wanted to publish my thoughts on Nietzsche. To my surprise, Josef Lienhart, president of the West German Richard Wagner Societies, invited me to show the video to the society in Freiburg in the autumn of 1988. Unfortunately, shortly beforehand, both my video equipment and the only copy of the video were stolen from the luggage locker at Hamburg Railway Station, and so I had to talk about the video without showing it, which proved extremely awkward because, in addition to some inveterate Wagnerians, there were also some open-minded people in the audience. Before and after the talk, Lienhart enthused about the time when my Uncle Wieland was the festival head in Bayreuth. This surprised me, because my father and his cohorts had taken great steps to banish his spectre. Lienhart also seemed to appreciate my critical examination of the Nazi past, in particular my intention to accept the invitation to Israel, and promised to do what he could after the trip to promote discussion in the Wagner societies.

However, I soon discovered that, despite my criticism of the Bayreuth Festival, he was under the impression that I would go to

Israel as a pro-Wagner propagandist. I made it clear that that was not my intention, and on my return from Israel I heard nothing more from him. In fact, he even spoke indirectly against my opinion of Wagner and the composer's antisemitism.

CHAPTER NINETEEN

ON THE ROAD WITH NIETZSCHE, WAGNER AND LISZT

At the end of October 1988, after making extensive preparations, I set off on a lecture tour that was to take me first to North America and then to Japan. My first stop was Washington, where I was to speak at the George Washington University. Before that, however, the historian Stephen Gallup threw an impromptu party, which was attended by stimulating academics from all over the world. From the moment I arrived I felt at ease in such an environment, with its atmosphere of great expertise and kindly tolerance, which was such a contrast to the gatherings of German academic circles. During the party, passionate discussions soon broke out both for and against Wagner, but they were always conducted graciously, with mutual respect for the opinion of others.

The hours I spent as a guest in the home of the Guenthers were equally stimulating. Roy was the head of the music department at the university and an excellent trombonist, and his wife, Eileen, was a music teacher and distinguished organist. Roy's personality is a happy mixture of scientific passion (which he easily conveys to his students) and pragmatism – he has the capacity to carry through efficiently any project to which he turns his hand. I had seldom, if ever, encountered this mixture of qualities in Europe, but I consider them to be vitally important for effective teaching. Roy helped me with the preparations for my talk on "The Cases Of Nietzsche And Wagner" and the post-lecture discussion.

My next appearance took me to Chicago, where I was a guest of the

Goethe Institute and the Chicago Opera House. Here, however, the conservative public reacted quite negatively to the recovered video of *Der Ring* and Nietzsche's criticism of Wagner. Their number comprised a powerful German contingent, which had expected a eulogy to Wagner and the Wagnerians in particular, and who were therefore disappointed. The discussion with some liberal intellectuals, who were particularly interested in the subject of Wagner and the Jews, was more constructive.

My last stop in the USA was of particular interest: in mid November I landed in Los Angeles, where I was the guest of Michael and Miriam Meyer in their beautiful home in Pacific Palisades, overlooking Santa Monica. Michael, who is a history professor specialising in the Third Reich and Richard Wagner at California State University in Northridge, was particularly interested in my theories on Nietzsche and Wagner, largely because of his own German-Jewish history (his Jewish mother had survived the Holocaust).

Cornelius Schnauber, head of the Max Kade Institute and the man who had suggested that I visit Los Angeles, had organised a series of events on the subject of Nietzsche and Wagner in various cultural institutions in the city. Because there was a large Jewish community in LA, as well as a Wagner society, the hall in the Goethe Institute proved too small and half of those who came had to be turned away. During my talk, the faces of those Wagnerians closely associated with Bayreuth grew stony, and the subsequent discussion was sparked off by a young man who apparently mistook me for a relative of Adolf Hitler and became quite abusive. After I had corrected him, various groups among the audience – many of whom were German or Austrian emigrants – engaged in an objective discussion on Wagner's and Nietzsche's conflicts with Judaism. This subject made the Wagnerians uncomfortable, although they kept quiet, many of them having only come to stare at me as a museum piece. Rather tactlessly I cut short the pro-Wagner eulogising, which I had witnessed so many times in Bayreuth, and the Wagnerians misinterpreted this as a typically overbearing Wagnerian character trait. It made me wonder what awaited me in Japan.

Leaving America at the end of November 1988, I was pleased to be met at Tokyo airport by two representatives of the Japanese Wagner

Society: the Germanist Tomoyoshi Takatsuji and Mrs Yasuko Miyake. Yasuko's husband is a musicologist, and he had provided an analysis of the structure of Wagner's *Tristan Und Isolde* for the Bayreuth Festival.

I had scarcely dropped off my bags in the guest room of the Goethe Institute when the Wagner Society's first reception took place in my honour. I finally met Tatsuji Ivanbuchi, with whom I had already corresponded and who had translated my book on Weill and Brecht, on whom he is an internationally-recognised authority, as well as a translator of German literature and much else besides. Now, however, I was able to meet him in person. He was a frail gentleman, wearing an elegant three-piece suit, and he shook my hand warmly and with a faint smile. He immediately offered me the *du* form of address which, from a Japanese man, impressed me. 'Buchi', as I was to call him from that point, is a cosmopolitan nomad in everything he does, thinks and feels. While I was in Japan, his presence served as a shield in a country that, despite all of the familiar Western influences, I found rather disconcerting.

My first talk for the Wagner Society in the Tokyo Goethe Institute, on Liszt and Wagner, was quite well attended and went smoothly, possibly because I refrained from discussing anything too inflammatory.

An excursion with the enchanting Yasuko, which began at five in the morning in Tokyo, was unforgettable. We sped to Kyoto by Shinkansen, the famous Japanese high-speed bullet train, to see the imperial residence. The weather was splendid, and the beauty of the palace, its gardens, its temple and its shrines fascinated me. Small, schoolgirls in black-and-white uniforms smiled at me irresistibly and asked if I would have my photograph taken with them, and when Yasuko told them something about me they beamed at me, humming 'The Ride Of The Valkyries'. It was neither the time nor the place to tell them my opinion of the necrophiliac opera scene, and for Yasuko's sake smiled and said "cheese" like a good European tourist.

On 29 November, in a marathon event at Gakushuin University, I presented both the talk on Nietzsche and Wagner and the video of *Der Ring* to an Japanese-European academic audience. When I subsequently showed the video at the Keio University, the reaction of the female students surprised me: at the erotic scenes they began to giggle behind their hands, which spread and became general amusement. The finale, however, where the dropping of the atomic bomb on Hiroshima symbolised the end of the *Götterdämmerung*, visibly moved the students.

CHAPTER TWENTY

HITLER AND WAGNER?

Early in 1989, preparations began for the centenary of Hitler's birth. Leo Haffner, a leading producer of cultural programmes for the Austrian radio channel ORF Vorarlberg, had pre-recorded a discussion with Karl Lubomirski and myself back in autumn 1988 on the subject of German culture, tradition and politics, on which it was impossible to avoid the subject of Hitler and Bayreuth. As Haffner was not one of those Austrians who turns Hitler into a German, he proposed that I deliver a talk at the beginning of April in their studio on the subject of Hitler and Wagner.

Hitler and Wagner?

While I was preparing the talk, I became increasingly aware of the implications that this subject had for me personally. It's the most painful chapter of my family history, which I tried to face then for the first time. I didn't want to take refuge in the art world, like Father and Uncle Wieland, and attempt to separate Wagner the operatic genius from Wagner the ideologist. Enough generations of Wagners before me had exercised such a fateful repression, ultimately denying their own responsibilities, so I had to ask myself why I hadn't been able to speak more openly to my grandmother and my father on the subject. After all, if my grandmother had accepted Hitler's proposal of marriage, I could have been called Gottfried Wagner-Hitler! (Historian Robert Wistrich records the proposal in his *Who's Who In Nazi Germany*, 1982.)

Hitler and Wagner are part of my life. Because of this intrinsic connection I experienced an identity crisis, which I was only able to resolve by working it through doggedly. At that time I had serious doubts about my identity as a Wagner, a German and a post-Holocaust Christian, and decided – not without a degree of uncertainty – to deliver a lecture with the title in the form of a question: 'Adolf Hitler And Richard Wagner?'

The lecture was my first (and, as it happened, an unsuccessful) attempt at separating Wagner's antisemitic writings from his musical works – in particular *Parsifal*, which is open to several interpretations. In doing so, I applied suppressive methods that were disturbingly typical of New Bayreuth. I quoted a line from Wagner's regenerative article 'Heroism And Christianity', in which, concerning his *Parsifal*, he wrote: "The blood of the Saviour, the issue from his head, his wounds upon the cross – who would impiously ask its race, if white or other?"[32]

Despite the historical connection between the quotations from Great-Uncle Chamberlain, Grandmother Winifred and Hitler, from November 1923 up until his official statement from the 'Wolf's lair' in January 1942, I still didn't understand – or more accurately, in hindsight, didn't want to understand – the full and terrible implications of the big picture: that Richard Wagner himself had already contributed his part to the unbreakable link between Bayreuth, Theresienstadt and Auschwitz. At that time I didn't want to regard Richard Wagner as being connected with Hitler.

Today I must acknowledge that I cannot uphold the final sentence of my talk of April 1989 in the ORF's Vorarlberg studio: "Wagner and Hitler? I hope the 'and' strikes you as odd…Wagner belongs to art, Hitler to the criminal records file."

That month I embarked on my first lecture tour of Norway, Iceland, Denmark and Sweden. Animosity concerning the subject 'Wagner And Nietzsche' and the *Ring* cycle was noticeable everywhere, as Richard Wagner was still bound together with the memory of the Nazi invasion and occupation in the 1940s. However, once people understood that I was neither a member of the master race nor intended to harp on about Wagner's unique greatness, the ice began to melt. After I had made it clear that I rejected not only the Wagner cult in Bayreuth from 1872 to 1945 but also the repression of the Nazi period in the New Bayreuth era, I was mostly received with openness, warmth and interest.

In Iceland, in particular, I realised that Wagner's use of Nordic mythology only very superficially corresponded to that in Scandinavian culture. I also learned that Nordic mythology has nothing whatever to do with Hitler's image of the Nordic race.

On the subject of the politico-cultural phenomenon of Wagner and Nazism, the less conventional the audience the more open the discussion appeared to be. The media also demonstrated sincere interest. It was only in Arhus and Stockholm that I met Wagnerians who didn't want to talk critically about their 'Master'. As I flew back to Milan from Stockholm, I realised how much the Wagner affair is overshadowed in Scandinavia by the fact that they haven't yet been able to come to terms with their connection with Nazism.

In July 1989, while I was preparing for my trip to Israel, I attended the premiere of my father's new production of *Parsifal* with Teresina in Bayreuth, as guests Helmuth Jungbauer, the managing director of the Upper Franconian Chamber Of Industry And Commerce, and his wife, Helga. Helmuth supported the opposition theatre group Studiobühne Bayreuth, who had made a name for themselves through their refreshingly disrespectful treatment of the Bayreuth Wagner tradition.

On the *Festspielhügel*, word had got around about my invitation to Israel, to deliver talks about Wagner, and the usually cool tolerance of our presence now turned icy. The Jungbauers picked up on the atmosphere, and their friendly attitude towards us became warm and open, in public as well in private. As we were escorted by them, even my father's staff had to accept our presence at official receptions in the opening week of the festival. Whereas in previous years Teresina and I had been invited only to the state reception, we now found ourselves at the table of the guests of honour after the premiere, which all of the other invited guests had to pass, including my father and his wife – although they managed to avoid see us.

I was asked for my opinion of my father's *Parsifal*, and I answered with careful objectivity, aware that the tabloid press was within earshot. I referred to the end of the opera, in particular the words "redemption for the redeemer", in which, according to Wagner's instructions, Parsifal – as the new, Aryan Christ – celebrates the last supper as a message of salvation. Contrary to Wagner's conception, Father had allowed Kundry to survive in the Christian temple of the Grail knights. Also, despite the writings and directorial instructions of his grandfather, Parsifal had disappeared among the crowd of Grail knights. Such misinterpreted democratisation meant that there was no individual, but only the knights' collective responsibility – a concept which appalled me. Clearly my audience understood my point, for they kept silent and changed the subject.

In 1994, Peter Deeg informed me that Father had changed the finale of the opera yet again. This time, Kundry, as female Messiah, offered the goblet to the knights of the Grail as redemption. This was New Bayreuth repression at its most extreme.

After this, we saw a production of *Der Ring* which was directed by Harry Kupfer and conducted by Daniel Barenboim. Watching the absurd opening scene, where trampling hordes of chorus members in a thick mist laboured under a figure – which, as insiders later informed me, was supposed to be Wotan, without the *Das Rheingold* music – I realised that the festival no longer had any meaning for me. The whole concept of the work was portrayed as an 'eco-swindle' story of Messrs Wotan and Alberich between two fictional atomic world wars. Unsurprisingly, the finale of this most absurd interpretation was in keeping with the rest of the production: in accordance with the theme of redemption through love, drunks and drug addicts burped together in some kind of East German railway restaurant.

After the performance of *Götterdämmerung*, I bumped into Barenboim in the Bürgerreuth Restaurant. He expected me to compliment him on his brilliant production, but I had to tell him I had never seen such nonsense. He feigned interest in my opinion and promised a meeting in the following days. He didn't keep his word.

CHAPTER TWENTY-ONE

ISRAEL

My first meeting with Professor Herzl Shmueli, in Zurich on 3 August 1989, was a complete contrast to my visit to the Festspielhügel. The musicologist had dared to hold seminars on Wagner in Tel Aviv in as far back as the 1970s, arousing great public interest, and we had first started corresponding in May 1988. The early Romantic period was one of his main areas of study, so he couldn't avoid "the Wagner case".

Shmueli had grown up in a traditional Jewish family in Istanbul, and had attended the German school there, emigrating to Israel at the beginning of the 1930s. He studied Mathematics, and then Musicology in Zurich from 1950 to 1952. Why Zurich? I asked him. He replied: "Despite my love for all German culture, instilled in me by my education in Istanbul, it was impossible for me to study in Germany after Hitler."

At our first meeting, he asked me about my life. "Doctoral thesis on Kurt Weill in Vienna, eh? That's not exactly a predictable choice for a Wagner after Hitler." And so a critical, intimate dialogue began, at the end of which he invited me to deliver a group of four lectures in Israel in January 1990.

At the beginning of September 1989, I accepted an invitation from the Montreal International Music Festival to deliver a multimedia talk on "Faust, Goethe, Wagner, Liszt: Poetry And Music". I informed my cousin, Winifred Arminjon-Lafferentz, of my arrival. Winifred, named after my grandmother, was the second daughter of my father's younger sister, Verena Lafferentz.

We had only met each other briefly, as children, after which my family had made all further contact impossible. (My father spoke of Aunt Verena's family in Nussdorf on Lake Constance as disparagingly as he did of Aunt Friedelind's. On one of our walks at the beginning of the Sixties, in Arosa, he had told me that Aunt Verena had been "a favourite of the Führer", and that her husband, Bodo Lafferentz, had organised the wartime festival as assistant of the chief of the Labour Front, Robert Ley. I never quite believed this version of history.

And so now Verena and I met again, weighed down by the family burden and encumbered by a web of lies from our childhoods – and just before my trip to Israel, of all times! After some general chat about my talk on *Faust*, the conversation finally turned to the crucial subject: the family's past. I found that I could speak openly with Winnie; the humiliations that she and her family had suffered on visits to Bayreuth shamed me. We both knew that *Festspielhügel* politics had made human intercourse impossible, even within our generation, because of the formation of the Wagner Foundation and the war of succession. The discussion on the succession was one subject which we avoided.

Like me, Winnie is haunted by our Nazi past. As a painter, she is keen to assert her own individuality. We both view a critical handling of family tradition, and a search for one's own identity through one's work, as a constructive alternative to repressing one's past as well as a chance to open a dialogue between us in the future. Deeply sensitive to the spectre of our family's Nazi connection, Winnie herself has studied Jewish history as a result.

After returning from Montreal, I continued working on my lectures. I had applied to the Ministry For Foreign Affairs and the Goethe Institute for financial support for the project, but still hadn't received an answer. In fact, after much toing and froing, nothing came of it: evidently neither body would sponsor my work towards a reconciliation with Israel.

At the beginning of October 1989, I presented Herzl Shmueli with my proposed topics for my lectures at the University of Tel Aviv: the video *The Ring Of The Nibelung, Or The Consequences Of The Misuse Of Power*, "The Fall Of The Gods or *Epatez Le Bourgeois* –

The Anti-Wagnerian Musical Contemporary Theatre Of Weill And Brecht", "The Cases Of Nietzsche And Wagner", and finally "The Wagner I'm Talking About – An Approach To Wagner's Personality And Work". Explaining my choice, I wrote: "My intention remains to calmly and patiently make my contribution to the furtherance of a continuing dialogue on the subject of Wagner and German culture. I am fully aware of my responsibilities, and cannot understand why the West German institutions in Israel (the Goethe Institute and the West German Embassy) do not support my conciliatory work, in which I have been engaged now for two decades."

Fortunately, I received help from Shai Burstyn, the head of the music department at Tel Aviv University. I had already apprised him of the content of these lectures, as I didn't want to cause any offence. I also asked him what, to me, was a critical question: "Would it be very tactless to present a few small musical examples from Wagner's music at the university?" He agreed that that would be fine, although he anticipated protests.

Finally, everything was ready, and on 2 January 1990 Teresina and I flew to Tel Aviv. There was a confusion of tongues in the crowded plane, of which modern Hebrew predominated. We listened, fascinated and uncomprehending, but secure in the knowledge that we could always have made ourselves understood in English or some other language. Travelling as I did at the invitation of the university, I didn't feel like a tourist, but instead felt rather privileged. Reading through the questions on the Israeli landing card for German visitors, I came upon the following question: "Were you a member of a party in the period from 1933 to 1945?", which I interpreted as: "If you're a German, were you a Nazi?" – a perfectly justified question, I felt. Even so, guilt and shame flashed through me, and I became uneasy when the pilot announced that we would soon be landing at Ben Gurion Airport. Despite the evident trust that our hosts Shai Burstyn and Herzl Shmueli (Shai's retired predecessor) had shown us in correspondence, I was still a descendant of the antisemitic Wagner family from Bayreuth. Who would I meet? How would they react to my grandmother's, father's and uncle's Nazism? Would they regard me as a Nazi Wagner?

Herzl and Shai greeted us with a friendly *shalom*, and from the beginning showed us nothing but a determined readiness to talk, which assuaged most of my fears of embarrassing myself by behaving wrongly. They talked about the itinerary ("our forthcoming Wagner events"), which Shai and his colleagues had planned down to the smallest detail for every day of our stay.

We agreed that I should refrain from touching immediately on critical subjects in my talks – such as Wagner's antisemitism, Hitler, Bayreuth and the Holocaust – since Herzl and Shai knew that the audience would address these subjects without our help. I understood that these lectures were in fact a starting point for further discussion. Added to this was the fact that I was appearing in Tel Aviv and Jerusalem only two months after the fall of the Berlin Wall.

Shai and Herzl rushed us to the Grand Beach Hotel, where immediately on my arrival I gave an interview to Hanoch Ron, from the main evening newspaper *Yediot Acharonot*. Hanoch Ron was well prepared for the discussion, setting the tone and the content of the interview, which was then followed (with minor variations) by other interviews and seminars, until I flew back on 14 January. For him, his colleagues and his readers, my opinions on Wagner's article 'The Jews In Music', on Hitler and my family, on my post-Holocaust upbringing in Bayreuth and on whether Wagner should or should not be performed in Israel were important. While I was covering these points, I became aware of the responsibility which I had to this country from this point on. I was no longer in the position where I could show any consideration for the opinions of my father, who had viewed my trip to Israel with grave misgivings. (I had told him about my intended lectures, suspecting that they would have repercussions both for our relationship and for myself personally.)

The interview with Hanoch Ron opened the floodgates. The journalists were mostly understanding – even sympathetic – about my desire for a continued dialogue with their nation, which helped me to answer difficult questions in a more relaxed and balanced way. However, I still found it difficult to answer the question of whether Wagner's works should be performed in Israel; I stressed that I had no right to interfere in Israeli domestic policy, but people were unconvinced by this and so I suggested that there should be a democratic vote on it in the music institutions. I also expressed understanding for the victims of the Nazis, who no longer wanted to hear Hitler's favourite composer. I also criticised the particularly undemocratic actions of the conductor Zubin Mehta, who in 1981 had wanted to perform Wagner during a concert against the wishes of most of the audience The public stopped his performance with shouts and booing after only a few bars of music.

During all of these discussions, my exhaustive research on Weill was considered sympathetically, as it had been in New York. The Israelis even grasped the significance of such an explosive mixture – Weill and Wagner! – and were even amused by it. Weill's dismantling of the Wagner cult in Bayreuth had much in common with my own attempts to knock my great-grandfather off his pedestal.

I grew less afraid to face the Israeli media, thanks largely to the efforts of Teresina, who supported me devotedly and had faith in my trip to Israel. Her steadfast support was clear to other members of the audience, including the interviewers. People often addressed her in Hebrew, because it was assumed that she was Jewish. She then said, smiling: "I'm only an Italian, from a Catholic family." When I related this to Herzl, he said: "Your story is so extreme that people assume that you could only be married to a Jew." Just as Teresina's help was important to me, so too was that displayed by the few friends and acquaintances I had made in Israel, who offered their open support both during and after this decisive time.

The discussions in the first afternoon and evening became increasingly intense over the next few days, even though my series of lectures didn't begin until 7 January. The idea that we could quietly tour Israel beforehand proved to be so much wishful thinking – even during our two-day visit with Herzl and Shai to Cesarea, Massada, a kibbutz and some Arab villages, we talked constantly about my lectures. Herzl, who was an expert on this area, convinced me that, in Israel, Richard Wagner was intrinsically linked with Hitler and Nazi Germany, but his principles would not stop him from organising seminars and lectures on this 'aberration' of music history at the university.

During these conversations, I began to realise how much I had changed. In order to rescue the reputation of the antisemite Richard Wagner, I had tried to place the blame on his children and grandchildren. I now understood that this didn't hold water. I have since learned that other Jewish friends, who are Wagnerians, found themselves in a similarly contradictory situation. Today I realise that it's impossible to split Wagner into the genius composer and the ideologist, as his *weltanschauung* [philosophy of life] belongs inextricably to his work and his life.

We gradually came around to discussing my experiences and responsibilities. I realised that, in Israel, I could no longer simply articulate my political and moral position indirectly, by grappling with German-Jewish culture; my time in the ivory tower of liberalist thinking was over. I had to win personal credibility through acting. In Israel there were limitless opportunities for undertaking this seriously, as time and again we came to talk about individual destinies, about people who had been driven out of Germany by persecution and suffering, fleeing to Israel and elsewhere.

As my hosts, their friends and lecture audiences described their life stories, I became more and more open about my own. Out of the dark, vague and frightening shadows of the six million victims of the Holocaust, individual stories emerged. I became determined to adopt a clearer position on our shared history, and on our joint responsibility for both present and future. I began to see Israel as a central pattern in the mosaic of my life. I remembered my time in the Kurt Weill Foundation in New York, and the links between German history, the chronicle of my family and my contrary lifestyle finally became clear to me. I wanted to translate the trust and understanding so constructively offered, by canvassing in future among my own countrymen too, for German-Jewish dialogue. My fear, insecurity and anxiety dissolved as my insight developed.

One of my first important public appearances was in Jerusalem, where I had been asked to give an interview for Israeli radio. The producer, Danny Or'Stav, welcomed me warmly and informed me that he would first introduce me to the listeners in Hebrew. He later told me that the introduction had focused on my life and the lectures. He also commented on my book on Weill, and on the time that I had spent working at the Kurt Weill Foundation in New York. The only thing I understood of the introduction was the repetition of my grandfather's first name, which Danny had obviously confused with my name. When he asked me how I liked it here in Israel, I answered: "I like it here very much, but my name is not Siegfried. It's Gottfried. I am Richard Wagner's great-grandson, not his son!" I didn't want to be identified with either my grandfather or with the blond beast and mad heroic figure from the opera of the same name. My reaction caused general amusement, and it could have been because of this that my first radio interview in Israel went so well.

Later, I was very pleased to hear that, only two months after this interview, Wagner's music was once again played on Israeli radio. Unfortunately, it was 'The Ride Of The Valkyries', which I rank among the most sinister and questionable of compositions. And yet our mission had proved to be a success: Wagner was no longer an emotive, taboo subject. Now a separate politico-cultural discussion developed. This was probably the most I could have hoped to achieve for Wagner's music in Israel.

Four days later I was interviewed in Jerusalem by Ram Evron for Israeli television. Before recording started, he told me that he was in favour of Wagner's works being performed in Israel. I disagreed, which amused him and prompted him to ask more about my rebellion against my family while the cameras were running. After discussing Weill and my grandmother, we eventually came to the question of how to deal with Wagner's essay 'The Jews In Music'. I categorically condemned the work, advocating a more discriminating historical approach.

The effect of the television interview was immediately noticeable: the following day in Tel Aviv, total strangers came up and addressed me. When I reacted to this with surprise in an optician's, the optician said in perfect German: "Herr Wagner, don't you know how small our country is? We show our guests Israel in the morning, and in the afternoon we wonder what on Earth we can do with them. So don't be surprised that we saw you on television yesterday. Your coming here is important, and not just for the 'Jeckes', the German Jews. Keep up the good work!"

My first lecture took an unusual course. My introduction to the film *The Ring Of The Nibelung, Or The Consequences Of The Misuse Of Power* had been planned to take place at noon at the university. However, a university employee discreetly informed me that there had been phone calls from fanatics protesting against my visit, so they were considering either giving me a bullet-proof vest or protecting me behind bullet-proof glass, and I had to refuse. Teresina asked me to take some steps to ensure my safety. "I am not Eichmann," I reasoned. "I have confidence in my hosts." It didn't make Teresina any calmer, but she accepted my decision.

Instead of the planned audience of 80, over 400 people turned up and we had to move to a larger hall. Security measures were also increased: the audience were searched, and two young Israeli soldiers were posted with guns in the larger (but still crowded) hall. Despite the crush of people, however, the first row remained unoccupied, through fear of coming into contact with a descendant of Wagner. I remembered a book that I had been given shortly before the talk, titled *Who's Afraid Of Richard Wagner?* Without really thinking about it, I said: "There are still some empty seats down here. Who's afraid of Gottfried Wagner?" Cathartic laughter broke out, and I joined in, easing the tension. The audience continued to laugh during the film, even at those parts where, when I'd played the film at previous talks across four continents, I'd been the only one to get the joke! Shai's introduction in Hebrew had seen to that – he presented my text on the history of Wagner's tetralogy faithfully: as a story of the criminals Wotan and Alberich in a struggle for supremacy.

The following day, my lecture on Weill and Brecht went quite differently. The fact that someone with my family background had the *chutzpah* to talk on Weill's contemporary musical theatre as a counter-model to Wagner's *gesamtkunstwerk* [total art work] at the biggest university in Israel filled the hall. The famous Israeli singer Adi Etzion sang songs by Weill at the end of the evening, accompanied by her husband Jonathan at the piano. It was all very much like 1920s Berlin.

An elderly lady from Berlin, who introduced herself only by her first name, Isolde, asked me: "Herr Wagner, why don't you give your talks in our German language? It's so beautiful."

"Because more people here speak English," I answered, confused.

She approached me again later that evening. "You can imagine why I'm called Isolde?" She asked. "Yes, you're right, my family loved Wagner's music, and I love him too. I still remember the wonderful productions in the Kroll Opera, under Otto Klemperer. And Bruno Walter's *Walküre*." She turned out to be an accomplished Wagnerian, such as I have only seldom encountered. She beamed at me like a kindly grandmother, and said: "You can't imagine what your visit means to us Berlin Jews." We hugged in silence, fighting back tears.

My last lecture, with the title 'The Wagner I'm Talking About', was a crucial test. Following Herzl's advice, I tried to explain Wagner's significance for European music theatre and music history. Before this, however, I tried to come to terms with my own Bayreuth past. Today I can see that it reflects my insecurity of that time, when I was trying to come to terms with my family's history and my own development, which were inextricably linked. I'd started to understand the course that my life had taken, but still separated Wagner's ideology from his opera. What I said about the composer at that time no longer had anything to do with my state of mind.

I'm still surprised today by the generosity demonstrated by my audiences. Anyone casting a critical eye over what I'd said at that time, reading nervously from my notes, could quite rightly have accused me of not having considered Wagner's antisemitism carefully enough. In particular, with hindsight I can see that what I'd said about "the purely human, the myth" and "redemption and pity" was a direct result of my own repression, an unsuccessful attempt to trivialise Wagner's antisemitism in order to make my own family's past more bearable. It was probably also my last (unsuccessful) attempt at self-repudiation, in an attempt to comprehend my father's position.

At the end of my lecture I quoted from Richard Wagner's letter to his friend Mathilde Wesendonck, from 1 October 1858. Based on an imperfect understanding of Arthur Schopenhauer's philosophy, he presents himself as the saint of universal pity, writing:

"After all, we know what exists around us only inasmuch as we picture it in our imagination, and as I imagine it, so it is for me. If I ennoble it, it is because I myself am noble; if I feel the other man's suffering to be deep, it is because I myself feel deeply when I imagine his suffering; and in contrast, whoever imagines it to be insignificant reveals in doing so that he is himself insignificant. Thus my fellow-suffering makes the other person's suffering a reality, and the more insignificant the being with which I can suffer then the wider and more embracing is the circle which suggests itself to my feelings.

"But here lies an aspect of my nature which others may see as a weakness. I admit that unilateral actions are much impeded by it; but I am certain that, when I do act, I act in accordance with my essential nature, and certainly never to cause pain to anyone intentionally. This consideration alone can influence me in all my actions: to cause others as little suffering as possible. On this point I am totally at one with myself, for only in this way can I hope to give others joy as well: for the only true, genuine joy, is to be found in the conformity of fellow-suffering."[33]

Here, Wagner has repressed his own pitiless antisemitism, which was later to culminate in the demand for a Jew-free Germany.

Following this, I declared:

"Here [ie in Wagner's egocentric definition of pity] lies also the key to the final artistic message, which we find in the closing bars of *Parsifal*. To me, this statement represents the distinct possibility to interpret Wagner's work responsibly, which of necessity contradicts his existence as an artist in a 'human, all too human' theatre world. Mixing up biography and work means, in Wagner's case, to manipulate the interpretation of his stage works, as well as falsifying his personality. This happened in the past when his work was abused for reasons both ideological and political, and Wagner's artistic aims were disregarded. I regard it as my duty, as a music journalist, opera director and as Wagner's great-grandson, to refute this. By upholding viewpoint, I shall always fall between two stools in Bayreuth. So let us always approach Wagner as the man he was: as a genius of opera in the 19th century, without whom the cultural history of Europe is unimaginable."

On reading my text from January 1990 today, I can only shake my head at such a wilful disregard of the facts and an inability to judge the Wagnerian legacy as a whole. I was still firmly rooted in family tradition, and I had to extricate myself from it – that much I already knew, and it became clearer to me in Israel. At that time, it was more a matter of demonstrating through my talks that I was interested in an ongoing dialogue, that I wanted to escape my isolation and learn. Most of the audiences understood this message and accepted me without mistrust, in spite of my lack of clarity. In Israel, I began once again to try to come to terms with Wagner's antisemitism. I had to gauge his effect on the Bayreuth Festival as well, and acknowledge that I could no longer uphold my position.

During this painful re-examination of my own past and my conscience, I distanced myself from certain turning points in my childhood and student years. I felt removed from the interpretations of Ernst Bloch, Hans Mayer and Claude Lévi-Strauss, those prominent Jewish authors who had been misused in New Bayreuth in order to repress and distort the past.

More important than my lectures in Israel, however, were the discussions I held with my audiences, which unfortunately I didn't have time to record. Some important episodes remain in my memory, however, such as the time I met Alfred and Ester Frankenstein, in their beautiful house in Ramat-Gan, who brought me into contact with Herzl Shmueli. Not even my great-grandfather's antisemitism could dissuade Frankenstein from passionately venerating Wagner, and he returns to the festival time after time. And yet, surrounded by the classics of German literature with coffee, cake, music, discussing German culture, I felt so at home with them. It was a shame that this took place in Ramat-Gan, and not in Berlin. Germany suffered a terrible loss when it drove out or murdered people like Alfred Frankenstein!

The meetings with the American Wagnerian Harry Riss, however, went much differently. It was many years before he eventually told me that some of his relatives had fallen victim to the Nazis, although he himself had emigrated to Israel in the mid Fifties as a Zionist. He believed that he had discovered in me, Richard Wagner's great-grandson, much that had nothing to do with me and little with the "genius Richard". Today Harry accepts my rebellion against the Wagnerian legacy in Bayreuth.

My discussions with the musicologist Peter Gradenwitz were far more discriminating and complex. My mother had given me a copy of his book *The Musical History Of Israel*, which had been written at a time when he shared my criticism of Wagner and I was troubled by the tensions within my family – a subject on which I was only willing to comment up to a certain point.

On our only free evening in Israel we were invited to a concert given by the Israel Philharmonic Orchestra, founded in 1936 by the violinist Bronislaw Huberman. The programme included works by Edvard Grieg, Luigi Boccherini, Franz Danzi and Wolfgang Mozart, and was conducted by Mika Eichenholz.

Unfortunately, the evening was by no means relaxing: shortly before we entered the concert hall there was a bomb scare, and we all had to evacuate into a side street. After the 'all clear' was called, I went to the box office to pick up our tickets. We were warmly received there by the head of the PR department and taken to our places. The young lady then went onto the stage, where some of the musicians were already tuning up, spoke to the first cellist and pointed at us. He stood up and beckoned to us. Rather shyly, we approached him. He leant down, shook our hands and said in English: "I'm all in favour of performing Wagner in Israel. We're very glad you're here. Thank you."

"But under the right conditions and with broad agreement," I answered. He agreed, and invited me backstage after the concert to meet Mika Eichenholz and the cello soloist, Lynn Harrell.

I was even more touched when I received an invitation from the Tel Aviv Central Music Library, which also contains the Bronislaw Huberman archive. The director of the library at the time, Nehama Lischitz, and her colleagues proudly showed me around their treasured collection, where I found a picture of Arturo Toscanini and Huberman on the beach at Haifa in 1938, only six months before the *Reichskristallnacht*. The Palestine Symphony Orchestra (now the Israel Philharmonic Orchestra) also played Wagner's works until that night of pogroms, including the preludes to the first and third acts of *Lohengrin*. I told them about my grandfather's collaboration with Toscanini on a production of *Tannhäuser* in Bayreuth in 1930, and about Toscanini's consequent resignation. (After the Nazis seized power in January 1933, he refused to perform in Germany any more, although Hitler had personally asked him to conduct again in Bayreuth. Nehama cordially gave me a copy of the book *An Orchestra Is Born*, which comprised a unique collection of documents concerning the history of Jewish music and culture in what was then

Palestine. The book, inscribed with a friendly dedication, is one of my most treasured mementos of my first short trip to Israel.)

Despite the mad rush of attending interviews and becoming locked in discussions with members of the audience at my talks, we didn't want to miss out on a visit to the Diaspora Museum in Tel Aviv. Teresina and I had the privilege of being shown around by Judith Etzion and the composer and music journalist Benjamin Bar-Am. The display, comprising texts, photos and films of Jewish culture and history, impressed us with its clarity, as also did Judith's explanations. The connection between Jewish and German history and the part my own family played in that was painfully real. The Diaspora Museum also has an extraordinarily detailed and extensive database, which can be accessed by visitors. I typed in the keyword 'Wagner' and received four printed sheets of fascinating information. I learned, for example, that there were also Jewish families with the name Wagner, who were first recorded in the 17th century in Leipzig and Frankfurt Am Main.

I also learned that there had been a Jewish community in Bayreuth since the beginning of the 13th century. In 1933, 261 Jews were resident there, which at that time constituted 0.7 per cent of the population. On 10 November 1938, *Kristallnacht*, the beautiful synagogue, which had been built in 1760, was destroyed and the homes and shops of Jewish citizens were plundered and devastated by the Nazis. On the following day, the population of Bayreuth attacked their Jewish compatriots and desecrated and destroyed the Jewish cemetery. On 27 November 1941, 50 Jews were deported to Riga, and on 12 January 1942, the last eleven Jewish citizens of Bayreuth were taken to Theresienstadt.

I thought angrily of how my family and my teachers had deceived me as a child. Where were the good burghers of Bayreuth and my family on 10 and 11 November 1938? We left the museum in silence.

Our encounter with Moshe Hoch, the head of the Institute For The Preservation And Study Of The Jewish Museum Of The Holocaust and a Holocaust survivor himself, in Yad Letslilei was also distressing. His description of the way he was persecuted as a child by the Nazis rekindled images of National Socialism in all its cruelty. The old question nagged at me: how was it possible for such a highly-developed nation to turn into criminals?

The attitude of the German media during and after my stay in Israel was peculiar. Most of them knew very little about Wagner's antisemitism, as was evident in their reporting. They were concerned mainly with sensational headlines, presenting me as a kind of Siegfried, battling against Fafner. This didn't help me in my efforts to paint a more discriminating picture of Wagner in Germany and Israel, nor to come to terms with my family history, and the German reports from Israel only served to isolate me further.

There is little left to say about the Germans I met in Israel. Hans-Heinrich von Stackelberg, the West German cultural attaché was, in my view, the wrong man in the wrong place. Despite the success of my lectures, I couldn't persuade him to change his mind about me.

The Israeli media made much more of an effort to understand me and my concerns. The journalist Hanna Yaddor, for example, summed up my visit in the evening newspaper *Ma'ariv* in an article with the title "Thank You For Your Courage", published on 16 January 1990: "The talk of the music world in Israel in the last ten days has been the visit by Dr Gottfried Wagner, the great-grandson of the German composer Richard Wagner...He did not meet with any hostility, but with affection and friendship... People recognised him from the media in the street and gave him gifts. Someone wrote to him in a letter: 'Thank you for your courage'...He hopes very much to come back to Israel for a longer period. He has already gone through his baptism of fire here; now all that remains for him is to counter a few hateful remarks from members of his family."

Hanna Yaddor's prediction was to prove correct.

CHAPTER TWENTY-TWO

FATHER'S LAST LETTER

On my return from Israel in mid January 1990, I found it difficult to concentrate. I kept thinking of the possible consequences of my trip – I knew that Bayreuth would react soon after the first wave of reports in the national and international press.

At the end of January, Josef Lienhart, the president of the Richard Wagner Society, called me up from Freiburg, wanting to know more about my trip. I described the results I'd achieved and told him of my experiences, and the great interest which the Israeli media had demonstrated in my work. Finally, I confidently declared that a new stage had begun in the discussion about Wagner in Israel. I sketched down the themes of our conversation and faxed a summary to my father:

"Dear Papa
"This evening Herr Lienhart rang me and informed me of the following, 'to his regret and stressing his appreciation of my work and his kind regard for me': that you had – on the basis of a one-sided selection from various West German newspaper articles on my trip to Israel and on the basis of your right as head of the festival – demanded that either all existing invitations from Richard Wagner Societies to me are withdrawn and ruled out for the future or you would publicly distance yourself from those societies. He also says that your boycotting of the Richard Wagner Societies, if they should choose not to

observe your demand, would take effect from the next plenary assembly of the Richard Wagner Societies [on 25 May 1990]. Furthermore, you have been sending Herr Lienhart the said articles highlighted in yellow and with your comments attacking me since mid January, by express registered post. I cannot believe that you would have given such instructions. I ask you, as my father, to act in this instance, especially as your instructions affect firm offers from Richard Wagner Societies, both now and in the future. I request that you fax me before the end of the week, in view of the very slow postal service. Awaiting your reply, I remain with kind regards

"Your son

"Gottfried."

The official reply came two days later. Father wrote that he had informed the Richard Wagner Society and its local branches that he would refuse to take part in any of their events if I was still able to give talks under the auspices of the Society, as his participation could be construed as sanctioning my views on the development and the artistic standards of the Bayreuth Festival, which he found unacceptable. He referred me to an article which appeared in the 11 January 1990 edition of *Die Welt*, in which I had stated that, since Wieland's death, the festival had become a cross between a stock exchange and a scrap-metal market. Furthermore, I had emphasised that the festival was ruled by politics and commerce, to the detriment of music, drama and poetry. Of course, Father didn't want his threat to boycott the Society events to be understood as an ultimatum – for which, in fact, he had no legitimate right – but rather as an expression of his own personal preferences. None of this, he maintained, had anything at all to do with my lecture tour of Israel.

He dismissed the comments I had made on the possible implications of the Foundation document for the further participation of the Wagner family in the administration of the festival in *Süddeutsche Zeitung* (17 January 1990) with the remark that I obviously wasn't aware of the content of this document. He also said that, if I really did have such critical thoughts about my grandmother, I should have rejected my share of her will as "dirty money" back in 1981. At the end of his letter, with reference to his overall responsibility for the Bayreuth Festival, he drew a definite line of separation between father and son.

I tried to explain my position to him, in the hope of avoiding later accusations that I'd provoked him out of petulance, but to no avail. I sent copies to friends and officials whom I believed were interested in resolving what was now a public conflict. Even when I look at it today, Father's letter makes it clear that he was never interested in a genuine acknowledgement of his own past and duties, as both father and festival head. The newspaper quotations, which by no means always corresponded to my statements, were taken out of context, incomplete and based on an arbitrary selection of articles. An objective assessment of international press reports paints quite a different picture, but neither the *Festspielhügel* nor the majority of German media has any desire to acknowledge this.

One need only look at the press in Israel in the period from December 1989 to January 1990, the *Wall Street Journal* of 7 January, the *Repubblica* of 15 January, the *Aftenposten* of 18 January or the objective report of my Israel trip in the *Neue Zürcher Zeitung* of 8 February 1990 with the title "Richard Wagner In Israel: Signs Of A Rapprochement."

"Potential access to Wagner and his work will certainly continue to improve for future generations, and consequently opportunities will increase for the performance of Wagner's works again in Israel. That real steps have already been taken in this direction was illustrated at the beginning of this year by the invitation extended to Richard Wagner's great-grandson Gottfried Wagner (son of the grandson Wolfgang) by the University of Tel Aviv. In four lectures, this descendant of Wagner, a doctor of musicology and a director, was able to discuss his personal approach to his ancestor's works, and about his conflicts with those works. Gottfried Wagner was born in Bayreuth shortly after the war (1947), and from an early age he was confronted with the problems surrounding his family's political and cultural heritage. Of course, it was neither his nor his hosts' brief to resolve the questions about Wagner or the performance or non-performance of his music in Israel. For the university, it was the music which was most important, to keep discussion alive on this important composer, and on Gottfried Wagner's part there was a serious attempt at rapprochment, as expressed in his radio and television interviews. Without these intentions, the encounter could not have taken place in such a generally positive atmosphere. In particular, it should be noted that this encounter with Wagner's great-grandson took place in a much broader framework than the university had originally planned; interviews on Israeli radio and television, and reports by the national and international press, confirm the necessity and the significance of such steps. In Israel, too, in those days the word *glasnost* was used when referring to the reception given to Wagner."

At the same time I received an official statement from Shai Burstyn, in his capacity as head of the music department of the University of Tel Aviv, saying:

"I should like to thank you for your efforts in ensuring that your visit to Tel Aviv University was so successful. The capacity crowds which your lectures drew, as well as the interest shown by the press, are clear indications that the topics of your lectures are of great interest to the Israeli academic public and, indeed, to a large part of the Israeli population...[The series of lectures] was a project that was both well prepared and well delivered. I wish you every success in the future, in developing the ideas you conveyed in your lectures here."

Comparing these reactions with those of my father and his friends, I realised that it was pointless to expect any constructive discussion to take place. I had to continue what I had begun in Israel, despite all resistance. Amidst all the personal, cultural, political and ethical differences, I still hoped that he would be prepared to meet me one day just as a father. However, as he now showed little inclination to listen to my opinion, and in light of the fact that the ultimatum he had given to the Wagner Societies had led to the breaking of previously-agreed contracts, I felt that I had no option but to respond in kind.

In the middle of February 1990, with the aid of my lawyer and friend Inge Lehmbruck, I wrote to him:

"Dear Papa

"...So I must acknowledge that, exerting the most severe pressure – namely the threat to boycott all of the Richard Wagner Society's events – you have prevailed on the president, Herr Lienhart, to cancel any events in which I am involved, including three lectures in Freiburg, Baden-Baden and Karsruhe. In other words, you have thought it right not to discuss with me personally my statements, but have instead decided to act via third parties, which has had repercussions on my material existence. I must emphatically deny your remark that I accepted 'dirty money' (not my expression) as inheritance from my grandmother. What I received at the beginning of the 1980s was approximately 85 per cent (exactly DM 83,509.27, before tax) of my grandfather Siegfried Wagner's legacy, and the remaining 15 per cent (DM 12,500.00, before tax – the figures can easily be verified by the executor, Thorwart) from Grandmother's legacy, which I have always regarded as only a part of the Wagnerian property coming from great-grandfather Richard.

"Gottfried."

This registered letter was returned to me unopened, and so Inge Lehmbruck wrote to Father: "I have to draw your attention in due course to the fact that my client, whose livelihood is economically largely dependent on his lecturing activities, would not hesitate to defend himself with all legal means – including court action – if your attacks on his professional career should be repeated."

Father's secretary acknowledged receipt of this letter without comment. Breaking off the relationship with his own son did not stop my father from using his influence to make life in the music world difficult for me. Using his countless contacts and connections – always acting via third parties – he brought about precisely what Inge Lehmbruck had tried to warn him from doing. In his 1994 autobiography, *Acts*, he offered a coherent formulation and justification of his position, and inadvertently helped my own position, as people have since become interested in my version of events. In the blurb of the German edition, my father writes:

> "In the vast amount of literature on every conceivable subject relating to Wagner and Bayreuth, there persist – particularly where the 20th century is concerned – so many clichés, tenacious prejudices, half-truths and quite infamous lies. There are just as many blatantly uncritical voices in favour as there are unobjective voices against. Rage, violent love and hatred and explode, all on a relentless scale, so that often an adequately sober view is obscured, or at least clouded. It seems to me that it is high time finally to bury the legends and end the empty talk. My autobiography is intended in the widest sense to offer testimony of greatness experienced and pain suffered, of course from my quite subjective viewpoint, but at the same time substantiated by documentary evidence and accurate records, which have until now largely remained unpublished. The unusual, outrageous, not to say sensational is no figment of my imagination, but lies in the established facts themselves."

I read this text several times, as I didn't understand it. Father stresses that he is writing from his "quite subjective viewpoint" – in other words, he doesn't aim at any objectivity – and that its credibility is reinforced with documentary evidence. However, his choice of documentation and their sources remain open to criticism, as they are arbitrary and vague. His "subjective viewpoint" apparently includes a selection of "documentary evidence and accurate records" which, until today, were largely unpublished. *Acts* serves to be not even a subjective account, but is instead an arbitrary interpretation of Father's own life.

So much I grasped on a first reading. On a second reading, I covered the sections which were crucial for me – his interpretation of the antisemitism of Richard Wagner and our family, his interpretation of Hitler and the Holocaust and the consequences of these in terms of our relationship – and compared them with his statements in the blurb. I wanted to know the reasons for the repression of his own past and the past of his family, as head of the festival, as a Wagner and as my father.

Acts demonstrated to me how he had succumbed to the contemporary mood in repressing his own past by dealing far too arbitrarily with his grandfather's Romantic philosophy. It also became clear to me how, in judging Father's Romantically-written autobiography, I orientated myself with rationalism and the Enlightenment of the Classical era. I agree with the philosopher Karl Popper, who in his 1967 essay 'On The Subject Of Freedom', in his understanding of rationalism and Enlightenment against the philosophising of the Romantics, writes:

"As one of the last stragglers of rationalism and Enlightenment, I believe in the self-liberation of man by knowledge...For in my backwardness, I can see in the philosophy of the Romantics – and in particular in the philosophy of the three great leaders of German idealism, Fichte, Schelling and Hegel – nothing but an intellectual and moral catastrophe; the worst that has ever befallen the German and European intelligentsia. This catastrophe, this intellectual and moral chain reaction, I believe had a disastrous and stultifying effect, which, like an atomic cloud, is still expanding. It provoked what Konrad Heiden years ago called in his book on Hitler 'the age of intellectual and moral dishonesty'...What I mean, when I talk about reason or rationalism, is nothing more than the conviction that we can *learn* from the criticism of our faults and mistakes, and in particular the criticism of others and ultimately by criticising ourselves."[34]

Father refuses to acknowledge that only critical discussion allows us to see our own ideas from different angles and judge them objectively. For him, critical discussion based on the concept of give and take has no meaning. He will not recognise that, as Popper describes it, "the sensible, critical approach can only be the result of the criticism of others, and one can only achieve self-criticism through the criticism of others." Instead, Father wants only to impress, forgetting that in art Richard Wagner is not the only "guiding light of mankind".

His language is vague and complicated. In his attempt to

legitimise his own position – a running theme throughout his life – he inadvertently refers to the third, secret instructor: Heinz Tietjen, the Mephisto of the Nazi opera world. In Bayreuth and Berlin under the Führer, as Tietjen's assistant, he learned to find every means for holding onto power – which was at that time to smoothe the path to his becoming intendant of the festival for life. For the great organiser, there was no zero hour.

There is a recurring pattern of repression in his book. He trampled on the dignity of those who could not protect themselves, and who refused to subject themselves wholly to his will. One need only read the pages on which he passes judgment on his brother Wieland, my mother (who, when all is said and done, was a supportive wife for 33 years), his sister Friedelind, his sister-in-law Gertrud and the "unqualified" fourth generation. Here he applies the phrase "do as you would be done by" only to himself, when he talks of the pain he has suffered, and presents himself as a victim. One moment he's a martyr, the next a victor. Like a conjuror, he makes the mass murderer Hitler vanish in a fog of mythology. Thus "Uncle Wolf" remains the "kindly human being" that Winifred believed him to be – Winifred, with whom he steamrollered through the Foundation statutes.

He makes no mention of the historical connection between his grandfather's antisemitism and Hitler, despite the copious material evidence explicitly documenting the close relationship between the family and the Führer. So where is this among the "accurate records"? Neither has he included the correspondence with Wieland in his book, which is crucial in arriving at an understanding of New Bayreuth.

There are some crucial scenes missing from *Acts*, although those concerned know about them. In this way, Father threw away a great and unique opportunity to present himself to the world in a credible manner. It appears that he doesn't care for the solidarity of honest people, and values instead the praise of those who simply follow fashion.

I believe in Democritus' aphorism: "I prefer an austere life in a democracy to wealth under a tyrant." This knowledge also gives me the freedom to leave a door open to him. Why should we not be "able to learn through our faults and mistakes, and in particular by the criticism of others and ultimately by self-criticism"? In this way my father could discover himself.

CHAPTER TWENTY-THREE

THE BAN FROM BAYREUTH

My father's personal and professional attacks on me had both negative and positive consequences. One positive result has been that I now no longer focus solely on Wagner and Jews but also on the history of Christianity and Judaism. The cultural and spiritual enrichment which this has entailed has had a significant effect on my personal and professional development.

On the negative side, career opportunities for me in Germany dwindled. Word of the rift between Father and I spread quickly, and precisely in those places where I had previously had prospects. Everyone in the music world who wanted to offer me work now knew that in doing so they would be attracting my father's enmity. Why should they spoil their relations with the *Festspielhügel*? Fortunately, however, many people found my father's attitude towards me excessive and indefensible.

When set against the peculiar relationship that Germans have with Richard Wagner, however, my position turned out to be complicated. For Germans, the name Wagner is pregnant with meaning, and his works heavyweight and earnest. Irony and criticism have never been a forte of the Germans. For them, Wagner is either a sacred national relic or a Nazi monster. He is always taken seriously, and he arouses more emotion than any other composer on Earth. The reason for this lies in those conflicts contained within his works, his life and the jumbled philosophy of the man himself, who used music as a vehicle of propaganda: he plays with the German soul, which is constantly seduced by idealistic concepts of world improvement. As long as fundamental discussion on Wagner's attitude to the Jews is avoided in Germany, every aspect of the *zeitgeist* can be accommodated in him. But any post-Holocaust German who finds this wild mixture of theatrical "redemption", racism, chauvinism and Teutomania to be not only culturally outdated but also dangerous will meet with violent resistance – and not only among the Bayreuth Wagner cult.

Where arguments about Wagner are concerned, Germans very quickly lose their sense of humour, while the composer also causes the German soul to become exalted. Woe betide anyone who questions Wagner, especially if he comes from Wagner's family and thus commits the most terrible crime of fouling his own nest!

At the Federal Congress of the Richard Wagner Society in Mannheim, at the end of May 1990, my father and Lienhart succeeded in curtailing any discussion of my trip to Israel, although some members of local branches wanted to talk about it. However, the majority of those present obeyed Father and Lienhart for fear of losing their ticket quota for the festival, and moved quickly to the next item on the agenda.

A letter from the chairwoman of the Saarbrücken Wagner Society, Otti Maurer, was typical of this attitude. Once a close friend of my grandmother, on 6 June 1991 Frau Maurer informed me – after presumably having received the green light from Bayreuth – that, on the basis of the "shocking" newspaper reports from the last year, she had appealed to the working session of the Hanover Wagner Society, asking the main assembly to discuss whether it was still appropriate to invite me as a speaker at events of the Richard Wagner Society, after my "derogatory remarks" concerning the Bayreuth Festival, my father and my grandmother, whom she had loved very much. She wrote that she had to ask herself whether it was worth jeopardising the friendship of the head of the festival and of his sister, Frau Verena Lafferentz, for the sake of one young man, even if he was a member of the family. She herself, however, didn't participate in the session.

The final sentence of her letter is revealing, and reflects

Father's attitude. Here, as in his correspondence, I am reproached for having profited from the inheritance that Winifred Wagner had held together.

To be fair, the attitude of most chairpersons of the German Richard Wagner societies was mixed. They generally understood my critique of Richard Wagner in Israel and its consequences, but expressing their opinions to me in private – in their own local society, or even to President Lienhart – they lacked the courage of their convictions.

The Munich Wagner Society, however, proved to be a commendable exception, demonstrating great steadfastness. Its president, Jürgen Dreher, wrote to me and informed me that the announcement in the annual programme had led to renewed threats from Gudrun and Wolfgang Wagner, which would certainly have thrown the federal chairman and the local chairwoman in Hanover into a state of panic. In spite of this, it appeared that they were looking forward to my "rapprochement with Richard Wagner" and were not going to let themselves be bullied by the head of the festival.

Despite the topic of my discussions, the name Wagner caused some hostility towards me. After the lecture in Munich, in January 1991, a man was waiting for me outside in the street dressed in leather trousers, green Loden coat and a Bavarian hat, with an enormous Alsatian dog. I actually remembered meeting him before, many years ago. When I got into my car he shouted at me, pointing to his dog: "My Wolfi will get you yet, you Wagner swine!"

A member of the audience in Munich later wrote me a letter, describing a dilemma in which many Wagnerians found themselves. The Jewish Wagnerian Heinrich Frank advised me to stop criticising members of my family, especially Winifred Wagner and Chamberlain, and referred to the fourth Commandment. People knew of my views on the matter, however, and avoiding the subject in the future would convince no one that I had changed my view of the woman who had run the festival from 1933 to 1944.

In my reply to Heinrich Frank, I said to him:

"My statements – always based on public documents and facts – correspond to my understanding of tradition...and my

conscience and knowledge, as a Wagner in the shadow of
Auschwitz who will never be prepared to remain silent for
reasons of professional expediency or out of blind obedience
to a questionable family tradition...I have known since my
childhood that, in so doing, I find myself outside the norms of
the 'morals and tolerance' of a 'certain German establishment',
which represses its own past in self-alienation...

"You speak of the fourth Commandment in connection
with my grandmother...Anyone who claims to have been
honoured as father and mother must have acted convincingly
through a correspondingly responsible life and firm actions
as a private and public person, in the interests of the future
of their children...Why do you think I get no answer from
Bayreuth to my letters, and have been declared *persona non
grata* there?...The reconciliation with a certain
establishment cannot not rest in repression, as occurred in
the case of the 1984 'Wagner And The Jews' exhibition in Villa
Wahnfried...You could play a part in mediating my mission to
a different, open German establishment – which, thank God,
still exists."

Unfortunately, our positions remained irreconcilable. As a German
Jew, he wanted to suppress discussion about Wagner's antisemitism
because it would involve for him a large degree of self-criticism and
discussion about how Jews could admire the music of a man who
hated them. When Frank implored me to stop criticising my family, I
think that he was actually trying to prevent more profound
discussion about being a Jewish Wagnerian. However, I don't believe
that it's morally responsible to make a distinction between Wagner
the great artist and Wagner the antisemite. For that reason, it's
impossible for me to remain silent on the deeds of my grandmother
and Chamberlain.

One thing I did learn from my correspondence with Frank,
however, was not to use the word 'mission' as much in connection
with my activities. Even then I didn't view my work as being a
mission but rather as a search for the truth about Richard Wagner.

Another interesting episode took place in mid-August, at a

conference in Weimar on the subject of 'The Case Of Richard Wagner In Israel And Germany' in the middle of August 1991. Herzl Shmueli also took part, and before the discussion began, in the Autonomous Cultural Centre, the chairman of the Richard Wagner Society in Weimar, Eberhard Lüdde, asked me: "What line should we take? All national and international Wagner societies have been instructed not to invite you to functions."

"Thanks for the tip," I answered. "Whether you or other Wagner societies want to invite me or not must surely depend on yourselves."

Other representatives from Wagner Societies turned up to my *Lohengrin* premiere in Dessau in May 1995. Here, again, views were mixed. The Berlin Society obviously toed the Bayreuth line, while the *Neue Zürcher Zeitung* applauded my concept of a critical reading of the text and then poked fun at the organised booing against me. Two soloists fell in with the anti-Gottfried mood, after having made out for months during rehearsals that they agreed with me, and were later reluctant to be named in the documentary film *Herr Hitler's Religion*. This film, which was televised in a number of countries in September 1995, shows scenes from my production of *Lohengrin*, in which Wagner's 'New Christianity in the direction of *Parsifal*' is clarified, to the horror of Bayreuth. The administrative department in Dessau shared my opinion, however, along with most of the theatre staff.

I had a difficult time in Bayreuth, particularly in my correspondence with the mayor, Dieter Mronz. In December 1989, I had sent him the introductory texts to my lectures on Wagner at the University of Tel Aviv. On 26 March 1990, after having heard nothing from him for three months, I wrote again:

"Dear Dr Mronz

"In our talks during the opening week of the Bayreuth Festival at the end of July 1989 you expressed an interest in my desire for reconciliation in Israel (cf also the interview of 18.8.89 in the *Nordbayerischer Kurier*) and promised to send me your views on the 'case of the Chamberlain-Furtwängler-Strasse'. For that reason, I referred yet again, in my letter of 21.12.89, to my forthcoming trip to Israel and enclosed the summaries of my three lectures and of my video presentation of *Der Ring* with the intention of evoking some reaction from you...Your continuing silence on the matter...which surely also concerns the citizens of Bayreuth, gives me cause for concern.

"With kind regards

"Gottfried H Wagner."

A month later, I received a four-page letter from Dr Mronz, in which he congratulated me on the success of my journey to Israel. His remarks on the Chamberlain affair, however, were indicative of the intellectual climate in Bayreuth. In reference to Werner Kolb, the municipal council member of the Greens who in 1989 had bravely lobbied for a renaming of the Chamberlain Strasse, Mronz came to his position towards the Bayreuth municipal council: on the basis of the fact that the present generation must also be suffering under the heavy burden of the Nazi dictatorship, he pointed out that, in Bayreuth, a new and more profound sensitivity had developed toward this problem. This in turn had led to them confidently freeing themselves from such burdens as the disputed street name, instead of encumbering themselves with new guilt complexes and burdens on top of the old.

In July I replied to Mronz:

"I find it not only regrettable but scandalous in every respect that it has taken 23 years to change the name of the 245 Chamberlainstrasse. The example of the Chamberlainstrasse shows that we are not capable of 'confidently freeing ourselves of such burdens as this street name'. The words 'confidently freeing' in this context make me feel uneasy. Whoever 'stubbornly clings on' to names like Chamberlain in Bayreuth, and indeed anywhere else, shows what sort of person he is. 'New guilt complexes and burdens' will certainly continue to exist if these antidemocratic powers are not publicly opposed with personal courage and democratic means, and people are still not prepared – especially in the period of German reunification – for a thorough acceptance of the past and genuine mourning through firm action, without remembrance ceremonies, which often function as rather dubious alibis. The city of Bayreuth could, for example, find a twin city in Israel. After talking with people there, you would certainly alter your opinion and attitude to this fundamental subject of German history, as I did. I regret that my conscience forces me to acknowledge that, in this sense, neither the commemorative text on the *Reichskristallnacht* [in Bayreuth] nor the volume *Wagner Und Die Juden* [*Wagner And The Jews*] correspond to my ideas. With thoughtful regards and constant readiness for dialogue, I remain, your Gottfried Wagner.

"PS On the basis of my critical statements at the University of Tel Aviv, on my grandmother's leadership as head of the festival in the Nazi period, I have been declared *persona non grata* by those close to the festival (letter of 2.2.90), including the federal president, Lienhart; I have been black-listed in Germany, and my work has been slandered by many people, trying to settle private scores. The international professional world and the press – particularly the Israeli press – still has to deal with this. This will certainly not be awkward for me, because the biased selection of press quotations against me will probably have to be aired. It is true that I no longer have access to the *Festspielhügel*, but surely I can still read the archives held by the city of Bayreuth? And, if I am hindered in my researches, can I come to you? Also, on the question of whether or not we can confidently free ourselves from such burdens – I have to say that, on the basis of my experiences, I fear not."

Mronz never answered this letter. I was not surprised that I was unwelcome at that time in the Richard Wagner Archive, and that my work was not encouraged.

Another instance concerning the University of Bayreuth – which I naively believed to be independent of *Festspielhügel* politics – was equally revealing. In June 1993, Professor Walter Gebhard of the German Department wrote to me in connection with a "possible lecture", which at the time (before the university had awarded by father with a doctorate) he considered to be inappropriate, not least because of the unpredictable way in which the festival administration might react to a critical lecture.

I did well to cancel the lecture. The university's attitude was made plain not only by awarding my father an honorary doctorate but also by the content of the ceremonial speech which Walter Jens had given in January 1994 on the 800th centenary of the city of Bayreuth. Jens rejected the findings of independent research into Wagner's antisemitism, and told the representatives of the city and the *Festspielhügel* exactly what they wanted to hear. He delivered what the Wagner scholar Hartmut Zelinsky appropriately termed a "flight into vagueness".

Yet another icon of the German cultural scene joined the Bayreuth game: August Everding, Germany's most powerful intendant. In April 1990, I had written to him in the hope that he would support my discussion of Wagner in Germany, after my trip to Israel. Typically, the politician Everding reacted noncommittally. However, things did not stop there: against the wishes of Stephan Kohler, the head of the Richard Strauss Institute in Munich, and the chairmen of the patrons circle of the Richard Strauss festival in Garmisch Partenkirchen, Dr Manfred Frei and Christian Lange, he also managed to see to it that my invitation to a symposium on 'Richard Strauss, An (Un)Heroic Life' in July 1991 was cancelled. Word got around that I was "difficult, verbose and dangerous".

A lecture that had been planned to take place at the Academy Of Fine Arts in Munich in 1991, on "The Case Of Wagner In Israel And Germany", which had been championed by the composer Günter Bialas, also came to nothing. I had written to Bialas in May, enclosing numerous documents in connection with my trip to Israel. He had been very interested in the subject, but at the end of June 1991 wrote to say that he found himself unable to invite me to give a lecture at the Bavarian Academy Of Fine Arts without the my father's consent, because Father was a member of the Music Department. According to Dr Bauer, the academy's secretary, the tensions between my father and myself were still too great to invite me.

My experiences with the media weren't much better. In autumn 1991, Walter Jens' son Tilman rang me and asked to interview me about my trip to Israel and Wagner's antisemitism, but the interview was then broadcast under the sensationalist title: "The Inheritance War – Trouble In The House Of Wagner: Wolfgang Wagner Is Angry" in November, on the culture review *Titel, Thesen, Temperamente*. My cousin Nike was deputised as spokesperson for the fourth Wagner generation, although her opinions and mine diverged where Bayreuth was concerned. Shortly after the broadcast, I wrote her a letter to open up a dialogue with her after a several years of silence. Unfortunately, she didn't reply. For years she has argued her claim to the succession by criticising the festival under my father. In an interview in the summer of 1995, she stated: "In every institution, a period of government should not go on too long. There is an urgent need for new ideas, a new artistic will, a new vision. The future of Wagner is at stake. That is what I stand for, and I am ready to take it on." But she failed to present a programme which dealt with Wagner's ideology and antisemitism.

Until that point she had avoided being involved in the Bayreuth politicking against me, and in that respect she was a refreshing change from the other two women in the family, Eva and Gudrun. Both of these women have ambitions of inheritance; both worked closely with Father, as well, and were tarred by the brush of his power politics. My father has two principles which rule his pupils almost as much as they do him: *control from the rear*, and *when dealing with the public, leave your sentiments ambiguous*. Neither Eva nor Gudrun have the will or the ability to come to terms with Bayreuth's Nazi past, which Eva has already proven by allegedly losing the copies of the films with which I had entrusted her.

Tilman Jens should have reported this in his programme. Of course, he also gave my father the chance to make a statement: "I can't turn the Bayreuth Festival into a playground for Richard Wagner's great-grandchildren. I can only appoint someone here who in my view has something to offer Bayreuth. We are not a training centre for Wagner's great-grandchildren."

JENS: "Does that mean that you are the last representative of the great Wagner family?"

FATHER: "No."

JENS: "You are the last Wagner?"

FATHER: "No. I have never maintained that, and I can't understand why I'm blamed because my nieces and nephews can't understand that."

JENS: "Okay, but if you say that at the moment nothing will come after..."

FATHER: "Sorry. What I was trying to say was that there's no one from within the family who, based on their achievements so far, is any better qualified than an outsider...in terms of what they could contribute to Wagner's work."

JENS: "Do you see something like a conflict between the generations of the great Wagner family?"

FATHER: "I can only say that, from the beginning, my brother maintained that older and younger generations don't work well together."

About me, and the fact that I no longer receive festival tickets, he said:

FATHER: "In many of the public talks he has given on tour, my son has made very negative comments about the present structure of the festival. Among other things he has claimed that my colleagues are just 'alibi Jews', and that I have been indulging in negative nationalist tendencies. That is an arrogant and false accusation, and furthermore a denigration of my colleagues, and as such is totally unacceptable."

JENS: "So he doesn't get tickets any more?"

FATHER: "As I have said, I can't receive him here because of my colleagues. If he says such things, attacking everyone, including myself, then he shouldn't be allowed in the house."

JENS: "How do you feel, playing the role of wicked father, or wicked uncle?"

FATHER: "Excuse me, I am not wicked! I am only one of a very small group..."

JENS: "...your family..."

FATHER: "What do you mean, my family? Excuse me. Family is a community that is compiled haphazardly...which happens to have originated from the same root. At some stage, one's own personality emerges, one develops and then one makes up one's own mind about things."

JENS: "Herr Wagner, you are now 72. People usually retire at 65. Why haven't you retired yet? Do you have any idea when you intend to do so?"

FATHER: "Adenauer started to rule Germany at 75 and then retired – voluntarily – 14 years later."

JENS: "Is that some indication of your plans?"

FATHER: "You will see. You are young. One day you will read it in the newspaper, and I presume that the television will cover it, too."

In conclusion, Jens remarked: "The patriarch will decide on his successor jointly with a commission. One may assume that none from the circle of his children, nephews and nieces will feature among the candidates, and so a family tradition is coming to an end. It's a typical chapter in the Wagner story. 15 years ago, Wolfgang Wagner married for the second time; now there is Frau Gudrun and Katherina, their daughter. In a few years she will have reached her majority and would not be the first female chief in Bayreuth. Nothing changes. Rejoice! Wagner without end!"[35]

Interviews I had given in January and August 1990 had led me to believe that critical discussion of Richard Wagner's antisemitism might be possible on Bavarian Radio. A statement I had made during the August interview – "Post-Wieland Bayreuth has nothing to do with [Richard Wagner's] idea of the festival" – was then used as grounds to cancel all collaboration on the planned project. The relationship – that is, the long-term business association – between the local radio station and the Bayreuth Festival could not be jeopardised.

In February 1996, the Viennese journalist Hellfried Brandl managed to arrange a broadcast with me on the subject of Wagner, Bayreuth and antisemitism as part of Bavarian Radio family programming, without the knowledge of the staff at the radio station who were connected with Bayreuth.

An interview with Wolfgang Seifert, a former employee of West

German Radio and Free Berlin Radio, went less favourably. I knew of Seifert through his exculpatory article for West German Radio, "New Bayreuth's Zero Hour", which had appeared in print after it was broadcast in February 1970. Documentation for this had been provided by Dietrich Mack, Father's former assistant director and house dramaturg of the Bayreuth Festival.

At the end of October 1993, a programme was broadcast focusing on four decades of the 'Bayreuth workshop', which distorted my statements, taking them out of context. Seifert also dismissed my comments on the "multicultural future of Bayreuth", hitting me with my father's words: "That is not suitable for Bayreuth."[36] He also drew attention to Father's influence in the Foundation Council of the Bayreuth Festival.

My experiences with a number of leading German newspapers were similarly negative, in particular the London correspondent of the *Frankfurter Allgemeine Zeitung*, Gina Thomas, who whipped up public scorn against me in an article published in April 1995. Thomas was taking her revenge for remarks I had made on the programme *Wagner Versus Wagner*, which had been televised at the beginning of April 1995 by the UK's Channel Four. She did this without any knowledge of either my work or of modern research into Wagner's antisemitic writings, which I had quoted. Instead of engaging in an objective discussion, she vented her resentment and kept deliberately silent about the fact that other critical experts, such as *Wagner Compendium* editor Barry Millington, Paul Lawrence Rose and Dan Bar On had also been interviewed in this programme. But it was the following remarks in particular that caused greatest astonishment:

> "*The Times* devoted half a page to Gottfried Wagner's childish objections and left his assertions uncontradicted. As someone who likes to present himself as the victim of persecution, other newspapers gave him a lot of space...Not even the faintest doubt is expressed in his exaggerated assertions. His English interviewers blindly believe him. The opera critic of *The Times* sympathetically describes the extent of Bayreuth's influence: Gottfried Wagner, whom the

keepers of the Grail wrongly described as a 'nest-fouler', is even denied access to the German media...Abroad, however, those who commission him works are ignorant of this, and they are only too happy to have their own clichéd ideas confirmed."[37]

The German reviews of my May 1995 production of *Lohengrin* were of a similar tone, and were plainly influenced by Bayreuth. Since May 1977 (ie since since the reviews of my first production, Beethoven's opera *Fidelio*), nothing has really changed. Most of the reviewers aligned themselves with Bayreuth and wrote in a style devoid of all objectivity; unfortunately, they were also often completely devoid of of any competence in the field.

At this point, something far more ominous came to my attention. At the beginning of October 1992, the American conductor John Edward Niles, with whom I'd been in contact since 1990 regarding various projects concerning Jewish composers who were murdered during the Nazi period, informed me that his brother Thomas, a high-ranking official in the American diplomatic service, had received hints that my Italian family and I were on the hit list of some international Nazi organisation. "I'm very concerned for your personal safety. My brother and some of his colleagues were informed that there are people who want to bump you and your family off. I'm not alarmist, but I beg you to be very careful." He said that we would be in danger if I continued my lectures on Wagner's antisemitism, particularly in Germany. This information scarcely surprised me; since my trip to Israel I had been constantly pestered by phone calls and death threats in the middle of the night.

At that time I was preparing a lecture which the German Council Of Industry And Commerce had invited me to deliver in Bonn, introduced (at my request) by Ralph Giordano. Concerned about my family, particularly with the increasing activities of neo-Nazis in Germany at that time, I asked Niles to find as much information as he could concerning the various neo-Nazi groups. At the beginning of December 1992, I also asked for help from Helmut Schäfer, the State Minister from the German Ministry Of Foreign Affairs. I reasoned that, "Since my lecture tour to Israel in January 1990, I have regularly received anonymous and abusive calls from Germany, in which I am called a 'Jew-lover', and worse." After the publication of a magazine article on my trip to Israel, the *Nationalzeitung* attacked me viciously, and in the USA in March 1992 I received death threats from skinheads, so I ended up giving one lecture under police protection.

Niles told me of a discussion he had had in the USA with an extreme right-wing German lawyer, who apparently lives in Switzerland. He learned from this dubious gentleman that people in Germany are very angry with me, as I concern myself with matters concerning the Holocaust and Wagner. Minister Schäfer ensured me that I was quite safe, but it left a bitter taste in my mouth when, in December 1992, we were driven around Bonn and Cologne in an armoured limousine under guard.

CHAPTER TWENTY-FOUR

ANTISEMITISM AND THE OPERA BUSINESS

Wagner's antisemitism had been the focus of my research and my lectures since January 1990. Although my talks were in rather meagre demand in Germany, there was lively interest in them overseas, especially in Jewish communities, and so I increasingly distanced myself from Germany.

In other countries, where repressive regimes are not all-powerful, I found that I could discuss Wagner more freely, and discussions were even more objective when hosts and audience had nothing to do with Bayreuth. There was always confrontation if they did, but this seldom happened. However, I should describe a few exceptions, which illustrate how deeply antisemitism has penetrated everywhere.

A US Nazi called Max Orlando wrote to me a few days after my Israel journey. "The era of the 'American Weimar Republic' is coming to an end," he said. "Who needs Washington DC and Moscow? Our organisation, Biopolitics USA – E[ustace] Mullins, R[obert E] Kuttner and myself – welcome the 21st century. Wagner music is of no consequence...His anti-Jewish position was instinctual, as the host to the parasite – ie *The Biological Jew* [written by] E Mullins, published in 1968." Orlando enclosed with his letter the research of the results that the McArdle Laboratory For Cancer Research at the University of Wisconsin had carried out, although I doubted their authenticity.

Other fanatics tried to bring me back to the "right path" of

Wagnerian hatred of Jews, or simply threatened me. Being called up in the night and being accused of being a "dirty traitor and friend of the Jews" has become a way of life ever since.

In March 1992 I delivered a talk in Dallas on "Wagner In Israel And Germany", where my hosts were the Southern Methodist University, the Goethe Centre and the local Richard Wagner Society. Two ladies on the committee of the society, both of whom were keen visitors to Bayreuth, were eager to whisper to me in private what I should and shouldn't say: I should avoid politics, say not a word about Wolf and Winnie, and display lots of enthusiasm for the neo-Christian case of the redeemer Richard Wagner. I thanked them, and proceeded to deliver my lecture against Wagner's antisemitism with even more passion. One of the two ladies exploded and ran shrieking from the hall. Before slamming the door behind her, she screamed: "Scandal! Scandal!" Fortunately, however, most of the audience were on my side, and one member of the Wagner Society even apologised for the incident. At the end of the lecture, my hosts immediately invited me back to deliver another talk.

My experiences with the conductors James Levine and Daniel Barenboim revealed the extent of Bayreuth's influence. After a lecture on the same subject, at the City University of New York at the end of February 1992, the music historian George Jellinek – who also worked for the *New York Times* and the radio station WQXR – invited me for an interview. He asked me in particular about *Parsifal*, as the programme containing my interview was to be broadcast in the intervals of a radio transmission of a live performance, under the baton of James Levine on 28 March 1992. The interview went smoothly, and at the end Jellineck said that he was "very happy". I subsequently told friends about the interview – among them Pierre Béique, the founder of the Montreal Symphony Orchestra, and Larry Mass, a doctor and contributor to the New York magazine *Opera Monthly* – and that the North American media had covered the broadcast and my part in it.

However, on 28 March I was informed by Pierre that the interview with me hadn't been broadcast, because I had apparently been ill. Larry looked into the matter further, and in the October 1992 edition of *Opera Monthly*, under the title "Met Cancels

Gottfried Wagner", he wrote:

> "*Opera Monthly* has learned that Richard Mohr, producer of
> the Texaco-Metropolitan Opera Radio Station, cancelled an
> interview with Gottfried Wagner, the great-grandson of the
> composer and outspoken critic of Bayreuth. The interview
> was scheduled to have run during the broadcast of *Parsifal* on
> 28 March 1992. George Jellinek, who had interviewed Dr
> Wagner for his radio programme on WQXR and who had also
> conducted the interview, confirmed that the decision to
> cancel was made because Dr Wagner was judged to be 'too
> controversial'. While Jellinek didn't want to be quoted as
> opposing the cancellation, he referred *Opera Monthly* to
> Mohr, who gave the following explanation: 'It was a defective
> tape. You can interpret that as you wish.'"[38]

In May 1992, Jellinek informed me that the interview had been
considered to be too controversial, and the decision to cancel had
apparently had something to do with the connection between the Met
and Bayreuth. However, he enclosed a list of radio stations in the USA
and Canada who had broadcast the interview (33 in the USA, and a few
in Canada), which confirmed yet again how strong North American
democracy is – they aren't impressed by connections.

I was advised against writing a letter of protest to Mohr, but I
couldn't just accept attitude that he and Levine displayed. When I
received a cheque for compensation for six times the amount of the
agreed fee, I wrote to Jellinek: "I shall send the cheque from the
Texaco-Metropolitan Opera International Radio Network to UNICEF
and try in that way to turn something bad into something good. I hope
you understand why."

Despite my "too controversial" contribution, only three days after
recording the radio interviews I delivered a long talk on *Parsifal* in the
renowned music conservatoire at the University of Cincinnati. The
arguments that I used here were no different from those that I'd used
in the interview with Jellinek, but not one member of the audience
appeared to feel provoked, nor could anyone have had a reason to.
Afterwards, I received a friendly thankyou letter from the conservatoire.

I was also visited by Henry Meyer, the eminent violinist and former member of the La Salle String Quartet, who presented me with a copy of his autobiographical sketches. Henry, a Jewish survivor of the Holocaust, had been James Levine's teacher.

However, the case of Daniel Barenboim, the one-time pianist prodigy and protégé of Otto Klemperer, is much more complex. (There have been several critical studies of his brilliant career, such as Norman Lebrecht's *The Maestro Myth*, Klaus Umbach's *Geldscheinsonate* and Stephen J Petit's *History Of The London Philharmonic Orchestra*.) In an interview with the Israeli newspaper *Yediot Acharonot*, published in the summer of 1992, Barenboim took issue with a stance I had taken concerning Wagner, the Bayreuth Festival and Judaism. Regarding the xenophobic violence of the neo-Nazis in Germany, in June 1993 he had told the Spanish newspaper *El Pais* that, "if the Nazi phenomenon becomes widespread", he did not want to "stay a day longer [in Germany]". I would have had some sympathy for this statement were not for the fact that, in the previous year, German neo-Nazis had also been very prominent during the festival in Bayreuth. To this day I haven't heard of any statements issued by Barenboim concerning this, nor on the historically distortive exhibition in 1984, *Wagner And The Jews*, held in the Villa Wahnfried.

In November 1993, in an interview with the newspaper *La Repubblica* under the title "Daniel Barenboim Rejoices And Is King Of Berlin", he said: "But I, as a Jew, defend Germany." To compound this, in an interview with *Opera Monthly* (May/June 1993) he made every effort to understate Richard Wagner's antisemitism: "We must remember that Wagner's antisemitism was intellectually *à la mode* in the 19th century, and he cannot be held responsible for the atrocities committed half a century later by those who misused his ideas."[39]

Leonard Bernstein, whom I had met in April 1990, just a few months before his death, would never have said such a thing. On the contrary, he openly stressed his deep aversion to conducting at the Bayreuth Festival under my father's administration and never compromised himself with Wagner's antisemitism or accepted New Bayreuth's policy of repression, but instead enthusiastically supported my trip to Israel.

But Barenboim had said these things, and I decided to defend myself against his attacks. In a letter to the editor published in the July/August 1993 issue of *Opera Monthly*, I again presented Wagner's antisemitism, in a way that couldn't have been mistaken to be simply *à la mode*. I described the ultimately catastrophic effects of this fanaticism in Germany, criticised the Bayreuth Festival and even talked about the neo-Nazi gatherings in Bayreuth in 1991. I declared that, through his antisemitic and inflammatory writings, Richard Wagner was at least partly responsible for the horrors of Auschwitz. Moreover, I supported Elie Wiesel, who in the *New York Times* on 12 January 1992 had criticised the way in which Barenboim excused Wagner from guilt.

Eventually, Franklin Littell, president of the Holocaust, Genocide And Human Rights Institute in Philadelphia and co-founder of the universally-recognised organisation The Holocaust And The Churches, joined the argument. In an article which was printed in various American newspapers, he wrote:

"But what happened at Bayreuth, that major fortress of cultural revisionism? Gottfried Wagner, the great-grandson of the famous composer, has a letter in the July/August issue of *Opera Monthly* that probes some of the deeper issues in this revisionist stronghold. He responds to an article in an earlier issue of the magazine in which the vaguely Jewish Daniel Barenboim has attempted to lift the burden of wilful and wicked antisemitism from Richard Wagner's record...Gottfried Wagner will have none of it. He feels the bitter antisemitism of his great-grandfather as a personal burden. He knows the correspondence of Winifred Wagner and Hitler between 1923 and 1944. He knows the antisemitic passages in his great-grandfather's letters and in Cosima Wagner's diaries. He asks why, if his antisemitism was so harmless, did the skinheads choose Bayreuth for their major rally in August of 1991?...We know about Bayreuth's past, and we can be thankful that Gottfried Wagner and his allies won't let that record be hidden for commercial and political purposes. There is a great deal going on in and around the city of Bayreuth today."[40]

Among the reactions were the articles in the August 1993 edition of the *New York Times* and in the January 1994 issue of the English magazine *Opera Now*. In a long letter to James R Oesterreicher, the music editor of the *New York Times*, I criticised an article by John Rockwell on the festival and the family which had been very poorly researched, published on 15 August 1993, under the title: "The Gods Sit There And Wait For Another Ugly Twilight". Rockwell asserted that:

"Relations seem to be most bitter between Wolfgang and his son. Gottfried has taken to denouncing his family's history of antisemitism, most prominently on a visit to Israel, the first such trip by a family member – even though the two most prominent conductors at Bayreuth today are James Levine and Daniel Barenboim. Wolfgang, who called the practise of stigmatising the conductors as 'alibi Jews' shameful, banned Gottfried from Bayreuth in 1990. 'Henceforth, both in Bayreuth and elsewhere,' he wrote, 'an absolute distance must be maintained between us.' Now, Gottfried says, his letters to his father return unopened."

Part of my letter to Oesterreicher read:

"Mr Rockwell doesn't appear to have seen my recent letter, published in the July/August edition of *Opera Monthly*. In this letter I express my opinion of the roles of Daniel Barenboim and James Levine and the hypocrisy in which I view their involvement. Your report only quotes the shameful statement of my father's, ie that my criticisms constitute a shameful stigmatisation of Barenboim and Levine as alibi Jews, but you don't allow me to respond. Twice now, in my grandmother's and now in my father's time, the Wagners have denied any personal responsibility in the Nazi or post-Holocaust era. The former marauders have become the fake philosemitic heralds of today, thanks to people like Barenboim and Levine, the children of the victims, and to the huge business enterprise of the 'redemption' Bayreuth Festival. The article also fails to mention my 20-year struggle to help further German-Jewish relations, as well as my co-founding of the Post-Holocaust Dialogue Group. I have dedicated my life to fighting the evil of the Wagner legacy, and in attempting to provide the public with a better understanding and reconciling the important issues that still pull us toward my great-grandfather's art...Neither these events, nor my father's continuous scheming over the 'royal' succession to the Bayreuth Festival, can hide one brutal truth: that a re-unified Germany has a responsibility to admit to its past, to face up to the important cultural role that the Wagner family played in the Nazi tyranny and to fight discrimination against those who, like me, are unwilling to engage in such a profitable music enterprise."

This letter was not published.

In January 1994, a slanderous article appeared in *Opera Now*. In connection with my father's 75th birthday, and as part of the promotions for his biography *Acts*, Robert Hartford wrote under the heading "House Of Cards":

"It is Bayreuth's heir apparent, Gottfried, who is making the most mischief. Gottfried has adopted a fashionable theme, his family's attitude towards Jews, and on the profitable principle of telling people what they want to hear he has been lecturing his way around America – and Israel, too, being the first Wagner to set foot there – denouncing Bayreuth as still in the thrall of Nazi ideals and antisemitism. He has made especially vicious attacks on conductors Levine and Barenboim, both Jews, alleging 'Uncle Tom' compliance in working at Bayreuth."

At the end of January 1994, I sent my reaction to *Opera Now*:

"Mr Hartford's comments on me and my work are wrong, slanderous and reflect his lack of knowledge concerning the subjects involved. Here are a few examples of false statements made about me:

1. The issue of Judaism and Wagner has been troubling me for more than 20 years, and I am a co-founder of the Post-Holocaust Dialogue Group. As such, this issue in effect

constitutes neither 'a fashionable theme' nor indeed 'a profitable principle'.

2. The author is not informed about the places at which I have spoken or will speak on these topics – this year, for example, at the United States Holocaust Memorial Museum and at Ben Gurion University. Are the distinguished institutions which invite me not able to select their speakers, or are they just inviting me so that I can tell them 'what they want to hear'?

3. I have never said that Bayreuth is 'still in the thrall of Nazi ideals and antisemitism'. My critique is on quite another level.

4. With regard to Messrs Levine and Barenboim, the author is apparently ignorant of my comments, for example in my letter to the editor of *Opera Monthly* (July 1993) and my interview in the August 1993 edition of *Musica* Nr 4 (Kassel). I am also not alone in my criticism of either Barenboim or Levine – for example, see Elie Wiesel's criticism of Barenboim in the *New York Times* (January 12 1992).

Finally, I will patiently repeat to journalists who are either unwilling or unable to understand me, again and again: I do not claim any aspirations to be my father's heir at the Bayreuth Festival."

My letter was printed in full in the March 1994 issue of *Opera Now*.

CHAPTER TWENTY-FIVE

EUGENIO

W hile I was preparing for my trip to Israel at the end of December 1989, Teresina, Mamma Antonietta and I saw the arrest and execution of the Romanian dictator Nicolae Ceausescu and his wife Elena on the television. The feature was followed by the first reports on the ill treatment of children in Romanian orphanages. We could scarcely believe that, after Hitler and Stalin, a European state could have committed such crimes for two decades – even Western and Eastern politicians and humanitarian organisations being aware of the situation – without provoking a storm of indignation.

Not until 1991, in child psychotherapist Alice Miller's book *Breaking Down The Wall Of Silence,* did I find an explanation of the reasons behind such a barbaric development. She writes: "Ceausescu's deeds and his political career were ruled by the idea of redemption through destruction. Without having had similar motivation in childhood, one will not become a dictator. Just like Hitler, Stalin and others before him, Ceausescu must constantly have heard that it was for his own good that he was being beaten, tortured, and spied on and his soul destroyed. As a child he could never have been able to see through the lie. These unexposed lies later become the fundamental principles of the tyrant." Miller writes further on how the child who has to believe these lies in order to survive but does not repudiate them in adulthood becomes himself a tyrant, assuming the beliefs that they learned from their dictatorial parents. What the Ceausescus did as "loving parents" to their people – who were living in indescribable hardship – is well known today. However, during his lifetime, Ceausescu expected grateful homage. In childhood, his parents had failed to meet his need for love and attention; he represented the pain of their neglect and abuse. As an adult, he was unable to relieve that repression in a normal adult way; instead he abused his nation of children in the "guise of national salvation".[41]

And so I found myself thinking of the children of Romania and wishing that I could save at least one of them from his abusive home.

In early January 1990, we read in the *Jerusalem Post* that, since the execution of the Ceausescus, it was possible to adopt children in Romania. After much discussion, Teresina and I decided to apply to adopt a child from Romania as soon as we got home in mid January. The bureaucratic procedures dragged on for months, but eventually we flew to Bucharest with the necessary documentation at the beginning of June 1990, just a few days before the miners' revolt.

The squalor of the people and the city took our breath away. The depression of the post-revolution days – which was unfortunately nothing but a *putsch* by Iliescu, Ceausescu's one-time vassal, and his thugs – also had its effect on us. Damp, stinking soot penetrated even the shops, where we couldn't even find mineral water or milk to buy. Hordes of neglected children ran after us, begging, as they had seen by our clothes that we came from the West.

We spent the first night in the Intercontinental Hotel, right on University Square, where the students were camping out in protest against Iliescu. We were constantly ripped off because we didn't speak the local language, and when the hotel tried to charge us higher prices than those quoted by the official travel agency we decided to move to a simpler, cheaper hotel on the street leading to the university. The first floor was a bordello for child prostitutes, and from our room we witnessed a group of Iliescu's thugs attacking former members of the secret service, the securitate. The police arrived too late to prevent a murder.

Finally, the day dawned. On 6 June we drove to Orphanage Four in the workers' district of Bucharest with the wily Romanian lawyer

George Alexandru, who had been procured for us by the Italian embassy. The Ceausescu regime had left total desolation there too. The orphanage was a prison, surrounded by high fences and barricades, and the dark and filthy interior of the concrete building stank of urine and ammonia. There was not a single picture hanging on the walls. No toys were to be seen, nor any children's voices heard.

The office of the director was equally cheerless. In her contempt for "her" orphans, she was typical of the still-omnipresent spirit of Ceausescu, and she made it clear to us that if we didn't want any problems in getting a child there would be "little extras" – cash and presents – to hurry her signature.

The door opened, and three children were introduced to us one after the other: Elena, then Christoph, and finally Eugenio. Eugenio was in a pitiful condition. He was emaciated and his belly was distended. His skin was pallid, raw and dirty. His pale blond hair was thin in patches and his teeth were coated with some black substance. His muscles were so underdeveloped that he had to keep sitting down out of exhaustion: he reminded me of Jackie Coogan in Chaplin's film *The Kid*. He wore only a pair of underpants, which were several sizes too large, and a shirt of some synthetic material which was full of holes. His shoes were enormous, so big in fact that he could not walk properly. But he gave me a faint smile when he saw me, which marked our first moments of being father and son.

The reality of the situation was brought back to us by the harsh voice of the director, who barked: "As you're already 43, you could have Eugenio. He's one of our oldest children."

We could only guess what the five-year-old Eugenio had had to endure. His mother had given him up immediately after birth. The Ceausescu state classified him as a delicate child, of "the second category". The more robust children, who were in the first category, were later destined to enter the service of the securitate, while the delicate children who did not appear up to this "heroic" task were shunted off to squalid orphanages. We yielded to the director's blackmailing only in order to liberate Eugenio from this hell-hole.

At that moment he noticed Teresina, who was sitting on a chair in the cramped room. They looked curiously at one another. Teresina gave him some chocolate – for him a really special present! With difficulty, he climbed on to Teresina's lap and smiled, tucking into what were probably the first sweets of his life.

After an odyssey through a Bucharest court, where we had to sign further adoption papers, we finally visited Eugenio two days later as his new parents. He had suspected that something was going on, because he called us both "Mama". (As he had been brought up only by women, he had no idea what a father was.) We gave him a little plastic truck, which he hugged, beaming, although at the same time we could see the fear that someone would take the toy away from him.

We took him for a brief excursion outside the orphanage. He had clearly never been out of the orphanage; everything was new for him. He reacted with a mixture of joy and fear on seeing chickens, buses, cranes and the crowds who scurried silently past us with impassive faces.

He trembled with fear the first time I tried to pick him up. I put him down again carefully. (He later told me that the nurses had only ever picked him up to carry him off to a dark room after a beating.)

We had to return him to the orphanage that June because the documentation was still incomplete, and we were naturally afraid we would never see him again. Iliescu's mob of miners were beginning to 'cleanse' the streets of students, and foreigners were unpopular, despite the wealth that they represented. At one point we were worried that we wouldn't make it to the airport, and we had to bribe a taxi driver to take us there.

It wasn't until 30 August 1990, my father's birthday, that Eugenio became our son by decree of a Bucharest court, which was also my father's birthday. He was baptised in December of the same year. In fact, I sent Father a photo of Eugenio, which was sent back without comment.

In September 1990, before our second trip to Romania, I interpreted the strange coincidence of significant dates in the lives of grandfather and grandchild as a turning point for a new chapter in my life. On the basis of my own childhood, I knew that I could never allow the memory of Ceausescu to become an all-powerful spectre in Eugenio's life, as the shadow of Hitler had been for me.

I will always remember the day that we collected Eugenio from the orphanage. He clutched our hands tightly and left without a word to anyone, without looking back once. Thanks to the wife of the Italian ambassador, Giovanna Amaduzzi, and their helpful colleagues, we were able to fly back to Rome immediately.

A new period began in our lives, to which we gradually began to accustom ourselves. Whenever Eugenio spoke of his past in the first year of our life together, he always started his story with "and then I flew home with Papa and Mama." It was difficult for him to find his own identity. In everything he did he lacked the life experiences of a child who had grown up under humane conditions. For the first five and a half years of his life he had had no family, and had never experienced any kind of love.

Child therapists such as Jean Piaget, Alice Miller, Hans Aebli, Ashley Montagu, Alfred Adler and David Kirk, whose works I had read before Eugenio's arrival, described fascinating theories and models, but in our everyday lives we soon realised just how difficult it is sometimes to realise good intentions. I had a lot to learn as a father, and it was not just to come from books.

Eugenio had not learned any language, and in fighting to survive in the orphanage he had assumed several antisocial habits. We were faced with the task of first teaching how to live in a family, and his new cousin Alberto helped him. The boys were the same age, and they grew up like brothers. We tried to teach Eugenio about good and evil and right and wrong, which also meant that we had to test our own standard of values.

It was particularly difficult to get Eugenio out of the habit of cringing obedience, which he had been broken into and which was now reinforced by his fear of being sent back to the orphanage. His servile eagerness to obey was replaced with the need to learn how to cope with freedom. For myself, I felt like I was walking a tightrope between liberating knowledge and bitter experiences from my own childhood.

Following my own experiences, I also wanted to avoid any repressive teaching methods. The risks of a misunderstanding and of over-reacting were always present for me, and I had constantly to remind myself that Eugenio was experiencing everything that had been missing from his early life, and this affected the way he played, the way he learned and his need for love. In this way, we were able to experience things we otherwise would not have done with another child.

I also read him bedtime stories. However, Eugenio was not interested in Grimm's fairy tales; instead he wanted me to tell him his own life story again and again, but only from the moment he had called us Papa and Mama, and each time he heard this wonderful "fairy tale", he wanted more details. He was probably satisfying his backlog need for warmth – although he got plenty of this in our house.

Eugenio's integration into the family took place with the high drama and shifting emotions that are only possible in Italy. I envy him that: I would also like to have grown up in a *famiglia Italiana*. In raising my son, however, a new process of integration also began for me. My thoughts, feelings and actions all evolved greatly. Eugenio confronted me with the very real responsibilities of planning for a common future. Much of my life that had once seemed important to me, including my Bayreuth past, was given a new perspective or simply lost all significance. Above all, I had to learn to be patient.

Outside the family, the path of Eugenio's integration didn't always run smoothly. After a positive start in the family and kindergarten, on starting school he suffered periods of isolation, caused by his former passivity and lack of motivation. In everything he did, he had to use all of his energies not only to absorb the new experiences with which he was bombarded in school every day but also to fill the gaps that had been left by his upbringing. As his teachers didn't know how to motivate him, his five years at primary school often proved an endurance test.

Neither the teachers nor the nuns and parents of the other children showed us much support, and rejected any deviation from the syllabus or discussions on more liberal methods of education. This was often the cue for hidden resentments to surface. For example, it was maintained that a "foreign intellectual" such as myself, with my family background, could never understand the people of Cerro Maggiore. Fortunately, my family didn't let this upset them.

However, this climate was hardly conducive for Eugenio's development, which could only really take place at home. He immediately understood my criticism of what was happening in the school, and would ask: "And what do you think of the story I heard today in school?" He also understood the somewhat alienated position in which we found ourselves, and whenever I disagreed with the teachers before going into the consultation room he would plead with me: "Please, Papa, *piano, piano!*" – he was obviously worried that I would tell the teachers too plainly what I thought of them. And, of course, he had every reason to fear this: I grew very annoyed when they kept trying to tell me my son was at the bottom of the class. "We'll see how Eugenio will turn out!" I would tell them. "My teachers always tried to convince me that I was untalented, too. Even today, Eugenio's horizons are extending beyond Cerro Maggiore." Teresina and I weren't prepared to take such nonsense from teachers we believed to be inadequate, and the paediatric neuropsychotherapist Anna Maria Carugo, who was a close friend of ours, arranged for us to visit one of the leading paediatric clinics in Milan. One of her colleagues ran a test, and the result was very reassuring and gave every cause for optimism.

As Eugenio became more integrated in our family, he articulated his interest in his own past and in my family more clearly. Even though we had expected the questions with which he confronted us, we were still moved when they came. He gradually understood that he had had no family life before we adopted him. We could only soften the pain he felt on realising that he had lost an essential part of his childhood by pointing out that he was, after all, now living in our family. Although he showed amazing understanding, it's clear exactly how much he needs me and how much I still have to learn to be a steady and balanced father.

One day, as we were visiting Papa Antonio's grave, he asked where his other grandfather was buried.

"Grandfather Wolfgang isn't dead. He's living in Germany," I replied.

He wanted to know why this grandfather didn't come and visit us. I became nervous: I didn't want to paint a gloomy picture of my father the first time we discussed him, so I said: "Grandfather doesn't view things the way we do. His theatre, his friends and his new family keep him very busy, so he hasn't any time left for us."

Eugenio didn't say any more, and then disappeared up to his room for some time. When he came down, he declared angrily: "If Grandfather Wolfgang doesn't have any time for us, then I don't want to see him, his theatre or his new family either!"

His reaction moved me deeply. I picked him up and said: "Who knows? Maybe Grandfather will talk to us one day." He didn't believe me.

On that October evening my work on this book faltered, and I felt like giving up. That evening I wrote to Ralph Giordano:

"I ask myself more and more often for whom I am actually writing my obituary – this book – in my isolation in Italy, which prevents me from living. In one respect you have perhaps deluded yourself: that I could write my book as well as doing other things. I find working on it such a strain that I have little energy left for anything else. I have severely overestimated my strength for this constant breaching of inner walls...I stare into the past of a family that was never mine, and to my horror this isolates my own loving family from the present too often, and I see no opportunity to build up a future for myself that corresponds to my needs...It all seems more and more uncertain, and I'm finding myself increasingly isolated. For a long time my concern has been not for myself but for the future of my son, whom I would like at least to ensure an education. For his sake I shall continue to hold on. On him I project my hopes for a better tomorrow, and he will always be confident of my love."

Ralph faxed me immediately:

"I have been aware of your growing despair...You are right to 'take stock'. You are running up against brick walls and only injuring yourself in doing so – that is one thing. The other is your social and financial situation, and that is depressing enough. The worst thing is that your gifts are lying fallow, as it were – there is apparently no demand for what you are, do and want here in Germany. You yourself have already distanced yourself very much from it, and I don't know whether you would be up to the constant guerrilla warfare you would have to wage here. I've been born into it, so to speak, and so I'm used to these conflicts with the outrageous, albeit only up to a certain point. I also sometimes think about running away to a different, less problematic place, to find a job that I enjoy, but at the same time I know that I am attached to this country, and will never escape from it. The same holds true for you: even if you aren't actually living in Germany, nevertheless the whole weight of it is squatting on top of you, as it were. And that isn't going to change...

"I, too, was only able to stop the wheel of fate at 41, so I lived long enough on the outskirts. And yet without that time, nothing would have turned out well afterwards. Life's like that – it's the hardships that form us, not the strokes of good luck. Of course, that doesn't mean you have to be mired in difficulties all the time, but it does mean drawing useful lessons from it in overcoming it. Don't see things as too black or too rosy, but try and remember that your book could really achieve something. Keep at it, and you may achieve something real and purposeful at a crucial stage in your life. I know how difficult it is when you're oppressed and harassed by so many other things, but I also know how a degree of fatalism can save one...Once you've finished it, you'll be a different person, the *status quo ante* will be biography, life story, and you will continue to hang onto the threads of that, but in a new stage...To try is the essence of life – if you know why you tried. All of these things apply to you and your capabilities. You can do it. Don't give up. Fight! Use the time, for Eugenio's sake, and also for your own."

His words – the final sentences, in particular – strengthened my conviction that we can learn from our mistakes and the criticism of our faults, and in particular (as Karl Popper says) through the criticism of others and ultimately ourselves.

I thought of the grandfatherly letter Ralph Giordano had written to Eugenio on his eighth birthday, on 30 April 1993:

"I wish you all the best for your birthday today – presents and a lot of happiness, the greatest and most precious of which is, as I know very well, the love of your mother and your father...Their greatest happiness is to know that you love them with your whole heart...While I'm sitting here in my home in Cologne and writing to you for your birthday, I look over my shoulder and what do you think I see? You! On lots of photos that all have a place of honour and that I look at several times every day. I can see Eugenio laughing, I can see Eugenio alone, but then together with his father and mother, and all three of you are a wonderful sight! And that is the way it should continue to be."

A happy family has to be constantly worked at, as Eugenio and I both know: for us there is no other way but that of dialogue.

CHAPTER TWENTY-SIX

ON TOUR WITH RICHARD WAGNER'S ANTISEMITISM

The trip to Israel had a marked influence on my work, which is evident in the lecture subjects and articles I have written since 1990. Essentially, the themes were: "As A Wagner In Israel", "The Case Of Wagner In Israel And Germany", "Richard Wagner's Antisemitism: Contradictions And Consequences For German Politics And Culture" and "Wagner And Antifeminism". They are all closely interconnected, and document a constant process which is both complex and almost exhaustive development. These basic themes formed the basis of lectures about the way Wagner is received in and around Bayreuth. Complementary to these were the themes "Does Wagner's *Gesamtkunstwerk* [total art work] Idea Still Have A Future?", "Lamas And Kundry's Images Of Genius – Notes On Elisabeth Förster-Nietzsche's And Cosima Wagner's Falsifications And Their Consequences Up To The Present Time", "Toscanini, Wagner And Hitler", "Redemption For The Redeemer – Thoughts On Wagner's *Parsifal*" and "Wagner's Bayreuth – Bayreuth's Liszt: Art As Ideology And Liberation", as well as theories I had formulated on Wagner's *Lohengrin* during my production of that opera in Dessau.

The other main subjects – although still closely connected – form quite a contrast: my contributions on the subject of Kurt Weill and Viktor Ullmann, who was murdered in Auschwitz in October 1944 and whose epoch-making compositions I have been intensively researching since 1990.

In my lecture at the 1995 Bruckner Festival, entitled "The Destruction Of Creativity In The Arts: Conformist Music – Nazi Ideology And Music As Political Propaganda", I pointed out in particular the historical connection between Wagner's antisemitic writings, Hitler's racist lunacy, and culture, right up to Joseph Goebbels' guidelines on music.

Purely 'aesthetic' subjects, with psychological aspects such as lectures on Mozart and on Goethe's *Faust* as represented in compositions by Liszt, Schumann and Wagner, served to keep me financially buoyant and enabled me to study those subjects in which I was really interested. Central to my interests was the tension that existed between Wagner and Weill and Ullmann. For me it meant finally exposing the 2,000-year-old conflict between Judaism and Christianity and the Bayreuth temple cult as an expression of a mania of Romantico-religious redemption (according to Wagner), and with all its consequences leading up to Auschwitz. I increasingly understood the whole development to be the consequence of a perverted Christian antisemitism, which had culminated with Wagner in Bayreuth.

The Austrian Catholic historian Friedrich Heer opened my eyes to this painful knowledge. Reading his words helped me to come to terms with the antisemitic past of my family. In his book *God's First Love: Christians And Jews Over 2,000 Years*, Heer proves fascinatingly that "the concepts of hating and killing Jews were based on Christian theology, taught by the most eminent fathers of the Church".[42] He comes to the conclusion that "Auschwitz and Hiroshima are based on a 1,000-year-old theological tradition".[43]

The more knowledge I gained through ever more enthusiastic historical study, and in discussions on human experiences, the more I distanced myself from the false Christian traditions of my family in Bayreuth, traditions which had lost all credibility after the Holocaust.

The break also prompted me to search for new ethical guidelines. Any form of religion claiming sole powers of redemption, any fundamentalist ideology, became intolerable to me. My question is, based on my knowledge and experience, how can I achieve universal understanding with other ways of thinking, feeling and acting that are alien to me? I agree with Popper, in that it is through the pursuit of knowledge that mankind liberates itself. My view of the world broadened, and I accepted that there are many paths to paradise on Earth and in heaven. They should, however, be based on active sympathy with all those deprived of their rights, irrespective of sex, nation, colour of skin or belief. The word 'race' disappeared from my thinking forever. In Heer's words:

> "Christianity today is rather like a tree, or a forest if you will, on a mountaintop, uprooted by a storm…The reason for this alarming fact is that Christianity is not rooted in the soil from which it stems – from Jewish piety, the Jewish fear of God, love of humanity, love of earthly pleasures, joy in the present and hope for the future…A true renaissance, a rebirth of Jewish piety, could possibly depend on whether the synagogue would assume the role of mother in the Mother Church and elder sister of the younger daughter churches. The return of Jesus the Jew to the community of His brothers, who have borne His cross as crusaders from the fourth century to the 20th century, could be an event of extraordinary and vital importance."[44]

I found new ethical impulses in my studies into Reform Judaism, which interestingly enough arose in Germany, in the wisdom of the Psalms, out of Jewish historical experience and deep piety. For example, Psalm 142 of the Jewish Bible, an instruction from David, when he was in the cave:

> "I cried unto the Lord with my voice; with my voice unto the Lord did I make my supplication. I poured out my complaint before him; I shewed before him my trouble. When my spirit was overwhelmed within me, then thou knewest my path. In the way wherein I walked have they privily laid a snare for me. I looked on my right hand, and beheld, but there was no man that would know me; refuge failed me; no man cared for my soul. I cried unto thee, O Lord: I said, Thou art my refuge and my portion in the land of the living. Attend unto my cry; for I am brought very low: deliver me from my persecutors; for they are stronger than I. Bring my soul out of prison, that I may praise

thy name: the righteous shall compass me about; for thou shalt deal bountifully with me."[45]

Belief in God also contains disbelief. This is expressed, for example, in a passage from Psalm 139, in the Jewish version:

"Surely the darkness shall cover me; even the night shall be light about me. Yea, the darkness hideth not from thee; but the night shineth as the day...How precious also are thy thoughts unto me, O God! How great is the sum of them! If I should count them, they are more in number than the sand: when I awake, I am still with thee."[46]

The poem 'Prayer', written by Ilse Blumenthal-Weiss in 1945 after her time in the concentration camps at Westerbork and Theresienstadt, is inconceivable without Jewish piety. It summarises my thinking.

I cannot hate.
They strike me. They kick me with their feet.
I cannot hate. I can but pray
For you and me.
I cannot hate.
They throttle me. They pelt me with stones.
I cannot hate. I can but weep.
Bitterly.[47]

Ilse Weiss' husband and son were both murdered in Nazi concentration camps.

My quarrel with Christian antisemitism is also with Richard Wagner and his descendants. A letter from Marcel Silberstein of Basle, who wrote to my host, Shai Burstyn, at the Tel Aviv University in mid January 1990, only a few days after my lecture tour in Israel, sparked further investigation into the subject. He wrote: "Wagner's antisemitism can be segregated neither from his general personality nor from his music." He added this statement to Hartmut Zelinsky's 1978 article in *Musik-Konzepten*, "Richard Wagner's 'Ordeal By Fire', Or The New Religion Of Redemption By Annihilation". In 1990 I couldn't, and indeed wouldn't, believe Zelinsky's assertion that Wagner was partly responsible for the rise of Hitler and National Socialism in Germany. Today, I can only interpret my hesitation – and the unease that Zelinsky provoked in me with his revolutionary thesis, first formulated in 1975 – after years of grappling with the subject. It was fear of an irrevocable break with my own family – with my father, above all – but fear too of the end of a childhood nightmare: to go back to Bayreuth and take part in a critical appraisal of Wagner there. Fear, as well, of a losing of my identity, and fear of the international opera business, and the Bayreuth connections on which my career as an opera director would be continually dependent.

By 1992, after performing lengthy investigations into the connection between Bayreuth and Auschwitz, I became painfully aware that there was no way past Zelinsky's findings. Even so, I don't share his philosophical understanding of the historical link between Hegel and the politico-cultural phenomenon of Richard Wagner. Wagner's theories had no solid philosophical basis, and as such he was a dangerous, self-appointed armchair philosopher.

Apart from this, Zelinsky's work represents a turning point in international research on the subject of Wagner; his pioneering work is the courageous act of an ostracised loner, and he has my sympathy and respect. As he writes: "Present-day Wagner admirers deceive themselves on Wagner's antisemitism – either they ignore it totally, in order not to sully their image of the genius...or they treat it as a sort of whim of genius, which is rather embarrassing and curious, but certainly shouldn't be taken seriously."[48]

In recent years, the self-deception exercised by most Wagnerians has been repeatedly confirmed. However, since the publication of Zelinsky's article in 1978, Ulrich Drüner's doctoral thesis 'Richard Wagner's Artistic Creation Between Ideology And Myth', Paul Lawrence Rose's painstaking historical study *Race And Revolution* (1992) and above all Marc Weiner's inter-disciplinary standard work *Richard Wagner And The Antisemitic Imagination* (1995), a slow change has come about in a few Wagnerians and most of those who are critically interested in the man. The subject is being taken increasingly seriously, as Weiner provides a detailed illustration of the close connection between the composer's biography, theoretical writings and stage works by thoroughly analysing the music scores. As an essential part of the politico-cultural phenomenon of Wagner, the antisemitic writings cannot and should not be overlooked any longer.

My personal view, from experience and knowledge of the causes of the conflict, can be summed up thus: Wagner's concept of a festival and its realisation in Bayreuth signifies humanity's departure from reality. In this sense, as the composer's great-grandson I have become an anti-Wagnerian. As a descendant of Wagner, I found it difficult to present my knowledge on him objectively. At the beginning of my lectures I described my situation to my audiences. The following introduction to one of my lectures, which isn't particularly academic, reflects this:

"Anyone addressing Richard Wagner's antisemitism finds himself confronted by complex problems. It requires broad inter-disciplinary knowledge and a passion for individual responsibility, which must be put to the test in the selection and presentation of documents. It's also important to look into the researcher's personal motives in dealing with the subject, as here one is touching on deep layers of human experience and suffering."

About myself as a speaker:

"I am aware that I am speaking to you as a great-grandson of Richard Wagner, who was Hitler's cultural model. So I am speaking here not merely as a music historian. Richard Wagner's antisemitic writings cast a great shadow over my life. The subject contains fundamental questions such as repression, a reluctance to talk, denial and the falsification of the links between German culture and politics, in which Richard Wagner plays a decisive and inglorious role. Whether I like it or not, the subject is part of my existence. It is linked to something I consider typical of the German mentality: the separation of the private and the public sphere in the discussion and translation of fundamental ethical positions. I refuse to condone such separation, and consider it dangerous on the basis of historical evidence, and as a Wagner after the Holocaust. We are dealing here with humanitarian values and individual responsibility. Anyone demanding open, unbiased discussion on this theme, and humane dealings with those with a different opinion, will not only run up against resistance and rejection; he will also find himself exposed to slander, existential problems and threats, which are a mask for all kinds of intolerance."

My practise of projecting texts, showing films and weaving in musical examples in the lectures was also unacademic. Often the lectures were followed by lively and fascinating debate, but sometimes too by an icy silence.

Between 1990 and 1995 I toured as the anti-Wagnerian great-grandson of Wagner, giving lectures in Germany, Switzerland, Austria, England, Italy, America and Canada. I found that audiences were polarised by critiques which required critical comment from the listeners on basic ethical questions concerning art and politics. Their reactions were quite varied: they were either polarised, quietly, indirectly or in open criticism of Richard Wagner, or of my interpretation of his work and personality. Many were disturbed in particular by the fact that I, as a descendant of Wagner, was so critical of him.

Of course, the reactions of my audiences were influenced by their national, historical, political and cultural backgrounds and personal histories, as well as their religions (whether they were mainly Jewish, Christian or a mixture of faiths), their age ranges, and whether they were experts on opera or just fans. From the broad sweep of reactions, I learned to be wary of crude generalisations, and I slowly began to adjust for each particular audience. But one thing didn't change: a descendant of Wagner talking critically about him can always expect surprises.

Sometimes the reaction was extremely emotional, because of the Nazi past: repression, denial, silence, falsification. Wagner, his antisemitism and my family's Nazi involvement in Bayreuth clearly illustrates that each individual bears personal responsibility. Anyone talking about Wagner and the Germans has to question the self-confidence of many Germans.

Some Wagnerians, who only endured my criticism because I am a great-grandson, often retreated into personal anecdotes and experiences of Wagner and the *Festspielhügel*. In this way they didn't have to question their view of the composer. Instead they behaved like missionaries, trying to bring me onto the right path for the Bayreuth case. I always tried to stay polite, and didn't see much point in discussing the matter. However, a few German anti-Wagnerians behaved quite differently towards me. Despite their ideological aversion, they were interested in the composer and seemed surprised to meet an atypical Wagner. Consequently we had some very intense and stimulating conversations.

In the middle of December 1992, I received an invitation to give a lecture on "Wagner's Antisemitism: Contradictions And Consequences For German Politics And Culture" at the German Congress Of Industry And Commerce. There were political motives for this: Germany's international reputation had plummeted that year because of the crimes committed by neo-Nazis (the arson attack in Solingen, for example), and leaders in business, politics and culture wanted to create a liberal image. A critical Wagner who spoke against his great-grandfather's racism, presented by Ralph Giordano – one of the most important German-Jewish voices – seemed to fit the bill perfectly.

Before the lecture, the audience was confronted with pictures from my travelling exhibition *From Bayreuth To Theresienstadt-Terzin*, shown to the sounds of the music of Viktor Ullmann. This was followed by a visual analysis of a colour slide of Arno Breker's bust of Wagner in Bayreuth, accompanied by 'Ride Of The Valkyries'. Before introducing me, Ralph Giordano gave his opinion on Bayreuth and the connections of the *Festspielhügel* and the negative influence they had on my work. The lecture mainly concentrated on Wagner's antisemitism.

The reaction was one of discomfort, smattered with a few polite (but certainly not unfamiliar) objections. As usual, people congratulated me in private and promised to support me indirectly, because – as I was told many times that evening – one must take into account the sponsors: Bayreuth, Father, Barenboim and Levine. The press reacted well to the lecture, although in a garbled manner. Here, again, there was still no clear statement concerning my criticism of New Bayreuth.

It became clearer to me that talking about Wagner meant ending any meaningful professional future in Germany. When I mentioned this to Ralph Giordano, he said: "Criticism of German politics and culture can only be expressed in Germany, and in the case of Wagner only by a Jew. As an oppositional Wagner you have no chance here at the moment, but I hope that one day that will change."

"Just like German antisemitic philosemitism, like in Bayreuth?" I asked him.

He nodded.

To my surprise, an ongoing interest in my work has developed in Austria since 1989. Since 1992 I have also regularly given interviews on Austrian television. My friendship with Gaby Flossmann, who has worked for the cultural division of ORF 2 since 1968, has had a common theme: the plight of German-speaking Jews and coming to terms with the consequences of National Socialism in Germany and Austria. Wherever she has been able, she has managed to report in detail on essential stages of my work around the world, and that is by no means always easy with my field of study.

When I went to Vienna, I met the sociologist Michael Ley and his wife, the painter Charlotte Ley-Kohn, with whom I not only discussed the drastic effects the Holocaust had on the next generations of German, Austrian and Jewish people, but also carried out projects, such as the filming of my production of *Lohengrin* in Dessau, as part of the documentary film *Herr Hitler's Religion*, directed by Petrus van der Let.

In marked contrast to my experiences in Germany, in Austria the themes of my work are always received enthusiastically. In Vienna, and again at the Bruckner Festival in Linz in 1995, when I delivered by lecture on "Music And Nazi Ideology", I could be unrestrained in talking about Hitler, Vienna and the Austrian Nazis. Indeed, I encountered the special way in which they dealt with their own 1,000-year-old history: the insults – the derisive use of double-edged flattery – were always shot through with a caustic black humour and self-mockery, which is something of which most Germans aren't capable. This attitude is particularly prominent in Austrian Jewish culture. Looking back, I can see why I wrote my doctoral thesis on Weill and Brecht in Vienna rather than Berlin. Because of the mordbid humour of the two iconoclasts of the last days of the Weimar Republic, before the twilight of Hitler's master race (which can be directly compared with the aimlessness in the period after the fall of communism at the end of the 1980s) I prefer Vienna to Berlin even today.

So what do the Swiss – the Zurichers in particular – have to do with the antisemitism of Wagner, whom in 1849 they kindly granted nine years of asylum? It reminds me of Mathilde Wesendonck, and her immortalisation in *Tristan Und Isolde*. The Swiss? Antisemitic? Yes, here too there have been painful events that people don't like to discuss, particularly the Nazi period, when Switzerland turned away Jews fleeing from Germany and money stolen from them disappeared into their bank accounts. However, one should guard against prejudice.

In Switzerland people are prepared to come to terms with the dark chapters of European history, as well as their own pasts. This was demonstrated in October 1992, when my patron and friend Albi Rosenthal, the legendary musical antiques collector and patron of the arts, and Walburga Sia Strecker, daughter of the founder of the Nietzsche Colloquium in Sils-Maria in Switzerland, invited me to speak about Cosima Wagner's and Elisabeth Förster-Nietzsche's distortions of history. My talk was not only aimed at Cosima's and Elisabeth's falsifications (who at that time were still alive) but also at the fallacies perpetrated by Wagner's autobiography, and I pointed out the way in which my family had abused the history right up until today. Richard, Cosima, Winifred, Wieland and Wolfgang – they all used history in the interests of their political and economic aims. Elisabeth Förster-Nietzsche behaved similarly with the Weimar Archive.

After the lecture, several German academics in the audience remained awkwardly silent, but the Swiss philosopher André Bloch, organiser of the Nietzsche Colloquium, presented me with a key to the Nietzsche House in Sils-Maria as a token of his appreciation. "No one is ever forbidden to enter the house here. You're always very welcome," he said.

I was equally well received in Zurich in November 1993. At the Paulus Academy, as in Sils-Maria, I spoke to a group of Swiss who had great sensitivity to the historical study of Wagner and antisemitism. Right next to the lectern on a stage was a piece by the artist Thea Weltner entitled 'Children's Shoes And Breadbins', which served as a reminder of the murdered children of Theresienstadt. The *Israelitisches Wochenblatt* and the *Neue Zürcher Zeitung* reported the event objectively.

An orthodox Jew invited me to his home after the lecture, where we discussed my ideas on directing *Lohengrin*. He regarded Lohengrin as a Messianic figure, and showed me a painting of a tree in the desert with a church tower driven into its trunk, representing Judeo-Christian cultural history, with its dark shadows. This picture, coupled with the mysterious discussion, later inspired the visual concept of my production of the opera in Dessau: two pillars of a cathedral set on two tree trunks.

In Italy there is scarcely any discussion on Wagner and Judaism, and people in the country of the Vatican have shown only detached interest in my lectures, whether they touch directly or indirectly on the subject. Their confusion over Wagner has been fuelled by the influence of Bayreuth and inaccurate translations, and not much is likely to change this. Media reports are restricted to the occasional account of bomb attacks and violence in Israel, which don't help in promoting discussion about antisemitism. It's therefore little wonder that I have often had to pack my suitcases and leave in order to exercise my task, as an historian with the wrong subject, elsewhere in the world.

I still wonder at how unconcerned people are in Italy about coming to terms with their own antisemitism. It wasn't until 1994 that the subject became the focus for a discussion within the framework of a travelling exhibition, *The Lie Of Race*. The Catholic Church has been one of the most important bulwarks of European antisemitism since the fourth century, and during and after Mussolini its role was hardly commendable. It was 43 years before the Vatican granted Israel diplomatic recognition in 1993. Sadly, I never come across this in my son's history books.

On my many visits to North America I always encounter great public interest in my studies. Anyone who has ever lived there knows that the cohabitation of many ethnic groups from all over the world is based on the principle of diversity, while at the same time recognising equal rights for all. In spite of the criticism levelled at it, I consider the American model to be capable of development and improvement. There is still something of the pioneering spirit evident in the country – of curiosity, spontaneity and unaffectedness – and something of this was also expressed at my lectures and in discussions afterwards.

The quality and quantity of research regarding my subjects are particularly impressive: after Zelinsky and Drüner, all of the important work comes from the USA, and the works of Paul Lawrence Rose of Pennsylvania State University and Marc Weiner of Indiana University outshine anything that has been published on the subject in Europe. Also, in many colleges and universities the liberal spirit prevails in the sense.

Diversity and the integration of Jewish groups into the respective institutions – or at least the recognition of German-Jewish history as a subject – is instrumental in the acceptance of problematic subjects. By extending invitations to me, it was evident that North American German communities were still influential. Because of its Nazi past, Germany itself has aroused interest; people like hearing the rebelling clan member, not least because it reminds them of TV series like *Dallas* and *Dynasty*. A lot was expected of me, precisely because of my family background, and my performance was fundamental to the way in which my lectures were received, which was fair enough. I always look forward to going to America, just as I do to visiting Israel, my elective home, and returning to Italy.

I also feel at home at the George Washington University. The director of the musicology department, Professor Roy Guenther, whom I rate highly both as a colleague and a private individual, embodies the archetype of the liberal American. The fact that my lectures on "Wagner – Nietzsche", "Weill" and "Wagner In Israel And Germany" took place in the capital of the United States had many positive repercussions. I also appeared in a number of universities in Canada and the USA, and I still enjoy exchanging opinions with many academics I have met on my lecture tours.

The local Goethe Institute and American branches of German firms have also supported me in many cities. Two Jewish cultural institutions in the USA – the Hebrew Union College in Cincinnati and the United States Holocaust Memorial Museum, based in Washington DC – played a major role in my trip to Israel and my dispute with Wagner's antisemitism. In February 1992, when I spoke on "The Case Of Wagner In Israel" in the Mayerson Hall of the Hebrew Union College, a world-renowned Jewish theological institute, I knew that there had been resistance to inviting me. Thankfully, this was discreetly overcome with the help of Abraham Peck, lecturer in modern German history and Judaism, who is administration and programming director of the American Jewish Archive in Cincinnati and author of numerous articles on 19th- and 20th-century German-Jewish history. Cincinnati is not only twinned with Munich, with a populace of largely German extraction, but it also has a significant Jewish community. The city is inhabited by German and Austrian Holocaust survivors, who know the history of the Wagner family very well.

After the lecture, these people – who were particularly affected by Nazism – talked with me openly, and even warmly. The director of the Hebrew Union College, Alfred Gottschalk, was among them, and he said that he had no further objections to future collaboration.

Afterwards, James Levine's mother was introduced to me as a member of this group. To my surprise, she asked me if I thought it right that her son was conducting in Bayreuth. "Only your son can answer that question," I replied.

I was also invited to lecture at the the United States Holocaust Memorial Museum in Washington in March 1994. They were already familiar with my work before they had contacted me in autumn 1993, particularly a long article which had appeared in the *Washington Post* at the end of April 1993. This interview – by Judith Weinraub, who had researched her subject thoroughly from November 1992 to April 1993 – I believe to be one of the fairest accounts of my story.

The lecture evening itself further demonstrated the spirit of mutual trust and interest. The hall was well filled, despite the raging blizzard outside, and the discussion was of a high calibre, not least due to the presence of Paul Lawrence Rose, investigator of Wagner antisemitism. Here, as in other Jewish institutions in North America, I found sympathy and a desire for continuing dialogue, which actually gave me the energy to continue my work in Germany.

CHAPTER TWENTY-SEVEN

THE POST-HOLOCAUST DIALOGUE GROUP: AND IN THE BEGINNING WAS AUSCHWITZ

During my trip to Israel, I also founded the Post-Holocaust Dialogue Group. Franklin Littell had heard of my Wagner lectures in Tel Aviv through the media, and in the summer of 1990 he invited me to the 21st annual congress of his organisation, The Holocaust And The Churches, in Stockton College, New Jersey, which was to take place in March 1991. He asked me to speak on my experiences in Israel, on the story of the Wagner family and on German history in relation to Wagner as a politico-cultural phenomenon.

I was vaguely aware of the provocative nature of the other guest speakers and the organisation, having learned a little about it since the end of the Sixties from descriptions of friends and acquaintances and reading about the Holocaust. Until my trip to Israel, however, I had met no experts on the subject.

I began to understand the intellectual ambience of the meeting from the opening session on 3 March 1991. The open-mindedness of the organisers was evident in their choosing the Afro-American Christian Hubert Locke, professor of political science and sociology, as vice-president. But Locke by no means suppressed the problems of his own group. He is the author of numerous works, such as *The Detroit Riot Of 1967* (1969) and

The Care And Feeding Of White Liberals (1970). When I asked him why he, an Afro-American, had been elected vice-president of the organisation, he answered: "The Holocaust is the culmination of experience with totalitarian systems, which can always be repeated if we don't watch out. As such it is independent of categories such as skin colour, nation, religion and ideology."

At this first meeting in 1991 I took part in as many seminars as I could, and my own lecture was received with great interest. I had an unforgettable encounter with the respected liberal senator Paul Simon, who had been one of the most promising Democrat presidential candidates under Richard Nixon. We were introduced after his impressive opening speech on contemporary human rights, which he illustrated with references to the American educational system. He shook my hand warmly, and said: "Hey, Gottfried, I have a photo of you at home that I took in Wahnfried Park in 1951, when I was an officer in the US Army. I lived in the Siegfried Wagner House for a few weeks as a kid, and you were always hanging around. But how come you're talking here about your lecture tour on Wagner in Israel, with your family history?"

"I think it's high time we talked about the effects of the Nazi period in Bayreuth after 1945," I answered.

We subsequently continued our frank discussion, corresponding by letter.

In those three days in March, I met a lot of people with whom I either became friends or have since occasionally exchanged opinions. I became friends immediately with Franklin Littell, his wife, the historian Marcia Littell-Sachs, and the host and organiser of the event, Jan G Colijn, who is also Director of General Studies at Stockton College, and Henry Knight, Professor of Religion at Tulsa University. They introduced me into the various groups and to two participants who interested me in particular, and welcomed me warmly. One of these was Abraham Peck, and the other was the Reform rabbi Steven Jacobs, from Huntsville, Alabama, who has published a considerable number of quite revolutionary works on Jewish faith and history, most notably his book *Rethinking Jewish Faith After The Holocaust* (1992). Both men are sons of Holocaust survivors.

After Israel, my lecture on the evening of 4 March, to a capacity audience, was another baptism by fire. Later, Abraham and Steven approached me and we talked until early in the morning. We decided to organise ourselves, as children of both Nazi victims and Nazi criminals. What unites us even now is summarised in the six points of the Post-Holocaust Dialogue Group's statutes. We took as our slogan the words of the Jewish judge and Holocaust survivor Samuel Gringauz, who in 1947 said: "Our tragedy must become the starting point of a new humanity."

We presented our programme at the 23rd scientific congress of The Holocaust And The Churches in Tulsa, in March 1993. Another board member, the composer Michael Shapiro, then prepared it for future official registration as a non-profit-making organisation. The text of the statutes reads:

1. We, the children of the victims and the children of the victimisers, see the Shoah/Holocaust as a unique rift in Western and world civilisation, and the starting point of a new morality in terms of thoughts, feelings and actions.
2. We stand opposed to the repressing and silencing of any and all discussion of the Shoah/Holocaust and the continuation of any and all prejudices and hatreds resulting from the activities of our parents and grandparents both now and in the future and directly attributable to the trauma of the Shoah/Holocaust.
3. We fully believe that the sharing of our own unique burden of this tragic past in a continuing present and future dialogue is of vital concern, independently of any religious, ideological, and/or political group. With our dialogue we give concrete evidence how our generation, and those after us, will confront the challenges presented by the Shoah/Holocaust and its ever-present influences.
4. We begin our dialogue with tolerance, respect and self-

critical awareness as the children of the victims and the children of the victimisers. Our mutual willingness to share our burden is coupled with our unhesitating commitment to overcome our present ignorance, prejudices, and misconceptions, and to present to those who are open and receptive a model for present and future trust and understanding.

5. We see ourselves as an international activist organisation whose avowed purpose is not only to inform others of the Shoah/Holocaust through scholarly conferences and publications, but to fight both theoretically and practically against any kind of totalitarian dogmatism religiously, politically, and ideologically. We stand for the adoption of human rights for all human beings, fully believing that we are responsible for our own actions, ever mindful of the "different other".

6. We hope by our humanitarian actions and our scholarly work to influence governments and nation states, thus lessening fear of present or future repetitions of the Shoah/Holocaust, striving at all times to realise our goal of a world living together in peaceful tolerance and appreciative of all diverse humanity.

After establishing the group in Seattle in March 1992, we not only held annual meetings, with the aid of Franklin Littell's organisation, but also conventions with other internationally-recognised organisations: Remembering For The Future, Christianity And The Holocaust, National Workshop On Christian-Jewish Relations, The Evangelical Academy near Frankfurt Am Main and the international institute Au Coeur De La Communication (ACC). The international media (except that in Germany) has also shown great interest in recent years. Unfortunately, the percentage of Germans of my generation in our group is still much smaller than that of Jewish members, but we are growing and we now have members from three continents.

One of the reasons for its international appeal is the fact that we have developed mutual appreciation of the different

1953: Gottfried posing with papier-mâché swan, a prop used in his father's debut production, *Lohengrin*

Gottfried with his father and sister Eva. Gottfried deduced as a young child that a show of admiration for all things Wagnerian could render him acceptable to Wolfgang and by this means he would avoid being sent to children's homes whenever the festival organisation loomed. His older sister Eva lacked her brother's rebellious nature, although she too was sent away

Gottfried aged four with his black Scottish terrier, Pupsi. Taken in the grounds of Villa Wahnfried in 1953

Gottfried, aged nine, 1956: the year he was confronted with a documentary on Nazi Germany and his family's past

Gottfried (left) and Wolf-Siegfried (Wieland's son, nicknamed Wummi) with Hera, their Newfoundland puppy, at the main entrance of Villa Wahnfried in 1953. Although reality was to prove quite different, this fourth generation of Wagners was intended as *Festspiele* directors of the future

Villa Wahnfried, badly damaged by the RAF in April 1945. On the right is Siegfried Wagner House, where Hitler lived in the 1930s. From 1947 onwards it was used as a base for US counter espionage

1952. Herbert von Karajan (centre) twice became a member of the Nazi Party in Germany and Austria, then later created the Salzburg Festival, producing and conducting special performances of Richard Wagner's operas

Friedelind, Winifred and Verena in 1954, the year Friedelind returned to the *Festspiele* for the first time after her escape from Nazi Germany

Wolfgang (right) with Wilhelm Furtwängler (centre) in 1951

Ellen and Wolfgang after the *Lohengrin* premiere in 1953

Eva and
Gottfried
amongst their
mother's
friends, 1955

Wolfgang and Ellen at a Society Of Friends Of Bayreuth dinner in 1956 (Wieland standing). So wide
was the gulf between the brothers that they wouldn't share the same dinner table after productions

Wieland and Winifred
in the early 1960s

Winifred and Wolfgang at the stage entrance of the *Festspielhaus*, 1957. They were always in agreement on essential business decisions, usually against Wieland

Ellen and Wolfgang, 1957

Gottfried with Lotte Lenya, 1978: Gottfried was contacted by Lenya to work on the Kurt Weill archives, Weill having been the subject of his doctoral thesis

During a rehearsal of *Arlecchino* by F Busoni with the ensemble of the Trier Theatre in 1978

Gottfried next to Ralph Giordano and Hanna Jordan, a famous German-Jewish set designer who lost part of her family in Theresienstadt

Gottfried and his wife Teresina in front of the oldest synagogue in the world, in Massada, 1990. The invitation to lecture at Tel Aviv University was a turning point in his life

With Herzl Shmueli, the well-known
Israeli musicologist and Gottfried's
host at Tel Aviv University. Taken in
August 1992, Zürich

Abraham Peck, the Post Holocaust Dialogue Group
co-founder, with Gottfried in March 1994, Berlin

Gottfried in July 1996, photographed by Riccardo Bremer

Gottfried's farewell to Bayreuth and its Wagner cult on 29 July 1997 with his son Eugenio, wife Teresina and his nephew Alberto, following a passionate debate after publication of the German edition of *He Who Does Not Howl With The Wolf*. The reaction it caused surprised even Gottfried. Photograph by Fabio Tosca

Eberhard Wagner

Gottfried in 1997, photographed by Riccardo Bremer

Gottfried with Teresina, Eugenio and mother-in-law Antonietta Malacrida, photographed in 1997 by Fabio Tosca

psychological, historical and family backgrounds of our members. The organisation comprises women and men with very different professional, national, religious and political backgrounds, and the choice of our discussions reflects this. In a spirit of self-criticism, we also examine the statutes of our organisation when choosing topics. We have all had to come to terms with our past experiences and our family histories, so that we are now able talk about our identities as post-Holocaust Germans and Jews.

Abraham and I have been moulded by the liberal political developments at the end of the Sixties. As former '68ers' we have held common intellectual orientations, leaning towards such intellectuals as Max Horkheimer, Theodor W Adorno and Hannah Arendt, who were Jews of the Frankfurt school. But in coming to terms with our own pasts, we took efforts not to nostalgically romanticise our student years. Rather, we were self-critical and set new targets for the children of Nazi victims and Nazi victimisers. In spite of the differences in our background, this joint learning process went surprisingly smoothly.

However, at this time it also became clear to me that my idea of a reconciliation between Germans and Jews wasn't realistic – reconciliation is only possible between perpetrators and victims. No guilt can be bequeathed to us, the children of the victimisers, let alone a path of reconciliation.

Even so, Abraham and I have been corresponding almost weekly since March 1991. Our exchanges on life and reading matter are very intensely passionate, and we involve other members, or those interested in our organisation, as far as we can. Dan Bar On, for example, whom we met for the first time in March 1993 in Tulsa, has been important in this critical process of self-interrogation. He presented us with six questions about the effect of the Holocaust on our lives. When and how were we confronted with the Holocaust? How did we cope with our lack of roots? How do we deal with social alienation and being different? Can we empathise with the role of victims and victimisers? Are we living our own lives free from the shadow of the Holocaust? Have we found a balance between the desire to live and the desire to die, through knowing about the Holocaust? We needed time to answer such complex questions seriously, and finally wrote down our thoughts some months later. While I approached each question individually, Abraham answered Dan Bar On's questions in the form of an article.

The way in which Dan Bar On judges the dialogue between Abraham and myself is also instructive. He describes it as "a microcosm of the German-Jewish dialogue", and writes:

"Gottfried Wagner and Abraham Peck are brave people. Their parents would never have been able to talk with one another. Only 50 years have passed since the ancestors of one were deeply involved in the atrocious act of attempting to annihilate the ancestors of the other. The survivors gave a solemn commandment to their descendants: never to forget and never to forgive. Why does Abraham try to break this commandment? Why does Gottfried try to break through the silence which came over the German people after the crime became public knowledge? Silence that is a mixture of shame and the desire to shrink from responsibility for the murder, to forget and to be forgiven?...For their own sakes, they are looking for a dialogue which, though breaking their fathers' commandments, will help them articulate their internal quest for hope."

He then analyses the effects which the Holocaust has had on our lives: being uprooted in our childhood from our environment, combined with isolation and mistrust.

"Gottfried found...his intellectual harbour in the post-War Jewish and gentile writers who genuinely tried to grapple with questions similar to his own, about 'Who is Wagner?' However, he had to pay a high price for his courage and was ostracised from his family and his homeland. He has a new personal sanctuary [in Italy], which protects him from the storms awaiting him in the open sea...After describing painful childhood memories which have shaped [Gottfried's and Abraham's] life stories, they quickly disassociate themselves [from these memories].

"Gottfried does it by giving too conclusive answers to questions which have no final answers...Abraham tells us that he believes the future will be good for the next generation, but his last sentences indicate that he cannot really believe that whole-heartedly: 'Can we ever free ourselves of the need to be watchful? We must be ever watchful and not believe that there exists a simple answer, 'Yes' or 'No'. If we do not succeed, what may our children face?"

And he sums up:

"It is quite terrifying! There is no real sanctuary in the world after Auschwitz...Unlike building a house, there are many participants in this process. All these watchful eyes and ears of the living and the dead, all with such extreme and conflicting sensibilities that the possibility of failing is endless. The original discourse of yesterday may easily become the false 'as if' discourse of tomorrow. How can we know? How can we find our path?"[49]

My answer to this is clearer now than it was in August 1993. The dialogue between Abraham and myself is a continual process of learning and maturing. Looking at the situation at that time, Dan Bar On was correct in his judgment. Today, though, I would answer Dan Bar On's questions quite differently, and I suspect that Abraham would, too. Based on my experiences in our group, I would now evaluate the way in which the problems which have arisen for me through being a descendant of Nazi victimisers have been handled more positively: even the longest path through the darkness eventually leads to light.

In 1995 Abraham wrote an article entitled 'Germans And Jews In Dialogue: Is There Anything To Discuss?', in which he said:

"Yet half a century after Auschwitz an entire generation of

Germans and Jews continues to share a legacy and a burden that, in the words of Sabine Reichel, born in 1946 in Hamburg, 'is like an historical umbilical cord that can't be cut off and that pulls at the most unlikely moments.'

"At the heart of this cord is family history. It is an obstacle to both Germans and Jews. For Germans it remains the great divide between silence and dialogue. It is a diseased branch on the pages of far too many family trees.

"Every well-meaning German wishing to engage in a frank discussion of German-Jewish relations (and there are quite a number) is nearly always reduced to tears or to silence when the inevitable question is asked: 'What did your father or grandfather do during the Second World War?' To argue that he was in the German *Wehrmacht* or armed forces is no longer much of a rejoinder: the collaboration of the front-line troops with the racial ideologues of the SS in the murder of the Jews is by now a well-established fact.

"Even more disarming is the question: 'What did your parents or grandparents know about the Final Solution?' – the planned destruction of European Jewish life. Often the answer is one of genuine ignorance. German families in the main did not discuss this particular issue in the years after 1945. But we are beginning to learn that many more knew what was happening to the Jewish family who suddenly disappeared from their apartment building one day and never returned. Many more knew because their fathers, husbands, sons and brothers could not keep a *Reichsgeheimsache*, a state secret, which the Final Solution was always intended to be. In letters from the front, from the concentration camp, or in drunken, sometimes terribly guilt-ridden confessions while home on leave, these men told a great part of the home-front just what was happening in the 'east' to the Jews of Nazi-occupied Europe.

"But family history is also a problem for Jews. Children of Holocaust survivors, such as myself, have grown up in the eye of a hurricane, surrounded by the shadows of the

Holocaust. We have grown up knowing that the Holocaust is a part of our being but often do not know why. Many have asked next to nothing about the suffering of our parents during the Holocaust years or the absence of murdered grandparents, uncles and aunts. These children of survivors fear the trauma inherent in their parents' reply."

Perhaps it was my sensitivity to the sufferings of others which increased my need for justice and spurred me on to greater personal courage. Today, I see Abraham and myself increasingly as witnesses of the second generation, who neither deny nor suppress the fact that they are the children of Nazi victims and Nazi criminals. Describing ourselves as such, I see our responsibility as being part of the present and the future, and that we are making a tangible contribution to the prevention of another Holocaust.

How much there is still to do is illustrated clearly by events in Bosnia and Rwanda. But with this active, positive approach and commitment we will also be able to better come to terms with our personal heritage. Today I no longer find it so terrible that "there is no real sanctuary in the world after Auschwitz". I am at home, where people love, understand or try to understand me. This is a release from the tradition of my family in Bayreuth.

As a cosmopolitan, home for me – the husband of an Italian and father of a Romanian son – is first and foremost with my family in Italy, but as a nomad I can put up my tent anywhere in the world where a mutual acceptance of difference is regarded as enrichment.

Responsible conduct, in respect of others, also lends meaning to my life. This I acknowledge despite the uncertainty concerning my future, and I realise that my thinking seems strange to many and isn't necessarily beneficial to my career as freelance director and journalist.

Discovering that I am constantly making mistakes also influences my life with my son. I am slowly trying to make him understand that my work in the Post-Holocaust Dialogue Group is a constructive part of my existence. Through the group I am continually learning to respect being different in a particularly intense way – an experience which I want to impart to my son at all costs. I hope he will understand some day why I refused to become a typical Bayreuth Wagner and repressed memories of the Holocaust. This ethical position is obviously linked to my commitments in the Post-Holocaust Dialogue Group, and here Abraham and I are always in agreement.

Thanks to Sharon Gutman, a member of our group, the second international congress, "Remembering The Future", took place in March 1994 at Berlin's Humboldt University. We met after years of hospitality and superb organisation in the USA. For Abraham and the other Jewish members, the choice of location was anything but problem-free: Berlin was primarily the capital of Hitler's Third Reich, and the nearby Wannsee Villa the place in which, in 1941, the Final Solution was agreed. The Opernplatz is also only a few steps from the Humboldt University, where the book-burning took place in 1933.

The concert itself was preceded by a talk by Abraham and myself on the subject "From Monologues To Dialogues". Only a few people came to the discussion in the Auditorium Maximum, and yet those who came engaged in intense talks with us. The hall was only half full for the concert, but we weren't discouraged: Ullmann hadn't received media attention and the support of big record companies in Auschwitz, and this was clearly not an evening to celebrate German brotherliness between Christians and Jews. But for those in the hall, most of whom had a Jewish history, our efforts had been worthwhile.

The programme contained works by Ullmann, Weill and Michael Shapiro. The months of preparing and organising the financial, historical and linguistic details, as well as the content, eventually bore fruit. On the evening of 16 March, Shapiro, Abraham Peck, Sharon Gutman, Jan Colijn, Franklin and Marcia Littell and all of those who helped behind the scenes created a uniquely intense atmosphere on the stage of the Auditorium Maximum, with performances by the soprano Mildred Tyree, pianists Jerome Rose and Shapiro and the cellist Ithau Khen, for our "Zero Hour Of Dialogue" in Germany. We will always remember that evening. Whether our dialogue there can develop further remains to be seen, as the difficulties facing a group such as ours in Germany are still enormous, but I firmly believe in a future for our group in that country too.

In accordance with our statutes, dialogue between the different generations in our group is of supreme importance. This constant process of mutual educationis very important, as illustrated by my discussion with the New York-based psychiatrist Yehuda Nir.

I met Yehuda briefly in March 1994 at the 24th international scholars' conference, on "The Holocaust And The Churches", in the Rider University in Lawrenceville, New Jersey. He gave me a copy of his autobiography, *The Lost Childhood* (1989), which had been translated into nine languages. Yehuda's stories were very moving: a Polish Jew, he survived the six years of the Second World War with his mother and sister. I recall especially the sentence: "We were living in times when one had to be grateful to another human being for not exercising his option to kill."[50]

Despite the horror of what he experienced, he impressed me by telling his story without hatred or prejudice. After I had read the book, I kept thinking of the motto of his memoirs, from Samuel Beckett's novel *Malone Dies*: "Let me say before I go any further that I forgive nobody. I wish them all an atrocious life and then the fires and ice of hell and in the execrable generations to come an honoured name."[51] This epigram confused me considerably at that time because I found that it contradicted the humanitarian tone of the book, as well as that of our meetings and the international events we both attended. In November 1995, I wrote to him and asked: "How can you manage to be my friend in spite of the message implicit in your book...and my family history?"

Yehuda was thoughtful: "Yours isn't an easy question to answer, but I'm glad you asked, because it allows me to gain additional insight into my feelings toward the Germans, who murdered my father when I was eleven years old. By quoting Beckett, I'm trying to express what it means to have one's innocent father murdered while still a child. It doesn't mean that I'm not hopeful, that I don't believe in the possibility of creating a better, peaceful world."

Referring to the Dutch edition of the book, with a special introduction for students, he continued:

"My book intends to encourage young people not to be passive, but to take charge of their lives as I did under German occupation. The Germans robbed me of my ability to forgive, but I hope that my book will help young people create a world in which one can forgive. I see you, Gottfried, as a herald of that world. You are the Lohengrin who doesn't hide his past, the Lohengrin who says 'Please, Yehuda, ask me about what my parents did.' You describe yourself honestly as 'a child of perpetrators', born a 'post-Holocaust German'. You say that you've been crucified on the history of Germany, and I believe you. You don't even ask for forgiveness – all you want is to engage in dialogue to understand what has happened, how it happened, and to ask whether it's possible to prevent it from happening again. You're a German who can help create a world in which we, as Jews, can contemplate forgiveness."

With that letter I was given a great responsibility.

I was also greatly affected by Michael Wieck's autobiography *Der Untergang Von Königsberg – Ein Geltungsjude Berichtet* [The Decline Of Königsberg – A German Jew Reports], which, through its humane approach of its subject, became the basis of another important friendship in my life. I corresponded with Wieck about many things, among them my relationship with my father. A child survivor like Yehuda, first of the Nazi terror and then of the Red Army in the former town of Königsberg in East Prussia (now Kaliningrad in Russia), he has a unique understanding of the meaning of family and the historical consequences of the Nazi period. In addition, after a career as an internationally-successful violin virtuoso, Michael – a descendant of Clara Schumann-Wieck – is also able to appreciate my own politico-cultural conflict, as both a Wagner and a German born after Hitler's death. After talking with Yehuda and Michael, who met in 1995 at the premiere of my production of *Lohengrin*, I know exactly why my work in the Post-Holocaust Dialogue Group is meaningful for me.

In the autumn of 1992, during a short journey with the painter Toby Heifetz, who is the niece of the world-famous violinist Jascha Heifetz, I learned the true extent of how art can help preserve human dignity in the shadow of death and horror. The journey – Toby's first to Germany – began in Nuremberg with a visit to the Dürer House and the site of the Nazi rallies, and then moved to Bayreuth and the *Festspielhügel,* with its busts of Richard and Cosima and the relics of Hitler's favourite sculptor, Arno Breker.

Götterdämmerung was being performed on that day, conducted by Daniel Barenboim, and Toby wanted to see inside the theatre, so at the beginning of the interval we went to enter one of the auditorium doors. We were immediately intercepted. The situation was unbearable, and I said angrily to one of the attendants: "Either you let me show Mrs Heifetz from New York the auditorium, just for a few minutes, or I'll publish something about the policing methods employed on the *Festspielhügel.*" We were granted five minutes.

It was a relief to leave Bayreuth and move on to the next stage of the journey: Prague, the Jewish quarter, and then the citadel and the ghetto in Theresienstadt (Terezin). Historical evidence can only partially describe the hell visited on this area, leaving the visitor to draw their own impression from the "forecourt of Auschwitz". For myself, it was a shocking experience to witness the art exhibition in Courtyard Four, with prints of drawings and paintings of the condemned Bedrich Fritta, Leo Haas, Karel Fleischmann, Otto Ungar, Malina Schalkova, Hugo Sonnenschein, Sona Spitzova and Petr Kien, and in particular the drawings of the Theresienstadt children. The expressive intensity in the Nazi city of Jewish culture, of the "Theresienstadt Spa For European Jewry" as a waystation on the road to murder, was almost unbearable. Toby and I each photographed our impression of these pictures, the music and literature, and in mid December 1992 these were shown with critical commentaries in an exhibition entitled *From Bayreuth To Theresienstadt* at the

German Congress Of Industry And Commerce.

In 1995, the American magazine *German Life* asked Abraham and myself to write about our group as part of the 50th anniversary of the liberation of Auschwitz, providing us with another opportunity to reflect on our objectives. Abraham wrote about the problem of "silence and mistrust shared by Germans and Jews", and discussed our own efforts to engage in useful dialogue with one another. Our efforts, he admitted, came with many difficulties: "As Gottfried has stated, we have yet to reach the kind of 'objectivity' necessary to free us from the shadows of the past. He continues to feel shame at the thought of what happened to my family during the Holocaust…He feels angry and powerless at his inability to provide his family with the sense of mourning necessary to begin the steps towards understanding. Abraham spoke of my condition as one typical of Germans of my generation, who "suffer under the burden of history and the attendant sense of homelessness and rootlessness." For now, he writes, whatever our confusions or fears, we must continue to talk to one another.

He then questions the worthiness of our understanding, "especially when so many Jewish friends tell me that there is absolutely nothing to say to Germans. I was never certain of this until I met Gottfried Wagner…We tremble at the thought of all the shadows that lurk over us. But we also know that our post-Holocaust world has not changed enough to withdraw from the challenge.

He concludes: "The Holocaust has shaped us both. But we are responsible for helping to shape the way it is remembered by future generations, starting with our own children. Can we go beyond the hatred, guilt and shame of our generation to leave a different world for them?"

In July, I received a phone call from Lara Nuer, whose mother, Claire Nuer, had founded the Institut Au Coeur De La Communication (ACC) in Paris, Montreal and San Francisco. She had heard of the work that I had achieved and the Post-Holocaust Dialogue Group through Dan Bar On, and was planning an international meeting for August that year in Auschwitz under the heading of "The Turning Point". I asked Lara rather nervously how I could contribute to this meeting. She answered: "We at the ACC have read your articles, and we know and the aims of your group. Like you, we want to open a dialogue between perpetrators and victims and their children – not just between Germans and Jews but also between all conflicting factions, past and present. Your aims are very similar to ours. We'd love you and Abraham to come to Auschwitz to speak at our seminars."

I accepted without hesitation. Lara sent me the main questions to be discussed: "What created the conditions for such large-scale destruction in the 1940s? What elements of general human behaviour made the unacceptable possible? How does this type of behaviour affect all sections of society?" This was followed by more contemporary questions: "How can we avoid the large-scale destruction that sprang from these conditions? How can we construct a healthy, sustainable society instead, beginning with our individual actions within our families, our own work and in smaller communities? And how can our individual actions then be transmitted to all sections of society and become more effective?"[52]

Unfortunately, Abraham couldn't attend the meeting, but another member of our group, Tommaso de Cataldo, went with the ACC colleagues from San Francisco. For my part, I prepared various lectures and texts, as well as audio and video material.

Driving past the watchtowers of Auschwitz-Birkenau, I was shocked by the incredible size of this factory of death, brooding behind fences of barbed wire. I vividly remembered the words of my friend Harry Guterman from Tulsa, who had survived in this hell for years, and who said to me: "It was all a lot worse than you can possibly imagine." Dazed, I entered the garden of the Catholic Meeting House, only a stone's throw from the three concentration camps in Auschwitz. It's difficult to describe the intensity and diversity of what I experienced over the next twelve days, in three seminars.

I shared a room with Bernard Offen, who later proceeded to guide us through the concentration camps Auschwitz One and Auschwitz-Birkenau. A survivor of Auschwitz-Birkenau, Plaszow, Julag and Mauthausen, he had been told of my background, although I never sensed any resentment against me for one moment. Before the start of our harrowing tours of the camps he gave me two tips that I will never forget: "What you're going to see now is difficult to describe in words. It will beggar your powers of imagination. Follow what happened to me here, which I'll be telling to all of you, and the reality of six million murdered people will become clear to you. Don't leave the group, because you shouldn't try to come to terms with what you'll see here alone. Talk about it with your companions." I learned to follow his advice, but I had wildly overestimated my psychological strength. I had convinced myself that I could assist others, but now I needed help myself.

At the Birkenau railway of death, Bernard informed us how, on 24 August 1944, his father had been selected to join a group of new arrivals destined for the gas chambers, while Bernard had been sent to a group who, for the time being, were to survive. At Crematorium Four, he described how the SS sent around 2,000 people to their deaths at each gassing session. I started to cry. Bernard took my hand and, after saying a *kaddisch* [prayer for the dead] for his father, we silently walked together over to where he used to hide, near the latrines. Henry Knight supported me on the way.

I had imagined that on further tours I would be able to handle the confrontation better, but I was deceiving myself. Every time I visited the two camps it became even more unbearable, as I learned more of the horror of the place. Initially I had hoped to be able to protect myself, by acting as photographer, distancing myself emotionally, but this was a vain hope. Bernard, who had survived this hell, was like a father to me. With his help, I slowly started to grasp that I had to regard the reality of this death factory as part of being human. Only afterwards was I aware that the others were weeping as well.

I was further moved by Irit Weir, a young woman from Israel in her mid 30s, who lives in Napa, near San Francisco. During the third seminar, after we were confronted again with Crematorium Four and the murder of Bernard's father, the group went to sit in the shade of a willow tree which grew before the monument to Nazi victims. Irit stood up and declared to all those present: "First of all I'd like to thank Gottfried for kindly accepting me for who I am. Also, I'd like to tell him that here [in Auschwitz] we have switched roles: he is now the victim and I am the criminal. He is the one who is suffering here. If we now want to go beyond the denial of guilt [between us] and everything connected with it, as Claire [Nuer] suggested, then we will have to be more open with one another."

Claire threw in: "Take your time. Guilt doesn't stop us from being responsible for what we want to create."

I responded: "I feel I should point out at this time that we in the Post-Holocaust Dialogue Group have also been talking about guilt and shame. I myself am grieving, but I don't believe that guilt should be passed on automatically to the next generation, because this would start a tragic and terrible vicious circle. Even so, being here in Auschwitz made me feel deeply ashamed. However, you've helped me replace the words 'guilt' and 'shame' with the word 'mourning', and since yesterday that has been a new experience for me."

After our tours of the camps, I attended seminars held by representatives of conflicting groups: Jews and Palestinians, Romanies and Sinti, a Serbian woman, a Croatian woman and a Moslem woman. None of us – and we comprised people from 33 nations, all engaging in passionate discussion in a profusion of tongues – were seeking a scapegoat. Rather, we were attempting to create in others a higher degree of sensitivity for the suffering of all mankind.

The Germans I met in Auschwitz were people in a state of shock, who were unasahamed to weep for the millions of murdered Jews, Christians, Romanies and Sinti. We kept asking ourselves the same question: "What can I as an individual, and we as a group, do to fight forms of totalitarian behaviour around us?" There was talk of becoming more human through the common experience of Auschwitz, but never of expecting absolution and redemption of one person by another.

When I landed at the Malpensa airport in Milan, Eugenio leapt into my arms and said, relieved, "Papa! Thank God they didn't kill you there."

"On the contrary," I answered him with a smile. "I made lots of new friends. We all just want to learn to live in peace with each other."

CHAPTER TWENTY-EIGHT

EPILOGUE

W hen the original German edition of this book appeared, at the end of February 1997, I knew that it was likely to polarise public opinion on the subject of Richard Wagner in Bayreuth. As it was, I underestimated international media interest and the subsequent knock-on effect, mistakenly assuming that my autobiography would be driven into the background by other passionately-conducted discussions in the German-speaking countries on repression of the Nazi period. Fierce controversy had broken out yet again, over Daniel Goldhagen's book *Hitler's Willing Executioners* and over the exhibition in Munich of crimes committed by the *Wehrmacht*. Even "neutral" Switzerland was forced to face up to the repression of Hitler's barbarism, when overwhelming evidence against the Swiss banks aroused worldwide attention to the murky business done with Nazi gold – in other words, with stolen Jewish property. The increased international sympathy to the subject of repression helped foster discussion of my book.

On subsequent reading tours, from March to mid December 1997 in Germany, Switzerland, Austria and Belgium, I made myself available for discussion with both my readers and also the media, in interviews, round-table discussions and on talk shows. At the same time, I was confronted by published reviews of my book.

The pressure generated by a crossfire of opinions and the constant travelling made it impossible for me to come to any coherent conclusions on the reactions at the time. Like other authors whose books arouse public controversy, I was forced to recognise that opinions on my autobiography had assumed their own dynamic, which only seldom had anything to do with my intentions. At first, I found the profusion of reactions confusing because, apart from objective articles (such as those in the *Neue Zürcher Zeitung, Süddeutsche Zeitung, Deutsche Lehrerzeitung, Liechtensteiner Vaterland,* and *Die Presse*), others with a more conformist tendency appeared, based on vague claims to power, aimed at preventing constructive criticism of the existing politico-cultural situation within the 'Bayreuth Redemption Company Inc.'

The similarity this bore to the damaging tactics used by the various conformists in the media scene was striking – in particular, the simplification and trivialising of the subject matter – and reminded me of Milan Kundera's book *The Book Of Laughter And Forgetting*, in which he says: "The struggle of man against power is the struggle of the memory against forgetting."[53]

While I was trying to analyse the conformist journalists' opinions, I came across two books by the psychoanalyst Arno Gruen: *Der Wahnzinn Der Normalität* [The Madness Of Normality] and *Falsche Götter* [False Gods].

In *Falsche Götter* Gruen sees "the capacity of man from birth to decide over his life. Either his empathy becomes the kernel of his being, or he will constantly try to escape it." In this sense, for Gruen, "human development is always the history of the damage to his abilities". Hence he distinguishes between "the integrated man, who remains in contact with his inner self and acts accordingly, and the man who focuses outward, who has a divided consciousness and a divided perception. His actions will always be directed against the holistic and, in spite of technological progress, will offend against life."[54]

Meanwhile, in *Wahnzinn Der Normalität* he describes the fundamental inner schism experienced by conformists – including the media – when dealing with information thus: "In order to rationalise, they have to separate thinking and feeling from one another. Public power is a means for maintaining the inner split. But such a man does not seek power for its own sake, but to find support in it and in order not to disintegrate. Hence he cannot afford any compromises either. Every increase in control enlarges the inner vacuum and of necessity provokes an intensified need for domination. If such people are treated with respect, they will interpret any compliance as weakness, because for them there is no equality, for them there is only domination and being dominated."[55] Hence Gruen comes to the general conclusion that for the man "who has surrendered to power, there can basically be no equality in social relations...Dealings with other people are determined by strength and weakness. Therefore more and more power must be accumulated. The aim here is to become invulnerable and be able to prove invulnerability."[56]

But what do Gruen's perceptions have to do with the would-be 'Bayreuth Redemption Company Inc', with conformist journalists of all shades and with my autobiography? Anyone who has studied the striking ways in which such groups have reacted to my book will understand the connection.

On 28 February 1997, my father described my autobiography as "insulting, defamatory and slanderous", to the applause of the festival sponsors, the Bayreuth Society Of Friends, foremost among them President E Hilger and private banker KG Schmidt. With reference to the Bayreuth Festival, he called the book "a considerable impairment and an as-yet unassessable injury to its international reputation". As in the three-page open letter to the international media in his 1994 autobiography, *Acts*, he ignored Wagner's and Hitler's antisemitic influence on the festival and hence on himself and his work.

It was clear to me that the city of Bayreuth and the media, who were subservient to the *Festspielhügel*, would now have to take a stand against me, as my attack on the institution of the festival also applied to them. It came as a pleasant surprise to find that the mighty 'Redemption Company' and its circles could neither dominate the international press in their usual way – with furtive threats of legal action – nor proceed with demagogic counter-attacks. Instead, hitting out at me helped to attract even more international attention to my book. The reaction it had stirred up catapulted it into the bestseller lists in Germany, Austria and Switzerland, and it has been translated into six different languages.

On 10 March 1997, the mayors of Bayreuth issued a statement, in which my book was decried as "malicious agitation", and they refused to engage in any serious discussion concerning the consequences of Wagner's antisemitism. This ploy backfired, however, when discussion flared up anew and the international media exerted increasing pressure on Bayreuth's repressiveness. The contrast between my father's autobiography and my own grew sharper, and people listened with increasing respect to my pleas for a disclosure of the connection between my family and German history. In an April 1997, the *Neue Zürcher Zeitung* acknowledged that "[my] book had rendered a contribution to that critical history of Bayreuth that neither Wieland nor Wolfgang Wagner have provided or provoked".

On 24 April 1997, the very day of my reading in Bayreuth, I learned from the *Nordbayrischer Kurier* (which is loyal to the *Festspielhügel*) that an exhibition about my grandmother, an intimate friend of Hitler, had been cancelled by the festival. The official reason for the cancellation, as reported by the *Neue Zürcher Zeitung* at the end of April, was: "...a still-incomplete processing of archive material from all over the world, which has only recently become accessible. Wolfgang Wagner declared that this surprising new evidence would first have to be classified according to their historical background. Selected documents on that part of festival history which is accompanied by manifold prejudices [ie the Nazi period] will be published in this year's festival book." The truth was that, as a result of discussions inspired by my book, a German bank had withdrawn its offer to finance the planned pro-Winifred Wagner exhibition.

The international media was not fooled: they recognised the festival administration's intention to deceive and quite frankly expressed their doubts about the reasons given for the cancellation.

The deception continued at the opening of the Bayreuth Festival on 25 July, 1997. The festival book tried to hoodwink the world's media into believing that six postcards from Hitler to Winifred Wagner, sent between the years 1929 and 1936, was the sum total of the correspondence from the Führer to the great lady between 1923 and 1945. The atmosphere during the international press conference on 27 July was suitably charged, and there were some hard-hitting attacks from the international press regarding the irresponsible treatment of undesirable and incriminating documents before, during and after the Nazi period.

Despite this situation, sponsors and the festival administration continued to attack me. On 28 August, at the end of the festival, the *Süddeutsche Zeitung* printed the official, corrected version of events that took place during the press conference on 27 July: "By 'fascist and racist elements', which Wolfgang Wagner identified among many critics [on 27 July 1997], he meant the book by his son, Gottfried, not articles by journalists."

The media offensive continued in September when, in close co-operation with some members of the Bayreuth Society Of Friends, the chief dramaturg of the Bayreuth Festival attempted to bring their massive influence to bear on the opinions of Germans and the international public (*inter alia* in Austria, Britain, the Netherlands and Finland).

An article by the non-Jewish author Horst Seferens, which appeared in the *Allgemeine Jüdische Wochenzeitung* (AJWZ) on 2 May 1997, played a decisive part in the slander campaign waged against me by the Bayreuth faithful. The content of the article was revealing about the power games played in and around the festival: "What Gottfried Wagner Still Needs To Say To His Therapist: Wagner's book is a sometimes painful attempt at that grasping philosemitism, with which a certain type of German tries to effect a sort of change of front – an egoistic clutching at Jewish coat tails." Seferens viewed himself later as a victim of headlines that he hadn't written, rejected their connection with his essay and sought to escape all responsibility. He went even further: with reference to an anonymous editor in the *AJWZ*, he alleged that the critical views which had been voiced against his article in the *AJWZ* on 12 June had been "ordered". Searching questions to the board of the *AJWZ* and many wilfully blind Jewish Wagnerians both inside and outside Germany remain unanswered.

A similar personal defamation in the guise of psychoanalysis appeared in an article by Frederic Spotts, a faithful follower of Wieland Wagner, a pilgrim to New Bayreuth since 1957, and the author of one of the plethora of conformist books on the history of the Bayreuth Festival. In his article in the July 1997 issue of the London-based publication *Opera*, he states: "It is debatable whether such a story is appropriately discussed in a cultural publication or in a journal of clinical psychology."

I replied briefly:

"Frederic Spotts' criticism of my autobiography is based on an incorrect assumption with regard to the intention of my book. Contrary to the reviewer's book on the Bayreuth Wagner Festival, my autobiography doesn't focus on the aesthetic consequences of the theatrical work in Bayreuth since 1951 but instead mainly on its socio-political implications. Therefore, most of his review misses the essence of my book.

"The attempt to save 'New Bayreuth' with aesthetic arguments – which Spotts supports – forces him into an historically and scientifically untenable assessment of the political role played by the second and third generations of Richard Wagner's descendants.

"The work of observers such as Köhler, Hein, Naegele, Karbaum, Zelinsky, Schüler, Craig, Prieberg, Wulf, Meyer, Wistrich, Ley and others has convincingly demonstrated that Wagner's descendants and the Bayreuth circle developed Wagner's antisemitism to a level of normative space and politics, in which Hitler found it easy to operate after World War I. In my opinion, playing down the history of Bayreuth is a dangerous practise.

"With regard to the reviewer's suggested factual corrections, I have relied on information given to me by my grandmother, Winifred Wagner. Insofar as she – or I – may have erred, these points have already been considered for the English, American, French, Spanish, Italian and Japanese editions of my book, as well as for the third German edition.

"PS: The allegations which the reviewer makes regarding my inheritance are simply false."[57]

In summing up the handling of Wagner's antisemitism under the direction of Wolfgang Wagner, one can generally say that, from 1966 through today, my father continued to deny that it existed, interpreting it (along with his brother) as philosemitism. This is clear in his autobiography, *Acts* (1994). However, in response to the 1979 TV series *The Holocaust*, and particularly after the reaction on publication of my book, he developed a new strategy for marketing the festival, which he employed along with the old: the "koshering" of Wagner, which he has attempted by engaging the help of many prominent Jewish voices, such as Daniel Barenboim, Ami Maayani, Yoram Dinstein, Joseph Horowitz, the New Yorker Rabin Kenneth Shuster and others.

I also refer to the (very dubious) talks which the maestro Asher Fish promoted – in the sense of his mentor Daniel Barenboim on the Wagner case – in Tel Aviv in June 1998, as well as the international conference entitled "Wagner And The Jews" in Bayreuth in August of the same year. Of course, both events are part of a campaign employed by Bayreuth to improve its image and attract tourists, after the city was criticised harshly by the international community on its handling of Wagner's antisemitism and the scandalous abuse of materials in the Richard Wagner archives since 1945, including the correspondence and footage of Hitler with the Wagner family.

In June 1998 in Tel Aviv, after attempting to force his upset and unprepared audience to listen to Wagner's music, Fish compared the Wagner boycott in Israel with the Nazi practise of burning books, which for me was a disgusting comparison.

There was no serious media coverage of the event in Tel Aviv, which can be seen as the prelude to the international symposium held in Bayreuth a couple of weeks later, entitled "Wagner And The Jews". It is important to note that the title of the symposium had already been used for an exhibition in 1984 and for a booklet published in 1985, and it was a great way for New Bayreuth to deny Wagner's antisemitism. The symposium was held in Bayreuth between 6 and 10 August 1998, under the chair of former German president Roman Herzog, with the Universities of Bayreuth, Tel Aviv and Heidelberg, the Richard Wagner Foundation and the Howard Gilman Israeli Cultural Foundation, and was supported by the Bavarian Ministry Of Cultural Affairs, the city of Bayreuth, the Richard Wagner associations and the Bayreuth Society Of Friends. These groups convened in the presence of Avi Primor, the Israeli ambassador to Bonn; Ignatz Bubi, the former chairman of the Central Committee Of Jews In Germany; and Yoram Dinstein, president of Tel Aviv University. As usual, part of the New Bayreuth philosemitic attitude was rooted in the separation of Wagner the musical genius from Wagner the ideologist. Dinstein compared Bayreuth with the pilgrimage sites of Lourdes, Sanitago di Campostella and Jerusalem.

The true intentions of Ami Maayani, the symposium's organiser and the former president of Tel Aviv University, can be found in an interview which was aired on Bavarian television on 13 October 1998: "It isn't of the slightest importance if Kundry [in *Parsifal*] is Jewish or not. [Wagner's whole work] is only theatre...Music is for me a religious power, only through which can I be lifted up to heaven."

This programme ended with the following remark on *Parsifal*: "Jewish and Christian musical traditions are exposed in Wagner's Utopian sketch as an ideal community with equal rights and the music triumphs over ideology." This, of course, makes any serious research on Wagner's antisemitism completely absurd.

There is a great deal of documentary evidence on this issue – including the open controversy between Ralph Giordano and Ami Maayani regarding my autobiography between 5 and 10 August 1998 – which can no longer be swept under the carpet, even in Israel, where the debate was suppressed by the media.

When asked why a renowned scholar such as myself wasn't invited to the symposium, Maayani answered: "We have intentionally limited ourselves to inviting only scientists. Naturally, I am aware of the problems which are present within his family, and it was important for me to keep familial antagonisms out of this symposium. As well as that, not only did I want Wolfgang Wagner to take part in this symposium but I also wanted him to feel good about doing so, and I believe that he did. I did meet Gottfried Wagner once, years ago; he struck me as being someone who doesn't work primarily in a scientific manner but instead shoots from the hip." My father's Bayreuth connections are fully evident in his foreword to Maayani's whitewashing Israeli compendium.

On 12 August 1998, Ralph Giordano replied:

"When reading the interview, I can hardly believe my own eyes, especially the part 'As well as that, not only did I want Wolfgang Wagner to take part in this symposium but I also wanted him to feel good about doing so, and I believe that he did' – that is the tone and behaviour of a court lackey, paying lip service to the theme of Wagner and the Jews...And this was the reason why Gottfried Wagner, the only actual critical contemporary member of the clan, wasn't invited. What a reliable analyst! This Ami

Maayani, who met the man 'once, years ago', only received the impression that 'he works instinctually.' My dear fellow Jew, you have no reason to creep before the cross in the presence of 'official' Bayreuth when it comes to this topic, but should instead ask that question asked by Gottfried Wagner, which no one else asks as clearly and succinctly in the context of Richard Wagner's heritage: 'What was Bayreuth's connection with antisemitsm [based on Richard Wagner's ideology] under the shadow of the unholy Cosima and, later, Winifred Wagner and her friend 'Wolf', whom the world knows better as Adolf Hitler? And what about those who suppress and deny the Nibelungen keepers of the *Festspielhaus* between 1945 and 1949, and indeed right up to the present day? These are the questions which Auschwitz puts to both you and I, as Jews, and which you, Herr Maayani, must answer, even at the cost of your relationship with Wolfgang Wagner, who for the past 53 years must be shown as being responsible for the suppression of the truth, and whose sensitivities might possibly be affected...For you...it is important to keep family quarrels out of the symposium.

"In that, my dear fellow, you have apparently succeeded, even to the detriment of those who, through their horrific fate in Hitler's Germany, have the right to learn 'the whole truth and nothing but the truth' about Bayreuth before and after 1945. You say: 'Naturally, I am aware of the problems which are present within his family." Really? Then there is no excuse whatsoever for not also inviting Gottfried Wagner, author of *The Wagner Legacy*. Henceforth, I – a survivor of the Holocaust – will keep an eye on your activities in and around Bayreuth."

These two events must be understood as an exercise in *realpolitik* between leading business groups in Germany and Israel, in an effect to extinguish the shadow of the past. It was done also for the sake of those close to Bayreuth and the future tourist potential of the festival, distracting attention from any moral duplicity and any historical irresponsibility in connection with the war of succession, reports of which had been manipulated by the Wagner Foundation and its connections in the international media, according to the independent papers in the summer of 1999.

The national shrine of Bayreuth has still learned nothing from its history. When I think of this place, and family members of the same generation who continue to jockey for my father's position, I am reminded by a phrase written by the psychotherapist Arno Gruen in his 1993 book *False Gods: On Hate And The Difficulty Of Peace*: "History is controlled by those whose feelings are based on suppression, possession and domination."

However, there is another, more important aspect. Since 1998 it has no longer been possible to ignore Richard Wagner's antisemitism when discussing his opera, his life and his influence on German society – even in Bayreuth, the epicentre of the Wagner cult. Today the question is not "Was Wagner a militant antisemite?" but "What are the consequences of his antisemitism for his opera, his life, the Bayreuth Festival and politics and culture, both inside and outside Germany?" How can we handle Wagner's antisemitism, nationalism and antifeminism in a democratic society? Doesn't the intended destruction of Judaism, and its global importance for world civilisation, not also include implicitly the destruction of Christianity? How should we teach future generations of Wagner and of the lies and lives of their ancestors? So many questions still have to be answered.

In this new phase of discussion, one has to say goodbye to the hypocrisy involved in thinking that the beauty of Wagner's music is compatible with his ideological standpoint and his desire for redemption from evil. These events also mark the end of the New Bayreuth marketing strategy: the slow death of false philosemitism and the "kosherising" of Wagner. This autobiography, which also provoked recent discussions concerning the handling of Wagner's antisemitism, was absolutely necessary – a view which has been confirmed many times. I hope that this new edition will find broad public appeal in the UK, just as it did in Germany, France, Italy, America, Japan, and now also in Spain, Portugal and Eastern Europe.

NOTES

1. *Selected Letters Of Richard Wagner*, edited and translated by Stewart Spencer and Barry Millington, JM Dent & Sons 1987, p 888.
2. Zdenko von Kraft, 'Genius', in: *Das Bayreuther Festspielbuch*, Bayreuth 1951, p 5.
3. Arnold Zweig, 'Antwort an Béla Balazs', in: *Weltbühne*, No 1/1930, p 618.
4. Dietrich Mack, *Das Trauerspiel der Macht, Miszellen zur Ring-Interpretation (nach Gesprächen mit Wolfgang Wagner, aufgezeichnet von Dietrich Mack), Das Rheingold* programme of 1970 Bayreuth *Festspiele* 1970, pp 3-12.
5. Richard Wagner, 'The Jews In Music', *Wagner* [magazine], translated by Stewart Spencer, Vol 9, No 1, January 1988.
6. Richard Wagner, *Religion And Art* (Chapter 1, 'Know Thyself'), in: *Richard Wagner's Prose Works*, Vol 6, translated by H Ashton Ellis, University of Nebraska Press 1994, p 274.
7. Friedrich Nietzsche, *Human, All Too Human*, translated by RJ Hollingdale, Cambridge University Press 1986, p 80.
8. *Cosima Wagner's Diaries*, Vol 2 (1878-1883), translated and edited by Geoffrey Skelton, Collins 1980, pp 772-3.
9. Houston Stewart Chamberlain, *Richard Wagner*, translated by G Ainslie Hight, JM Dent 1897, p 176.
10. Houston Steward Chamberlain to Adolf Hitler, 8 October 1923, quoted in: Hartmut Zelinsky (ed), *Richard Wagner. Ein deutsches Thema*, Berlin-Vienna 1983, p 169.
11. Winifred Wagner, "Open Letter", in: *Oberfränkische Zeitung*, 14 November 1923, quoted in: Zelinsky, op cit, p 169.
12. Siegfried Wagner, letter to *Deutsche Zeitung*, Berlin, 6 June 1921.
13. Siegfried Wagner to Rosa Eidam, Christmas 1923, in: Michael Karbaum, *Studien zur Geschichte der Bayreuther Festspiele (1876-1976), Part II, Dokumente und Anmerkungen*, Regensburg 1976, p 65.
14. Adolf Hitler to Siegfried Wagner, 5 May 1924, in: Karbaum, op cit, p 65.
15. *Bayreuther Bund der Deutschen Jugend* (BbdJ), 'Proclamation', in: Karbaum, op cit, p 74.
16. Winifred Wagner, *Meistersinger* programme of wartime *Festspiele* 1943, Bayreuth, p 11.
17. Friedrich Nietzsche, 'The Case Of Wagner' in: *Basic Writings Of Nietzsche*, translated and edited by Walter Kaufmann, Modern Library, New York 1968, pp 638-9.
18. Foundation charter of Richard Wagner Foundation, Bayreuth, pp 8, 10ff, and 4, quoted from: Wolfgang Wagner, *Lebensakte*, München 1994, pp 446-463 [the statutes are omitted from English edition, *Acts*, Weidenfeld & Nicolson 1995].
19. Ibid.
20. Ibid.
21. Winifred Wagner in: *Zeit Magazin*, No 19, 30 April 1976.
22. Ibid.

23. Josef Herbort, 'Vom Junior Keine Konkurrenz', in *Die Zeit*, 3 June 1977.

24. Roy Koch, 'Special' [report on the *Fidelio* premiere], in: *The New York Times*, 30 May 1976.

25. Wolf-Siegfried Wagner, Interview with Karsten Peters, in: German edition of *Harper's Bazaar*, April/May 1985.

26. Immanuel Kant, *Critique Of Pure Reason*, quoted in: *Philosophisches Wörterbuch*, Stuttgart 1969, p 621.

27. Nietzsche, 'The Case Of Wagner', p 647.

28. Franz Liszt, 'Chopins Individualität' in: *Gesammelte Schriften*, Vol 1, Hildesheim-New York 1978, pp 94ff.

29. Uri Toeplitz, quoted in: *Neue Zürcher Zeitung*, 8 February 1990.

30. Karl Lubomirski, *Die Zeitpendel (I Pedali Del Tempo)*, Florence 1990, p 25.

31. Richard Wagner to Ludwig II, 14 October 1868, in Spencer and Millington (eds), *Selected Letters Of Richard Wagner*, p 732.

32. Richard Wagner, 'Hero-dom And Christendom', in *Religion And Art*, in: *Richard Wagner's Prose Works*, Vol 6, p 280.

33. Richard Wagner to Mathilde Wesendonck, 1 October 1858, in: Spencer and Millington (eds), *Selected Letters Of Richard Wagner*, p 423.

34. Karl Popper, *Alles Leben ist Problemlosen*, Munich 1995, pp 158ff.

35. Tilmann Jens, 'Der Erbfolgekrieg [the war of succession]', in: *titel, thesen, temperamente*, televised 10 November 1991.

36. Wolfgang Wagner, quoted in: 'Werkstatt Bayreuth im Wandel [workshop Bayreuth undergoing change]', WDR Radio, 3rd Programme, broadcast 30 October 1993.

37. Gina Thomas, 'Wagner Vs Wagner', in: *Frankfurter Allgemeine Zeitung*, 15 April 1995.

38. Larry Mass, 'Met Cancels Gottfried Wagner', in: *Opera Monthly*, October 1992, p 40.

39. Daniel Barenboim, Interview, in: *Opera Monthly*, May-June 1993, p 4.

40. Franklin Littell, 'Confrontation In Bayreuth', in: *Los Angeles Jewish Times*, 27 July 1993.

41. Alice Miller, *Breaking Down The Wall Of Silence*, Dutton, Toronto Ontario, 1991, pp 105ff.

42. Friedrich Heer, *God's First Love. Christians And Jews Over Two Thousand Years*, translated by Geoffrey Skelton, Weidenfeld & Nicolson 1970, dust jacket text.

43. Ibid.

44. Ibid, pp xiv-xv.

45. Sidur Sesat Emet, Edition B (Jewish Bible), Psalm 142.

46. Ibid, Psalm 139.

47. Ilse Blumenthal-Weiss, quoted in: Heer, op cit, p 2.

48. Hartmut Zelinsky, 'Die "Feuerkur" des Richard Wagner oder die "Neue Religion" der "Erlösung Durch Vernichtung" ['Richard Wagner's "Ordeal By Fire" Or The "New Religion" Of "Redemption By Annihilation"', in: *Musik-Konzepten*, No 5/1978, Munich, p 79.

49. Dan Bar On, Introduction to: Dr Abraham Peck and Dr Gottfried H Wagner (eds), *The Uses And Abuses Of Knowledge*, texts submitted at the twenty-third Annual Scholars' Conference on "The Holocaust And The German Church Struggle", 8 March 1993 in Tulsa, Oklahoma, *Studies In The Shoah*, Vol 17, pp 428-30, University Press of America, Lanham, Maryland, 1993.

50. Yehuda Nir, *The Lost Childhood*, Harcourt, Brace Jovanovich, New York 1989, from text on dust jacket.

51. Samuel Beckett, *Malone Dies*, John Calder, London 1956, p 2.

52. Information leaflet of the ACC, Paris, July 1995.

53. Milan Kundera, *The Book Of Laughter And Forgetting*, trans by Aaron Asher, Faber & Faber, London 1996.

54. Arno Gruen, *Falsche Götter – Über Liebe, Hass und die Schwierigkeit des Friedens*, DTV, Munich 1993, p 11.

55. Arno Gruen, *Der Wahnsinn der Normalität, Realität als Krankheit: Eine Grundlegende Theorie zur Menschlichen Destruktivität*, DTV, Munich 1996, p 189.

56. Ibid, p 139.

57. Gottfried Wagner, letter in *Opera*, November 1997, pp 1282-3.

INDEX